Dolomites *Selected Climbs*

Dolomites

SELECTED CLIMBS
by Ron James

General Editor: Les Swindin

ALPINE CLUB · LONDON
1988

Dolomites Selected climbs

First published in Britain by the
Alpine Club 74 South Audley Street London W1Y 5FF

First Edition (Crew) 1963
New Series First Edition (Brailsford) in 2 volumes 1970

Produced by the Alpine Club

Designed by John Bowler ARCA

Cover photographs
Front Tre Cime di Lavaredo (James)
Back Climbing on the South Face of Marmolada (Giordani)

Typeset in Plantin from author's word processor
by Factel Limited Cheltenham

Printed by L R Printing Services Limited Crawley West Sussex

British Library Cataloguing in Publication Data

James, Ron
    Dolomites: selected climbs.
    1. Italy. Dolomites. Mountaineering
    I. Title
    796.5'22'094538

    ISBN 0-900523-55-7

Contents

Map of the region *front end paper*
List of photographs and diagrams 7–8
General editor's preface 9
Author's preface 10

General Information 11–18
The Area (11): Using this Guide (13): Training and introductory
areas (15): Equipment (16): Other guide-books (17):
Abbreviations (17): Glossary (18)

Brenta (Group 1) 19–45

Pala (Group 2) 46–65

Catinaccio (Group 3) 66–89

Sassolungo (Group 4) 90–108

Odle (Group 5) 109–119

Sella (Group 6) 120–140

Marmolada (Group 7) 141–168

Civetta (Group 8) 169–207

Pelmo (Group 9) 208–212

Bosconero (Group 10) 213–219

Schiara (Group 11) 220–225

Lagazuoi, Fanis and Cunturines (Group 12) 226–237

Tofana (Group 13) 238–243

Cinque Torri (Group 14) 244–254

Pomagagnon and Cristallo (Group 15) 255–259

Sorapiss and Antelao (Group 16)   260–268

Tre Cime di Lavaredo (Group 17)   269–285

Paterno and Croda dei Toni (Group 18)   286–292

Index of climbs   293–303

Photographs and diagrams   304–368

Mountain rescue procedures   *back end paper*

List of photographs and diagrams

1	Torre d'Ambiez SE flank GB	304
2	Torre di Brenta SW face GB	304
3	Cima Margherita N face GB	305
4	Cima d'Ambiez SE face GB	306
5	Cima Tosa and Crozzon di Brenta NE face DM	306
6	Brenta Alta NE face GB	307
7	Campanile Basso diagram of routes	308
8	Campanile Basso SW flank GB	309
9	Croz dell'Altissimo SE face LS 11 Cima Brenta NE face GB	309
10	Sass Maor and Cima della Madonna NW flank LS	310
11	Cima Brenta NE face GB	310
12	Torre di Brenta N face GB	311
13	Cima Margherita S face GB	311
14	Sass Maor E face RJ	312
15	Campanile di Pradidali SE flank RJ	313
16	Cima Canali and Torre Gialla W flank S	314
17	Pala di San Martino SW face LS	315
18	Cima di Val di Roda W face LS	315
19	Cima della Vezzana and Cimon della Pala NW flank LS	316
20	Catinaccio SE face LS	316
21	Monte Agner NNE flank GB	317
22	Catanaccio North, Punta Emma and Torre Est SE flank PB	318
23	Roda di Vael W face GB	319
24	Cima Sud dei Mugoni SE face RJ	320
25	Punta Emma NE flank LS	321
26	Vajolet Towers (Piaz, Delago, Stabeler, Winkler) SE flank LS	322
27	Crepa di Socorda SW face LS	323
28	Spallone del Sassolungo SE face GB	323
29	Sasso Levante and Cinque Dita S flank LS	324
30	Sassolungo SW face AC	325
31	Sassolungo and Il Salame N face AC	326
32	Punta Pian de Sass and Sasso Levante S flank LS	327
33	Sassolungo NE face LS	328
34	3rd Sella Tower SW face LS	329
35	Odle Group S face AC	330–331
36	Sass Pordoi W flank GB	332
37	2nd Sella Tower N face LS	333
38	1st Sella Tower W ridge LS	333
39	Piz Ciavazes S face LS	334
40	1st Sella Tower S face PB	335
41	Sass Pordoi S flank LS	336

42   Marmolada di Rocca S face RJ 336
43   Marmolada d'Ombretta S face RJ 337
44   Marmolada di Penia S face MG 338
45   Torre d'Alleghe NW flank PB 339
46   Punta Civetta, Punta Tissi and Monte Civetta NW face GB 340
47   Cima de Gasperi, Cima Su Alto & Cima della Terranova NW flank GB 341
48   Torre Venezia S and W face GB 342
49   Pulpito di Pelsa and Punta Agordo W flank GB 343
50   Pan di Zucchero E face GB 344
51   Torre di Valgrande NW face SB 344
52   Pan di Zucchero and Punta Civetta NW face GB 345
53   Torre Trieste S face SB 345
54   Monte Pelmo and Pelmetto NW flank GB 346
55   Monte Pelmo S flank GB 347
56   Guséla del Vescovà NW face GB 347
57   Sasso di Bosconero NW flank GB 348
58   Cima and Torre del Lago SW face RJ 348
59   Sasso della Croce W flank GB 349
60   Rocchetta Alta di Bosconero N face GB 350
61   Sasso Nove S face PB 351
62   Lagazuoi North W face RJ 351
63   Cima Scotoni SW face GB 352
64   Tofana di Mezzo E face PB 353
65   Tofana di Rozes S face GB 354
66   Torre del Barancio S face PB 355
67   Pilastro di Rozes S face GB 355
68   Torre Grande Cima Ovest W flank PB 356
69   Cinque Torri plan of starting points 357
70   Punta Fiames S face GB 358
71   Testa del Bartoldo S face GB 358
72   Torre Quarta Alta E face PB 359
73   Torre Grande Cima Sud S face PB 359
74   Torre Inglesi SE face PB 360
75   Punta Zurlon N face RJ 361
76   Dito di Dio N face RJ 361
77   Antelao SW face GB 362
78   Tre Sorelle N face GB 362
79   Tre Cime di Lavaredo S flank AC 363
80   Tre Cime di Lavaredo N face GB 364–365
81   Tre Cime di Lavaredo SE flank JC 366
82   Paterno NW flank GB 367
83   Cima Una N face PB 368
84   Croda dei Toni N flank DM 368

Text photographs:
Paulo Bonetti PB,
Simon Brown SB,
Gino Buscaini GB,
John Cleare JC,
Maurizio Giordani MG,
Ron James RJ,
Douglas Milner DM,
Les Swindin LS,
AC collection AC

General editor's preface

This edition is the second of a new series of guide-books to the major European alpine regions being prepared by the Alpine Club. The changes introduced in the first of the series, Ecrins Massif, are retained in this volume. A further change, in this edition, is the replacement of two volumes of the long out of print guide-books to the Dolomites compiled by John Brailsford in a single volume, whilst at the same time increasing the number of routes described. An omission is the walking route through the Dolomites that appeared in the earlier volumes but now adequately covered elsewhere.

The purpose of this guide-book is to give a comprehensive selection of climbs of all grades to suit a wide range of abilities. The choice naturally includes all the classics but the trouble with such climbs is that they attract the crowds, so this volume includes a large selection of other routes which you should find much less crowded. The choice has been made by the author, Ron James, who has been able to draw on his vast range of experience of climbing in the region. Certainly for a modern guide-book to an alpine region it must contain a larger number of routes that the author has climbed than any other in the English language. Ron is well known amongst British climbers for his book, Selected Climbs in North Wales, but this is the first guide-book that he has written for the Alpine Club. In the preparation of the work I know that he has taken a vast amount of care to check the detail of route descriptions with as many sources of information as it was possible to obtain and has taken particular care with the cross-checking of grades. The finished product is something I'm sure he can be proud of and justifies the hundreds of hours work that went into its preparation, a true labour of love for an area that has given him so much enjoyment over the years.

As with all our guide-books the Alpine Club welcomes helpful comments about the climbs described and any worthwhile omissions that might be included in future editions. We also welcome offers of good quality photographs that might be used in the preparation of photo-diagrams. All comments and offers should be addressed to the general editor at the Alpine Club.

My thanks to those people who provided photographs for the guide-book, especially Gino Buscaini, Paulo Bonetti and Maurizio Giordani, to Jeremy Whitehead for his proof reading, to Ginny James for the excellent work in preparing the text for type-setting and to my wife, Barbara, for translating many letters into and from Italian.

Les Swindin

Author's preface

I first visited the Dolomites in 1953 and have returned to these fascinating mountains in summer and winter in virtually every year since. At one time they were quite popular with British climbers and the Sella Pass and Lavaredo hut were delightful places to be with an imported atmosphere more akin to Langdale or Llanberis than the Alps. However times changed and other areas and types of climbing drew people away.

The Dolomites have always been popular with continental climbers and recent developments have seen an increase in their numbers. A change in attitude to aid has led to new routes of great difficulty and beauty up some very fine walls and gradually many of the old artificial routes are being climbed free. Overpegged routes are being depegged and new lines climbed using chocks and friends rather than pitons for protection.

Whilst much of the material in this guide is based on personal experience a great debt is owed to Peter Crew and John Brailsford for their earlier volumes of Selected Climbs and Dolomites East and West. Obviously these still have an influence on this work as do the excellent Italian and German guide books now available.

My personal thanks must go to my friends who tolerated my fascination with the region and its more obscure areas. Peter Vaughan and Peter Benson joined me in the early days, John Wilkinson, Dai Rowlands, Chris Parsons, Dave Jones and Dave Siviter in the middle years whilst Barbara James shared many of the harder ascents.

In the actual production of the guide thanks go to the many climbers who have written to me about their experiences on Dolomite climbs and to the photographers who provided pictures.

Ginny James did all the word processing with innumerable re-writes as well as being involved with much route checking in recent seasons. Jeremy Whitehead tidied up my literary weaknesses whilst proof reading.

Finally special thanks to the series editor, Les Swindin, whose enthusiasm for the guide took him to the area in 1987 and drove me on in moments of lethargy or despair.

I hope users find amongst the 426 routes and descents just a fraction of the pleasure these mountains have given me for there is something here for everyone. Good climbing!

Ron James, North Wales, 1988

General Information

THE AREA

The Dolomites are a large complex area of limestone mountains situated in the North East of Italy. They are generally lower than the main Alpine peaks with Marmolada at 3342m being the highest summit. Valleys with good roads divide the mountains up into numerous groups and 18 of these are covered in this guide book. Although each group has its own special character they all have certain features in common. Vertical rock walls rising out of green alps are the norm and there is rarely much snow to climb. Glaciers are small and restricted to the northern cirques whilst the weather overall is better than in the Western Alps, although thunderstorms can present problems in the summer months. What the peaks lack in altitude they make up for in steepness and what they lose scenically in lack of large snow fields they gain in the rich variety of colour in the rock. It is the abundance and variety of rock faces which provides one of the best collections of mountain rock climbing routes in Europe whilst the general ambience provides some of the most pleasant walking. Most groups have excellent paths, frequent huts and quite fantastic via ferrata (ladderways) thus enabling the scrambler to pentrate deep into an environment once the sole preserve of the experienced rock climber.

In winter the Dolomites is an extremely well organised ski area and the chairlifts and cablecars provided for the skiers also aid the summer mountaineer by giving rapid access to many huts and faces.

With its popularity in both winter and summer the area offers a wide variety of accommodation. Tourism is the main business and everything is geared to this. In August the area is very busy but certain groups attract the crowds whilst others seem to be left as real wildernesses. The road system makes moving from group to group perfectly feasible so that the full range of experiences can be sampled in a short visit.

For the pure rock climber small low level crags are being developed and even in a poor season there is a lot to do whilst the big wall climber can find routes of all standards up some of the largest faces in the Alps. For those with modest aspirations the choice is unending with many gradations from via ferrata to numerous classic routes of medium difficulty.

The Dolomites had a reputation for poor rock and this is true in places. However, the popular routes are usually all on solid rock and the rock itself has characteristic colours which indicate its texture.

11

Red rock is the most loose, yellow less so, white quite good and grey very firm whilst black rock is excellent although sometimes wet.

Access to the area is straightforward by car from Dunkerque via the German autobahns past Munich to Innsbruck and then South over the Brenner Pass (old road or autoroute with toll) to Bolzano (about 1200kms or 750 miles). It is possible to go by train to Bolzano or Trento or fly to Venice or Milan then either hire a car (expensive) or use trains and buses (slow) to get into the area. Within the area the bus services are fairly good during the season (1st July to mid September) and movement from group to group is reasonably simple. Some huts have service roads which it may be possible to drive up or be driven up, at a price, by four-wheel drive vehicles.

Being a popular holiday area most of the climbing areas lie within easy reach of towns which contain all the facilities that a visitor would require. To the West of the Adige valley the Brenta are a fine separate group with the towns of Madonna di Campiglio to the West and Molveno and Andalo to the East with Trento only a few kms away. Bolzano is a large commercial town West of the main areas. Cortina d'Ampezzo is a high class resort to the East and Belluno is a typical Italian town to the South. Around the Sella, Catinaccio, Odle, Sassolungo and Marmolada groups the Val Gardena and the Canazei to Cavalese valley are dotted with resorts of various sizes and character. Marmolada's summer ski-ing has caused an increase in small resorts to its East whilst Alleghe and San Martino di Castrozza serve the Civetta and Pala groups respectively. The Lagazuoi group is best reached from the Val di Fassa from the North whilst in the Eastern Dolomites Cortina d'Ampezzo is the dominant resort, and together with the smaller villages of Cadore leading South towards Belluno, serves the Tofana, Cinque Torri, Pomagagnon, Sorapiss, Tre Cime, Paterno, Schiara, Pelmo and Bosconero groups.

Each valley and most of the towns have a tourist office (Azienda di Soggiorno e Turismo) from which details of banks, medical services, shops, accommodation, camp sites, transport and hut details including booking can be obtained. The major centres have hospitals, ambulance services, mountain recue teams and mountain guides bureaux. Hut guardians, with the police, usually arrange rescue and most are in contact with the valley by phone or radio. British guides (UIAA and BMG) are welcome in the area and may be booked in advance through the British Mountaineering Council or the Association of British Mountain Guides. Camping is only permitted on official sites and the positions of these sites are shown on the maps suggested and the end-paper map in this book.

Up to date information about the area can be obtained from the
Italian Tourist Office, 1 Princes Street, London, W1 (01 408 1254).

USING THIS GUIDE

THE GROUPS are described from the SW to the NE and each area
starts with general notes about its layout and character. All
information about hut approaches and paths is meant only to
supplement the suggested map. New issues of maps at 1:25000 are
appearing regularly and these are indispensible aids to movement
around the peaks. A map recommendation is made at the beginning
of each group description. Paths are almost invariably numbered and
sign posts are often found at important junctions.

HUTS in the Dolomites vary from large hotel types at popular sites to
small bivouac boxes on summits, descent routes, at the foot of isolated
faces or placed to assist walkers on via ferrata and the famous
Dolomite N to S walking routes. The huts mentioned in this guide
book are operated by the Italian Alpine Club (CAI) unless stated
otherwise and give the appropriate discounts. Private huts are found
sharing the same high passes and alps. There are also a sprinkling of
tourist hut/bars which do not usually encourage overnight stays.

HUT LINKS are described only when relevant to climbs described
with times for both directions given.

THE MAIN LANGUAGE of the area has been taken to be Italian
although in the Northern groups German is often more common
whilst in some areas a local dialect, Ladin, which is similar to
Romansch, is used. Hence some peaks are known by three different
names!

THE ROUTES selected have generally been chosen for their quality
and as wide a range of standards as is possible has been included.
They are numbered by group and in most cases the numbering has
taken a logical sequence around a peak or group.

DESCENTS are usually described as the final route on a peak.

ROUTE TITLES are those by which the route is usually known. As
faces have become developed the tendency has been to move from
names incorporating main features (eg South Face Route) via those
using names of climbers associated with the first ascent (eg South
Face - Vinatzer Route) to route names (eg South Face - Modern
Zeiten).

FIRST ASCENT DETAILS have been kept to a minimum serving only to give an impression of style and period.

INTRODUCTORY REMARKS to each route give some indication of the type of climbing and quality of the route. The remarks may also give an indication of the general line and seriousness of the undertaking.

BASE HUT is the most commonly used starting point for the climb described.

TIME TO START should suit a fairly average party.

ROUTE LENGTH indicates the actual distance to be climbed rather than the height of the face.

FINAL TIME indicates the expectations of a normal rope of two, climbing at the standard in good weather without traffic problems!

STANDARD of the climb is given in the margin and follows basically the UIAA pattern. For many of the harder routes two grades are given; the first reflects the modern approach of free, red point ascents as far as is currently possible and will obviously change as any remaining aid points are eliminated, the second reflects an ascent in traditional style using aid when needed. Popular hard routes are being depegged and so it is worth checking the state of these routes before embarking on them. Incidentally the grade shown for the route is the grade of the hardest pitch and the individual pitch descriptions will indicate how sustained the climb is.

PHOTOGRAPH NUMBER is shown below the grade. Each photograph has the route shown by its number within its group eg Marmolada South Pillar Route (7.05) will be indicated as route 5 on the appropriate photograph.

START DESCRIPTIONS have been written without too much reference to other routes on the face and with not too many details on how to reach the face. Maps and general orientation should facilitate this part.

ROUTE DESCRIPTIONS vary between detailed pitch by pitch accounts and more general statements. The method depends on the complexity of the route-finding and the information available. Nearly half the descriptions are based on the author's personal experience, many others have been produced by direct contact with those who have climbed them, in all cases linked to translations from Italian,

German and French guide books and journals. A few are legacies from the two previous Alpine Club guide books. Regardless of source and apparent authenticity all should be treated with care for the character of Dolomite climbing is such that variations are often feasible and actual choice of line may vary from one ascent to another. It is the general form and line of the ascent that is important and sound route-finding skills are as vital here as in any other Alpine area. It is also worth noting that routes do change on limestone both by weathering and by traffic and these factors must be kept in mind.

The terms R and L are always used with reference to the direction of travel.

PITCH LENGTHS, where used, err on the generous side and stances are often possible at other places on a pitch. On popular routes, particularly those used by guides or for training, cemented pegs may be found giving excellent belays and abseil points.

PITCH GRADES rely on four conventions. The UIAA numerical grades, I–X with + or -, are used with A0 to A3 grades for aid sections. A mixed grade eg VI+/A0 indicates mainly VI+ with some A0 whilst A0/VI+ indicates mainly A0 with some VI+. Varying grades on a pitch eg VI+,A0 indicates that the first part is VI+ followed by A0 climbing. When two styles of ascent are included the grade VI+ or A0 indicates a free grade of VI+ or an aid grade of A0. The table of grade comparisons is an attempt to convert free UIAA gradings into those commonly used by other rock climbing technical grading systems. It is only intended as an indication and problems can occur with traditional descriptions using VI for all hard sections regardless of style. These may be found to be harder than the equivalent grade in the table. Popular routes do become polished and may also be found to be harder than the stated grade.

TRAINING AND INTRODUCTORY AREAS

In most groups there are bouldering areas and smaller, low level, training peaks and crags which prove very useful in poor weather or at the start of a visit. Incidentally these areas often provide opportunities for meeting continental climbers thus acquiring up-to-date information about routes and styles. The following are worth consideration and most are included in this guide book.

Brenta	Croz del Refugio	(1.25 - 1.26)
	Corno Rossa below the	
	Passo Grosté cablecar	
Pala	Croda Paola	(2.08 - 2.09)

Catinaccio	West Face	(3.24 - 3.28)
	Torre Piaz	(3.47 - 3.48)
Odle	Il Pulpiti	(5.28)
Sella	First Sella Tower	(6.01 - 6.08)
Civetta	Babante area	(8.28 - 8.32)
Schiara	Pale del Balcon	(11.03 - 11.06)
Lagazuoi	Piccola Lagazuoi	(12.00)
Cinque Torri	Smaller towers	(14.12 - 14.24)

EQUIPMENT

On routes up to V- a single 40m rope is usually sufficient but with descents often needing abseils, a longer rope (45m) or a double rope will often speed up a descent and make it safer. For retreat double rope has obvious advantages.

On hard routes especially on the big faces double 50m rope is not unusual. The steepness of the climbs makes a harness essential whilst the presence of stonefall makes a crash helmet extremely desirable.

The actual rack depends on the route. On routes up to V- spikes and threads are often found and so slings are more use than chocks. Pegs only appear at this standard on hard moves. On some of the classic chimney climbs protection is scarce except for giant jammed blocks needing long slings. Once the standard passes V modern racks of hexentrics, stoppers and friends seem normal with tie-offs for pegs. If traditional style attempts are planned etrièr may be required. De-pegging means that fewer people carry pegs than in the past but a few plus a hammer may aid a descent or escape or be needed to replace a missing point of aid or protection.

Footwear also relates to standard and the orientation and position of a face. Sticky soles for the climb and trainers for the descent are popular in some areas but boots are still the vogue in others. Watch out for snow on descents as this can cause epics for a light-weight party.

On the N side of the larger peaks axes and crampons may be needed just to get onto the rock whilst on hard long routes bivouac gear must be considered. Thirst is another Dolomite problem and sunny faces get very hot and lots of liquid must be carried.

Equipment decisions depend on the party and style of ascent. It is not unusual on the NW face of Civetta to find parties in boots with etrièr, bivouac gear, ice gear and plenty of food and drink being overtaken by two chalk bag toting climbers equipped for outcrop climbing. Speed diminishes exposure to risk but in either case sound mountaineering judgement must be involved in the decision. If short VI- routes on the Sella Towers take a party more than the suggested guide book time they should be very wary of embarking on flash ascents on the big faces whatever their technical ability.

One final item of equipment is worth considering for use during the pre-route stages. Binoculars can help you find out many of the obscure details of routes, spot variants and identify features and the Dolomites are such that face viewing is often much easier on an off day than in the Western Alps.

GRADING COMPARISONS

UIAA	UK	France	USA	Australia	E.Germany	Czech.
III	Hard Dif		5.0	4		
III+	V Dif		5.1	5		
IV−	Hard V Dif		5.2	6		
IV−	3a		5.3	7		
IV+	3b	4a	5.4	8/9		
V−	3c	4b	5.5	10/11		
V	4a	4c	5.6	12/13		
V+	4b	5a	5.7	14	VIIIa	VI
VI−	4c	5b	5.8	15	VIIb	VII
VI	5a	5c	5.9	16 / 17	VIIc	VIIa
VI+	5b	6a	5.10a	18	VIIIa	VIIb
VII−	5b	6a+	5.10b	19	VIIIb	VIIc
VII	5c	6b	5.10c	20	VIIIb	VIIc
VII+	5c	6b+	5.10d	21	VIIIc	
VIII−	6a	6c	5.11a	22	IXa	
VIII	6a	6c+	5.11b	23	IXa	
VIII	6b	7a	5.11c	24	IXb	
VIII+	6b	7a+	5.11d	25	IXc	
IX−	6c	7b	5.12a	26	Xa	
IX	6c	7b+	5.12b	27	Xa	
IX	7a	7c	5.12c	28		
IX+	7a	7c+	5.12d	29		
X−	7b	8a	5.13a	30		
X	7b	8a	5.13b	30		

OTHER GUIDE BOOKS

Via Ferrata - Scramble in the Dolomites, Cicerone Press

Classic Climbs in the Dolomites, Cicerone Press

Both the above are English translations of Italian guides.

Italian Alpine Club guide books cover many of the areas and contain good diagrams or photographs. German Selected guides from Bergverlag Rudolf Rother, Munich have good photographs and, in the more recent editions, good topos.

In the Rébuffat series of big glossies Gino Buscaini, Les Dolomites Orientales, gives excellent browsing and reading and is published by Denoël.

Finally there are a number of private, selected guides appearing for popular groups eg Pala, Civetta and Cinque Torri and these can be bought in tourist shops on the Dolomite road passes and in Cortina. Some appear a little competitive in their grading, brief in detail and biased in their choice of routes.

ABBREVIATIONS

The usual abbreviations for the points of the compass, directions and distances are used as well as those listed below.

B: *Bocca*　　　　　　　　OH: *overhang*
d: *di, del, delle*　　　　　P: *Passo*
F: *Forcella*　　　　　　　S: *Sella*

GLOSSARY

Bocca: *narrow col*
Buco: *hole*
CAI: *Club Alpine Italiano*
Camino: *chimney*
Campanille: *sharp peak*
Canale: *gully*
Canalone: *gorge*
Cengia: *ledge*
Chiodi: *peg*
Cima: *peak*
Cresta: *ridge*
Dente: *tooth*
Diedro: *dièdre or corner*
Fessura: *crack*

Forcella; *col or pass*
Ghiacciaio: *glacier*
Guglia: *needle*
Parete: *wall*
Pilastro: *pillar*
Punta: *minor peak*
Sentiero: *path*
Sella: *col or pass*
Spigolo: *steep ridge or buttress*
Strapiombo: *overhang*
Vetta: *summit*
Via ferrata: *route equipped with fixed ropes, ladders etc.*
Zoccolo: *base rocks of a buttress*

Kompass 1:50000 sheet 73

The Brenta is the most westerly group and is separated from the main Dolomite region by the Adige valley. The mountains are three to five hours walk from the valley bases and they have a wilder and more forbidding aspect than the other Dolomite groups. There are several chains of massive peaks with vast rock plateaux between and small glaciers and snow gullies. They have a wide range of climbs of varied lengths and standards on sound rock. There are superb via ferrata which often give good access to and from the peaks for the rock climber and also interesting and often exciting ways of travelling from hut to hut. The Via delle Bochette Alta is a series of via ferrata crossing the Brenta from N to S and it is divided into several named sections. All paths are numbered or named and are generally clearly marked.

HUTS

Brentei Hut 2182m. Winter room, goods lift. Approach from Madonna di Campiglio to Vallesinella hut(1hr or car) then 317 to Casinei hut then 318 to hut (handrails and rock tunnels) (2hr)

Alimonta Hut 2580m. Private. Goods lift. Approach from Brentei hut by SOSAT path(1hr)

Tuckett and Sella Huts 2272m. Winter room, goods lift. Approach from Madonna di C to Vallesinella hut (1hr or car) then 317 to Casinei hut then 317 or 328(2hr) OR Funivia del Groste to top station then 316 (1½hr)

Pedrotti and Tosa Huts 2491m. Winter room, goods lift. Approach from Molveno 319 (4½hr)

Agostini Hut 2410m. Winter room, jeep for goods. Approach from San Lorenzo in Banale (S of Molveno) hire jeep (expensive) or car/walk to Scale bridge (45min) then 325 to Cacciatore hut, follow road then L on 325 to hut (4½hr)

12 Apostoli (Garbari) Hut 2488m. Approach from Pinzolo (S of Madonna di C) by 307 (4½hr) OR Dos del Sabion lift then 357,324,307 (3hr) OR car from San Antonio di Mavignola (between Madonna and Pinzolo) to Malga d'Agola on (323 and 324) then walk past lake then 307 to hut (2½hr)

HUT LINKS

Brentei to Alimonta SOSAT path 1hr ←45min

Brentei to Tuckett 318,328 1¼hr←1½hr OR SOSAT via S face P d Campiglio 3hr←2½hr

Brentei to Pedrotti 318 via Bocca di Brenta 2552m 1¼hr←1hr

Brentei to Agostini 327,304,358 via B d'Ambiez 2871m 3hr←2½hr

Brentei to 12 Apostoli 327,304 via B d Camosci 2784m 3–4hr←3hr

Alimonta to Tuckett Bochette Alte via S d Massodi 2998m 5–6hr←6hr

Alimonta to Pedrotti Bochette Centrale via B d Armi 2749m and B d Brenta 2552m 4–5hr←5hr

Tuckett to Pedrotti 303,ORSI via B d Tuckett 2648m Popular path, excellent views 3½hr←3hr

Pedrotti to Agostini 320 via F d Noghera 2423m 2½hr←2½hr OR 320,304,358 via S & B d Tosa 2864m 4hr←4hr

Pedrotti to 12 Apostoli 304 via S d Tosa & B d'Ambiez 2871m 4hr←3½hr

Agostini to 12 Apostoli 321 via B d Due Denti 2859m 2½hr←3hr OR 358,304 via B d Camosci & B d'Ambiez 2871m 4hr←4hr

Torre d'Ambiez 2840m

This small peak is immediately behind the Agostini hut and is one of the pinnacles below the Cima d'Ambiez. The climbs being short and accessible are very popular.

SOUTH FACE
Armani, Gasperini-Medaia, 1938.

This is a short exposed route on good rock in its upper part.

Base hut – Agostini 40 min to the start 200m 2hr

1.01
II+
1

Follow the footpath (Via ferrata Castiglioni–321) round the foot of the ridge and climb up ledges and scree R to a large terrace under the S face near a deep block chimney well seen from the hut.

    After an initial scramble climb a chimney on the R made by a detached flake to a stance at the top (II). Move 2m R and climb a short 5m crack (III+) then traverse R and climb a steep, exposed wall on good holds (III). Continue in the same direction by walls and shallow chimneys to a niche & finally climb a small bulge to reach the summit.

EAST DIÈDRE
Armani, Gasperini-Medaia, 1938.

A very popular route up the obvious dièdre in the E face of the tower.

Base hut – Agostini 30 min to the start 250m 3hr

1.02
V+
1

Follow the path up towards the Cima d'Ambiez and then scramble up the screes to the foot of the wall. Start at the foot of a groove which leads to the dièdre.

1 35m Move R up slabs and ramps to a crack leading to a dièdre on the R of a grey wall (IV+,IV-)

2 20m Climb the dièdre either by the grey wall (V) or direct (IV) to a stance on the R

3 20m Continue up a higher corner (IV)

4 20m Climb a vertical corner (IV/IV+)

5 25m The next corner leads to a good ledge (IV,IV-). Route 1.01 is near here so move 10m R to the line of the obvious upper dièdres

6 35m,40m,35m Three good pitches up dièdres (IV+) to a stance near the ridge

7 15m Easily to the summit.

DESCENT

1.03 Either descend Route 1.01 or better continue the traverse of the
pinnacles. First descend to the col between the Torre and the fourth
Dente. Go round this on the E and climb the third Dente (III+),
cross the summit and descend a chimney (III-) which leads to an easy
ledge leading to the col between the second and third Dente.
Continue descending on the W Face until an ascent leads to an abseil
to the col between the pinnacles and Cima d'Ambiez. The descent
from Cima d'Ambiez also reaches this col and now leads down the E
face to the great ledge leading across to the screes and so down to the
hut. (2hr)

4

Cima d'Ambiez 3017m

SOUTH-EAST FACE

Fox, Stenico, 1939.

*This is a classic climb of the Brenta, elegant and popular. Difficulty lasts
about 200m and the first pitch is the hardest.*

Base hut – Agostini 50min to the start 350m 4–5hr

1.04
V+
4
A large ledge cuts across the E and SE face of the peak. Go up to the
R(E) end of the ledge by the path up scree and snow and follow it
across round to the SE face and the start of the route. (Also possible to
climb direct to this point from below – often wet). Scramble up 20m
over easy ledges to a narrower ledge with a big leaning block. Start of
real climbing. Climb 1m L of the block up a shallow vertical
yellow/black dièdre. After 10m (V+ or A0) reach a narrow ledge,
move R 2m and then follow a faintly marked dièdre (10m,V+) to a
stance. Continue directly in a crack to reach a larger ledge (15m,V).
Next fine climbing up a rather open yellow dièdre (V-,V) leads to a
good stance in 40m. From here climb 3m direct (V), traverse 2m
delicately L and follow an oblique crack L (20m,V) to reach a large
stance on a ledge. Follow a yellow open corner for 15m (V-) to reach a
stance on the R and then climb a slab R for 20m (IV+,V) to a wide
ledge. The steep rock above has two characteristic parallel corner
cracks beside two large rock ribs easily seen from below called the
'ears'. Climb either of these cracks (IV+/V-) for two pitches to reach
less steep and less solid rock leading L to the ridge S of the summit.

EAST FACE (VIA DELLA CONCORDIA)
Aste and Miorandi, Aiazzi and Oggioni, 1955.

This excellent route follows a series of well marked cracks which cut the central part of the east face. Not recommended after wet weather.

The rock is good, the lower section of the route is free but the upper part may need some artificial moves but can be climbed at VI+.

Base hut – Agostini 50 min to the start 350m 6–8hr

1.05
VI+
V+/A1
4

From the hut take the path up scree and snow to the R-hand end of the ledge which crosses the bottom of the face. Walk along to the start of the route. Start at the R-hand edge of the black rock near a short corner about 15m R of the actual crack line. Up the lowest step either by a wet crack (20m,II) or by a crack moving up and L to a stance at R edge of black corner (20m,IV). Climb diagonally R by an OHing crack in grey rock to a resting place under a yellow OH (25m,V/V+) then traverse 10m horizontally L on small holds until it is possible to move up near the black water stripe to a good stance (V).

Climb several metres L of the water then L on less difficult dry rock (25m,IV+, IV). Recross the water streak a little higher to reach a terrace on R. Direct for two pitches (IV) to large ledge under a yellow OH. Take a tiring yellow chimney (20m,V). An ascending traverse to the R under the OH on yellow friable rock leads to a ledge (16m,VI or V+/A1). Direct for some metres then steadily L over a series of OHs, the last being black and wet (20m,V+/A1). Climb the deep chimney behind the large pillar (IV+) then two pitches up a series of cracked corners (VI+ or V/A1) to a good ledge on the R. Ignore the corner and climb the grey wall on compact rock for 40m finally moving R to a large ledge (IV+/V) and the end of the difficulties. The summit can be reached direct up 200m of scree covered rocks (II).

EAST FACE DIRECT
Barbier, Masè, 1961.

This route goes by chimneys to turn the large roofs on the R half of the face and then continues by cracks and dièdres direct to the summit. A ledge at half height allows an escape. Sustained free or mixed free and artificial climbing.

Base hut – Agostini 50min to the start 350m 13hr

1.06   Start 80m R of the Concordia Route (1.04) at the beginning of the
VI+   approach ledges. Climb several metres in a chimney (III), take a rib
V+/A1 on the L returning to the chimney for some metres then traverse to L

4   and climb to a small stance under the big roof. Climb the roof on the
L and then by traversing R turn the arête to reach a niche (VI or
A1,V). Climb out of the niche and continue for 20m past two difficult
OHs (VI+ or A1). Go R with less difficulty (IV) to reach the first
ledge. (Escape R).

Continue easily for 20m (II) towards a yellow OH and climb a
faint dièdre for 15m (IV) to a small ledge. Climb the wall to finish up a
yellow OHing dièdre (VI+ or A1) and then follow OHing cracks for
5m to a very small stance. Traverse 5m horizontally R (V) then climb
obliquely L (VI or A1) to return to the crack which is followed to a
larger ledge. (Bivouac.)

Climb a large yellow roof (VI+ or A1) on the R and continue for
8m (VI) up a small chimney to reach a niche. Follow an OHing crack
then a pronounced crack to reach a second ledge. Climb a dièdre
finishing on a ledge formed by a detached flake (IV). Move R to climb
an OHing wall (VI+ or A1) and finally L to reach the S ridge, near
the summit.

DESCENT

1.07   Follow a well cairned path down the S ridge to reach ledges and
4   gullies which zig-zag down on good rock to a massive cairn. Then
follow a slanting chimney to the gap between Cima and Dente
d'Ambiez and hence by a gully going L(E) descend to the large ledge
which leads back to the start of the routes. (II,2hr)

Cima Tosa 3173m

NORTH-EAST FACE DIRECT
Castiglioni, Detassis, 1933.

*A strenuous route which follows the line of chimneys cutting the face and
isolating the Torre Gilberti. Loose rock during the first 100m but its length,
unavoidability and variety make it one of the most satisifying climbs on the
mountain.*

Base hut – Brentei 1½hr to the start 750m 8–10hr

1.08 Cross the scree slopes to the steep snow cone at the foot of the wall.
V From the top of the cone (danger point) climb a deepening chimney
 with a difficult OH. After 40m take a gully on the R to a ledge, above
which the wall OHs. Climb this for some metres on the L, a bit
OHing and loose, to reach a crack which leads to a smooth gully.
Follow this for a few pitches to a ledge overhung on the R by a large
roof with a tower on the L which is climbed for a short distance.
Follow the crack defining the L side of the tower to reach a hole, go
through this and up a smooth groove and chimney to the top of the
tower.

Take an oblique crack to a gap on the L then by a steep smooth
wall to a higher chimney to the L. Follow this chimney and a series of
smooth gullies to a terrace under an OHing wall on the R of which is a
small tower (cairn). Go round the OHing arête where the wall meets
the tower and climb a crack behind the arête then a long series of
smooth slabs to reach the foot of the yellow wall of the Torre Gilberti.

Now follow a gully of scree and snow for 60m obliquely L until
a deep gully is reached. This gully, which separates Torre Gilberti
from Cima Tosa is followed for 100m to a fork. Take the steep, deep R
branch as a chimney for 60m. Good climbing up the drier inside leads
to the gap behind Torre Gilberti (easily climbed by its ridge).

From the gap take the R-hand groove which is narrow at first
but opens out after 100m and leads to the summit snow-fields. Much
of this section may be iced up, especially the final chimney.

NORTH CANALONE DELLA TOSA
Neri, 1929.

Base hut – Brentei 1hr to the start 1200m 4–6hr

1.09 This ice gully has a slope varying from 45 to 55 degrees. It usually has
AD three main sections of difficulty, two crevasses and an ice bulge. It is
considered one of the best ice climbs in the Dolomites but is very
prone to rockfall and snow slides from the summit. Early in the
season on a cold night is best.

DESCENT
1.10 This is by the normal route up the SE face. From the summit follow
the snow ridge W, then curve round to the S and descend easy slopes
to a rock step (many cairns) split by a 20m chimney (II or abseil). A
path then leads to the Vedretta della Tosa inferior and continues to the
Pedrotti hut. (1½hr in descent, 2½hr–3hr in ascent, a scramble with
just one 20m pitch of II)

Crozzon di Brenta 3118m

NORTH RIDGE
Schneider,Schulze, 1905.

A long fine classic route. Aluminium bivouac hut on summit, 4 beds. The route follows the ridge mostly by easy climbing with occasional deviations to the R.

Base hut – Brentei 50min to the start 1000m 8hr

1.11
IV+
5
From the path which leads round the valley head, start some metres to the L of the ridge. Reach the ridge by a large dièdre of good grey rock and then from the first ledge go obliquely L (III) then R onto the ridge to reach a large scree terrace. Continue, taking the easiest line, with only occasional difficulties (IV-), for about 600m to reach two-thirds height on the ridge. A yellow wall gives the crux of the route. First climb on the R by a small easy cleft to a dark niche. Traverse a narrow ledge L, climb a short vertical wall (IV+) to reach a large chimney which splits the wall. Start on the deep R-hand side and climb by strenuous bridging past OHs for 80m to reach a rocky terrace and so back to the main ridge. Now follow the line of least resistance mainly on the L of the ridge to the great shoulder, from whence the summit is reached along a long rocky ridge often snow covered.

NORTH-NORTH-EAST FACE (ASTE DIEDRE)
Aste, Nevasa, 1959.

An interesting route with either hard free climbing or artificial pitches. Enjoyable because of its length and situation – no very hard pitches, good bivouac sites, good stances. The best descent for a competent party is the descent of the N Ridge (1.11) with 6 or 7 abseils (2½hr)

Base hut – Brentei 50min to the start 850m 13hr

1.12
VI+
VI–/A2
5
Follow the path round below the wall until directly below the dièdre immediately R of two large blocks. Climb diagonally R up a series of cracked chimneys and small grooves (III,IV and one pitch of V-) for five pitches (180m) to a ledge near the foot of a long chimney on the L. Traverse L on this ledge (V,V+) for 35m to reach the chimney. Climb it (poor rock) for 45m (V+,V). Traverse again to the L for 30m on a ledge (IV) to reach an easy gully which leads in 140m to a more difficult section. Either climb the back of the gully (IV,A1) or an easy chimney further R (IV). This leads to a scree ledge and the start of the real difficulties. Start a little to the R of the line of the great dièdre up

an easy ramp and then a narrow chimney (IV). Move 15m L (IV) to a
Ledge under a large roof. Go up to the L up a loose wall (IV) and then
over the roof (VI+ or A2) to a good ledge. Trend L and climb a steep
grey wall (VI or V+/A0) to gain a large ledge.

Continue direct for 35m (IV,VI or A1/V) then easily diagonally
R to reach the back of the dièdre. Climb a pitch up the wall on the R
(IV) then diagonally L into the corner for a few m then leave it on the
R by a little OH to a ledge (VI or V/A1). Traverse R and then climb
straight up (IV+) to a large ledge. Climb a small corner, trend R and
go up a second corner to the roofs, then under these to the R to an
uncomfortable niche on the R wall (VI or A1). Leave the niche to the
R (VI or A1/V) and after 15m (IV) reach a platform on the L. Climb
the roof above direct (VI- or A0) and continue for two pitches up a
broken chimney to join the N ridge. Follow this (IV+,III) to the
summit or descend by it.

NORTH-EAST PILLAR (FRENCHMAN'S PILLAR)
Frehel, Leprince-Ringuet, 1965.

*This excellent free climb follows the steep pillar L of the Aste Dièdre. The
rock is excellent, stances good and situations superb.*

Base hut – Brentei 1hr to the start 830m 7–10hr

1.13
VI–
5
It is possible to start as for the Preuss route (1.14) and then traverse
easily R to reach the pillar but a more fitting approach takes the
cowl-like spur directly below the pillar. Two easy pitches go up to the
R of the subsidiary spur and then a steep wall (IV) leads to a crack (V)
which leads L (V-). Go direct for two pitches (III,IV) to reach first
one then a second large terrace (150m) (cairns). Join the original route
at a snow patch. Go R to a ledge quite near the line of the Aste Dièdre
about 60m below a yellow roof on the crest of the pillar. Climb L up
an OHing chimney which dominates the terrace (IV+) and continue
direct to finish on a large stance (III) at the base of a grey wall with
two yellow roofs on the L. Traverse a little R to climb a thin crack
then traverse R again and finally direct onto a great detached flake,
level with and to the R of the roof (30m,VI-). Step 2m L to climb a
grey wall (VI-) or a little OHing dièdre (15m,A0,V) then continue
direct to finish R over a yellow OH (V+) and finally obliquely L (IV)
to a good stance (30m). A short pitch leads to a good stance. Climb
some m (IV+) then traverse L (V-) to reach a ridge which leads to a
vertical corner capped by two small roofs. Excellent climbing up this
corner for 40m (V) then continue slightly R by a crack (IV,III) then

move 2m R to a ledge and finally via a dièdre to reach a small stance (35m,IV+,V). After going some m to R continue direct up a steep pitch and then slant L to reach a big ledge (35m,V,V+) at the end of major difficulties. Follow the ledge L for a few m then go direct up a dièdre which starts steeply then eases (35m,IV+,IV,III) to reach a terrace below a gully on the L of the pillar. One pitch diagonally R (III+,IV) then direct for a few pitches on good grey rock (IV,III) on the ridge leads to the top of the N ridge.

NORTH-EAST FACE (PREUSS ROUTE)
Preuss, Relly, 1911.

One of the best routes of its standard in the Brenta. The start described was added later making a more direct route. Difficulty is not continuous and the rock is generally good.

Base hut – Brentei 1hr to the start 800m 6hr

1.14
IV+

5

Follow the path from the Brentei hut to a snow patch in the middle of the face.

At first climb straight up a smooth wall which leads to an easy angled but smooth gully. This eases and leads to a small hollow below a barrier of OHs (100m,II). A steep ramp of grey rock leads up to the R and forms a narrow chimney with OHs (120m,II,III). Climb a smooth slab to reach the chimney which leads strenuously to another barrier of red OHing walls. Continue up a steep wet chimney, which is 90m high and has several OHs (120m,III,IV+). Now climb L wards to the large amphitheatre half way up the face. The original route reaches this amphitheatre from the L by a series of chimneys starting from the foot of the Guides Route (1.15).

Move up and cross the amphitheatre R below a black wall along easy ledges to its centre and move R to a higher ledge under a smooth vertical wall (120m,II,III). Follow a wet ledge towards a band of bulging rock, then climb a steep wall, on small holds, for 35m (IV+) towards a chimney. Enter the chimney by a shallow OHing crack and follow it to easy rocks and the large ledge above the steep band above the amphitheatre.

Follow this ledge to the L for 100m, 15m beyond a wet, shallow gully. Climb diagonally R towards a deep gully which higher up becomes an ice couloir (III). Follow it until it becomes a chimney again, then move L along a ledge and climb up easier ledges and gullies, keeping L, to reach the ridge near the summit (III,II,III+).

EAST-NORTH-EAST FACE (GUIDES ROUTE)
Detassis, Giordani, 1935.

A classic free climb on good rock following the R-hand of the black water streaks which mark the convex buttress between the NNE and E faces.

Base hut – Brentei 1¼hr to the start 800m 7–9hr

1.15
V+
5

Start near a red marking at the foot of a line of chimneys on the E side of the buttress up the screes above the path round the cwm.

Cross the bergschrund and climb the L-hand chimney, first by a crack, hard to start (V), then R to a wider crack which becomes a groove and is then closed by two blocks. Avoid these on the L and climb five pitches up a dièdre (III,IV) finishing with a section on the L wall to reach a ledge that runs right across the spur. Move a little L and climb a good pitch up the pillar.

Continue straight up a chimney and finally through a hole to a ledge at the foot of the R-hand of the two black water streaks (IV+). The route now follows this streak with sustained difficulty.

Step 5m R up a crack slanting L then straight up, passing an OH on the R to a red niche. Climb a dièdre on the L to a terrace, then climb diagonally L to a small ledge under a large OH, visible from below. Climb up for 5m, traverse R for 4m on a narrow ledge, then go back diagonally L to another dièdre which leads to another red niche. Move R and continue straight up for 40m, then slant diagonally L to an OHing dièdre , which leads to a small terrace where the angle eases. Continue more easily for 45m to a scree terrace, then straight up the wall above; the first 35m, OHing, is taken on the R (IV), the final 35m wall on the L. Easy rocks lead to the summit in 170m.

DESCENT
1.16 1–2hr to the Cima Tosa then 1½hr descent as for Cima Tosa.

From the bivouac hut on the N summit descend (abseil) to the col and then ascend the Central summit on the NW flank. Continue via another gap to the S summit and then descend onto the W face (snow gully) and traverse across to the col between Crozzon and Cima Tosa. Continue traversing on the W flank until a ridge (III-) leads almost to the snow covered summit of Cima Tosa. (See Cima Tosa for descent from here (1.10))

This route can be followed in reverse to give an easy ascent of the peak. Grade II 1½hr–2hr from Cima Tosa. In bad conditions it can be complicated with snow and poor rock.

Cima della Vedretta 2670m

EAST FACE
Goedeke, Linde, 1964.

This route and the next (1.19) lie on a lower group of peaks usually called the Fracingli clearly visible to the SW of the Brentei hut. The route follows an obvious ramp across the face of the L-hand peak with good rock on the harder pitches.

Base hut – Brentei 1hr to the start   350m   4–5hr

1.17
V
To start take the Sentiero Martinazzi towards the 12 Apostoli hut until near the Vedretta dei Camosci. Cross the glacier tongue to the foot of the wall. Start directly below the summit, 5m to the L of a hollow. Climb direct to a niche of red rock (IV-). To the R of the niche climb easily to reach a deep slanting chimney. Enter this via blocks on the L and climb to below a yellow wall (IV-). Go 60m L up scree covered rock to a gully ramp running L under a yellow wall. Follow this for two pitches then climb a crack (IV+) in the same line to its end. Traverse L past a pinnacle and go up to a scree covered ledge. From its R-hand end climb diagonally R over pleasant slabs (III) for 20m to a stance by a small pillar. Climb up a little, then traverse R (V) for 10m to reach a hollow in the wall. Climb this by a crack (IV) to a stance (cairn). Move diagonally R to the end of a large scree covered ledge to a ramp and climb the ramp (IV+). Continue up a loose, yellow corner, past an OH (IV+) and then follow a chimney on the R to finish 10m S of the summit.

DESCENT
1.18
Go down ledges on the SW face for 30m and then traverse, walking up and down when necessary, round the ridge of the Cima di V Stretta (the next peak S) to reach the path from the 12 Apostoli hut to the B d Camosci. From here descend the Vedretta dei Camosci to meet the path taken on ascent then to the Brentei hut. (3½hr)

Cima della Farfalla 2660m

NORTH-EAST WALL
Maestri, Claus, 1967.

This route is on the peak to the R (NW) of the previous one. The face is defined by two yellow walls which resemble the outstretched wings of a butterfly and give the peak its name. It follows, in the main, the vertical

*line between the wings. The rock is mainly sound and the route deserves to
become a classic.*

Base hut – Brentei 1hr to the start 380m 8–10hr

1.19 Start as for 1.17 then across snow to the bottom R-hand side of the wall.
VI–/A2 Follow an easy gangway 120m past a good bivouac cave to reach
a series of grooves leading vertically upwards. Climb the grooves to a
small stance under a yellow OH (60m,VI-). Climb the OH and the
wall above on bolts to an etrier stance (27m,A1). Continue on bolts
(A1) then free (IV) to a large flake. Ascend L to a groove and up this
to a stance in a grotto (35m,V). Climb the wall on the L on bolts to a
poor stance (35m,A1). Climb the crack for 5m then step L into
another crack and climb to the top of a flake (V). Step L and continue
to a small ledge (VI-). Go L again to a good ledge then follow a ramp
to a bulge (A1) and R to a good belay (35m). Traverse R to a crack
which is followed (A1) to a good stance under the final OH (30m,V).
Follow bolts to the OH, step L to a groove and a poor stance
(40m,A1,A2). Climb the groove for 10m to a good ledge. This marks
the end of the sustained difficulties.

Climb easily R to the bottom of a wide chimney/crack which is
climbed (moves of VI-) on doubtful holds for 35m. Continue to a
ledge (10m) and traverse delicately just below the ledge to reach easier
ground. Either continue direct (hard,20m) or traverse 100m L, climb
easily up to a small cave in a diagonal crack (10m) and continue R to a
higher ledge then traverse 100m R. Climb a difficult crack (VI-) to a
stance just below the summit. Reach the top by a delicate pitch on
small, friable holds (12m).

DESCENT
1.20 Follow the ridge S to join the descent as for previous route. (4hr)

Cima Margherita 2845m

SOUTH-SOUTH-WEST FACE
Videsott, Tassin, 1926

*This exposed, classic route, interesting and often climbed, follows a
characteristic oblique crack which leads direct to the summit on good rock.*

Base hut – Pedrotti 40min to the start 300m 3¹/₂hr

1.21 To start follow the Cima Tosa path then bear R to the base of the wall.
III Start on the R.

Climb direct on good rock to reach the oblique crack (40m,III-). Now follow this L for 80m (II) to a terrace from which the route goes steeply for 30m obliquely L(III) to reach a ledge below the steep upper wall. Start gently L (10m,IV) then diagonally R (3m) to reach a stance at the foot of a dièdre. Climb the dièdre (III) finishing R and continue up a higher dièdre to the base of a detached flake (III+) which leads to a higher ledge (stance 4m R). Climb obliquely L for 30m up a cracked dièdre, situated to the R of an area of white rock, to a terrace. Climb the final wall direct (30m,IV-) to the summit block.

SOUTH-SOUTH-WEST FACE (DETASSIS CRACK)
Detassis and others, 1932.

An exposed climb up a long, narrow, vertical crack cutting the S Face. Numerous OHs with the crux at the top. Difficult to find!

Base hut – Pedrotti 40min to the start 300m 4hr

1.22
V–
13

From the Cima Tosa path ascend R to the face. Start to the L of its centre. Follow an easy chimney for 50m to the second of two terraces. Continue up a second chimney to a niche and go over a slight OH to the base of a difficult, grey wall. Climb L to a little white niche and traverse R (3m) to another niche (peg). Continue L up the OHing wall to a terrace (escape L). Follow the ledge R for 25m to the base of a long, narrow, vertical crack – the object of the route. (This point could be reached by a traverse L from 1.21). Climb the crack to an OH and turn this on the L. Above, return to the crack and pass several small OHs to reach a comfortable niche (IV). Continue directly up the crack. The hardest pitch, with the crux, is right at the top (V). From terraces above follow a crack, then a chimney, more easily to ledges near the summit.

NORTH FACE
Frismon, Steinkotter, 1963.

One of the hardest routes in the area which could involve a bivouac, although the lower wall can be avoided.

Base hut – Brentei 1½hr to the start 600m (430m from the ledge) 10–12hr

1.23
VI/A2
3

To start follow path 318 towards the B d Brenta for 30min then turn R (W) climbing debris and snow patches, to the foot of the N face.
Start 10m R (W) of the lowest point (cairn). Take the easiest route up the lower wall following scree ledges first L then R to reach a chimney (cairn). Follow this, traverse 50m L (cairn), climb an easy wall for 30m to a ledge and continue for 20m to the R to a stance.

Climb an OH and then a crack (40m,V+) to a large ledge. Continue R along the ledge to a peg. Start of the route proper.

This is just R of the line of a large dièdre which cuts the upper walls and can be reached by walking in from the L. From the peg climb one rope length diagonally R, using a belay to the L, into a niche (40m,IV). Leave the niche to the R and climb up to a crack/dièdre. Climb the dièdre and go R to a stance (35m,VI-). Now traverse R and climb a crack to a good stance (25m,II,IV). Continue R up a crack then move R to a stance(25m,V). Climb L into a white dièdre, continue up it and traverse R. Go up for 5m on bolts and bear L to a stance in a niche (30m,A2,V+). Follow the crack out of the niche, traverse on to a ledge on the R and cross a short wall (20m,V,VI). Continue R over compact rock to a knob (30m,VI-). Bear R for 30m to a stance on a ledge (IV). Traverse 4m R and go across a short wall to a ledge (20m,IV+,III+). Go for 40m along to the L (III+). Climb an overlap (V) and a yellow wall then L to a poor stance (25m,A2,V+). Climb 5m to an OH and then R to a good stance (15m,V+,A2). Now climb a thin crack and traverse L (20m,A2,V+) to a crack/dièdre. Continue up the dièdre (25m,VI), up a crack beneath an OH and climb up L to a good stance (25m,VI). Climb for 4m, traverse R and climb a crack to the R to a stance (20m,V+) and the end of the major difficulties.

Climb a crack for 10m and bear L to a stance on a rock knob (25m,IV). Move L to reach a crack to the R of a tower. Climb the crack and go L for 10m to reach a ledge (25m,IV). Climb a gully (III+) and continue on the R to reach a scree terrace (35m,III+,II). Continue in the gully for 30m and at the end climb up to a knob (III). Climb the N ridge (II) for 30m to the summit.

DESCENT

1.24
3
First go W along the ridge down to the Bocca Margherita between Cima Tosa and Cima Margherita. From the gully turn S to a path and descend this. (2hr)

Croz del Rifugio 2615m

SOUTH-WEST BUTTRESS (CAMPANILE TERESA)
Detassis, Fox, 1935.

This is an isolated peak to the E of the Sella del Rifugio and close to the Tosa hut. This training climb follows the ridge seen in profile from the

Pedrotti hut. The normal route climbs the WNW ridge starting on the R flank. It gives an elegant and exposed climb of Grade II and is rather popular. It can be used for the descent.

Base hut – Pedrotti 15min to the start 150m 1½hr

1.25 Reach the SW buttress by the path below the W face. Start from
IV behind the ridge, to the R of two parallel black dièdres, and climb 25m to a terrace. Continue up a small dièdre on the edge of the ridge and slant obliquely R across a wall on small holds to another ledge. Return to the ridge and climb to a terrace with a yellow niche on its L. Continue for 10m up a yellow dièdre, traverse 2m L into the final dièdre and climb easier rock to the top of the Campanile Teresa.

Descend to the gap & climb an easy chimney to the main summit.

DESCENT

1.26 Descend to the col between the main peak and a subsidiary peak to the W and either reverse the WNW ridge with one abseil, or descend the gully S from here with one abseil. (30min)

Brenta Alta 2960m

NORTH-EAST FACE

Detassis, Battistata, Giordani with Pisoni, Leonardi variation, 1934.

One of the hardest pre-war routes in the Brenta. A very exposed free climb on very compact rock. The route starts near the R-hand edge of the face, traverses to the middle of the face at half height and finishes up the final walls direct to the summit. Variations are possible for both the traverse (20m below) and the finish.

Base hut – Tosa 40min to the start 500m 8hr

1.27 Start about 25m to the L of the NNE ridge.
V+

6

1 35m 3m up the obvious crack, traverse 3m L then 5m direct up a dièdre until a traverse some m L leads to a ledge. Climb direct to a terrace below a corner (V-,V)

2 35m Climb the corner for 7m, then direct to reach a roof, turn this on the L and trend R to a stance (V,V+)

3 35m Go gently L to a peg, traverse 15m R to a ledge (V,V+)

4 35m Traverse some m R, climb a 4m corner and continue more to

the R to a higher ledge, finishing by climbing a crack, OHing at the start(IV,V)

5   40m Obliquely L, a little to the R of a dièdre, to a niche under a yellow roof. Climb the roof on the L and then go direct on black, compact rock to a ledge (V,V+)

6   35m Traverse L on the ledge (II)

7   25m Continue L by a hand-traverse (IV,V)

8   30m Follow a dièdre R, then a smooth slab to a stance in a red niche on the R (V,V+)

9   25m Traverse 10m horizontally R, descend slightly, and then climb to a large terrace (IV,V)

10   35m Climb direct, then slightly L, then R and finally traverse down L to a large niche (V)

11   35m Follow the crack on the R of the niche, then bear L and from the last peg traverse 3m R (V,V+)

12   25m Return 2m L, climb a steep crack, then delicately R to a narrow ledge and then climb to a good stance (V-,V)

13   15m Climb obliquely R to a peg, direct for 6m, then a crack on the R (V)

14   30m Go direct to a little yellow roof, traverse R and climb a dièdre. Finally move R to a stance in a cave (V,IV+)

15   40m Continue up an OHing chimney, then L over a yellow bulge (IV,V) to a ledge and the end of the real difficulties.

It is now possible to traverse well L for two pitches (III,IV-) and then finish up a long gully (III,IV) to reach the E ridge and the summit. Alternatively it is possible to continue first diagonally L to the centre of the upper walls, then by a black wall, a dièdre, a series of ledges leading R, a crack and finally a chimney.

NORTH-EAST DIEDRE
Oggioni, Aiazzi, 1953.

A very good route, comparable in difficulty to the Cassin route on the Cima Ovest di Lavaredo (17.19). Good free climbing with a few, straightforward, artificial sections.

Base hut – Tosa 40min to the start 450m 8-10hr

1.28 Start at the L-hand side of the NE face directly below the great V+/A2 dièdre.

1 35m Climb the L flank of the dièdre to reach a deep niche which continues to the R as a chimney (IV,V)

2 30m Climb the black chimney R (V/A1)

3 35m A vertical crack (A1,V+) leads to a wet OHing chimney. Follow this for 10m (V-), then move 8m R (V+) to a stance

4 30m A grey layback crack (V,A1) to a roof, over this (IV) via a hole on friable rock

5 25m Move R and climb a black crack (V,A1) to a good stance

6 20m Climb a yellow, OHing dièdre a little to the L (A1), then L to ledges at the foot of a large dièdre (IV+)·

7 35m Take the L wall on grey rock (IV,IV+)

8 30m Continue by a black crack in the back, first L then R to a good stance (V-,A1)

9 30m Take the crack on the R of the OH, first yellow, then black and vertical (V+)

10 30m Continue to a roof which is turned on the L, then direct to another OH which is climbed on the R (A2,V+)

11 Climb the black OHing chimney crack at the back of the corner to reach an easier chimney (A1,V)

This is the end of the main difficulties and whilst it is possible to continue up the dièdre (VI-) it is usual to move out L onto the rounded rib and to follow this to the final gully and the E ridge (150m,IV,III). 15 min up the ridge to the summit.

DESCENT

1.29 Well marked by cairns down the S face, first over short walls and ledges to a gully which leads down to the first scree terrace. Move L and down easy chimneys, then R to the second terrace. Now descend the L-hand chimney and traverse across to the B d Brenta. (1hr)

Campanile Basso (Guglia di Brenta) 2877m

ORDINARY ROUTE
Ampherer, Berger, 1899.

*This is the easiest route up the most famous and spectacular peak in the
area. It starts on the S face, crosses the E face, traversing the N side and
finishes via the W shoulder and the NW ridge.*

Base hut – Tosa or Brentei 45min or 1½hr to the start 270m 3hr

1.30
IV

7
8

Follow the Bochette path to the B d Campanile Basso and descend a
few m to the L to attack the easy rocks on the S side of the Campanile.
Scramble up easy rocks on the S face to follow a chimney obliquely to
the R without difficulty (III-) for 30m. Climb the yellow wall above
(the 'Pooli Wall', one of the more difficult pitches (IV)) to a small
terrace on the ridge on the R. Continue R along ledges and up
chimneys L to reach the 'Stradone Provinciale', a large scree ledge
running across the N side of the Campanile.

Traverse along this ledge to the W shoulder, then climb the
chimney running up the summit tower for 60m (III) to a scree ledge.
Slant L for 12m to another terrace a little higher ('Terrazzino
Garbari') below the final wall. Gain a small pulpit on the NW edge
('Terrazzino del Re del Belgio') then make an exposed 8m traverse on
the N wall to the foot of the 'Ampferer Wall'.

Start up the wall immediately L of a little niche, climb straight
up for 6m, then traverse L for a few m and continue up a vertical
dièdre to finish on a narrow ledge (IV). Traverse R again and climb up
easier angled rocks to the summit.

EAST FACE
Preuss, 1911.

*An unusually fine climb on small but sound holds; exposed. The climb
follows a narrow, grey wall rising vertically above the
'StradoneProvinciale'.*

Base hut – Tosa or Brentei 45min or 1½hr to the start 120m 2hr

1.31
V

7

Follow the Ordinary Route to the 'Stradone Provinciale' at a point
just L of the middle of the E face. Now make a delicate ascending
traverse from L to R towards a yellow, OHing dièdre. Then by a grey
wall climb straight up towards a yellow stain. Just before the stain,
traverse L by a long step (V-) towards a small terrace situated above a

little protruding roof split by a thin crack. Climb the roof by means of this thin crack and continue up a sort of a shallow groove. Then take to the wall itself, passing a series of steps ascending to the R in the direction of another yellow niche (cairn). From the niche a narrow traverse leads off R towards a small hollow in the wall. Continue to the R on the less steep rocks in the neighbourhood of the N ridge. Return L and from one traverse line reach another higher one, which leads L into a black chimney leading to the summit.

SOUTH-EAST RIDGE (FOX ROUTE)

Fox, Costazza, Disetori, Golser, 1937.

Hard free climbing or some A0.

Base hut – Tosa or Brentei 45min or 1¹/₂hr to the start 200m 4hr

1.32 Follow the Ordinary Route to the top of the 'Pooli Wall'. Climb 70m
VI+ of easy rocks (IV) then an open dièdre on the R of the ridge to reach,
V/A0 in 45m, (V-) the 'Stradone Provinciale' at the foot of the E Face
[7] Preuss Route. Climb up towards the L edge, about 2m R of the ridge. Ascend directly for 22m to a small stance and traverse 5m R to avoid a large OH. (30m,VI+ or V/A0)

Climb direct for 5m to a niche and directly for another 22m to a sentry box (V+). The ridge OHs slightly here, so climb R (IV+) to reach a ledge 30m up, which extends to both sides of the ridge. Follow a narrow dièdre (V-) and easier rock steps to the summit.

SOUTH-WEST DIEDRE (FEHRMAN ROUTE)

Smith, Fehrman, 1908.

A satisfying climb; well maintained in standard, on good rock.

Base hut – Tosa or Brentei 30 or 45min to the start 550m 5hr

1.33 The climb starts in the cwm below the B d Campanile Basso between
IV+ the Guglia and the Brenta Alta. It is reached from the footpath joining
[7] the Brentei hut with the B d Brenta up scree to the foot of the huge
[8] dièdre formed by the SW Wall and the W shoulder of the Campanile. The route lies up this dièdre. The dièdre's lower end is formed as a kind of pillar facing L and forming a narrow, steep, cracked ramp, running up from L to R.

Climb for 90m up the pillar to a ledge (III,IV,IV+,IV) then two pitches up the ramp to another ledge (IV). Move R to the edge of the ramp and continue up to a scree ledge at the base of the dièdre proper.

The route follows the deep cleft of the dièdre which, after 50m, changes into an OHing yellow corner. Above the corner traverse diagonally R towards the edge of the R wall over easier rock to a niche. The wall becomes vertical again, but a little to the L of the niche is a crack formed by a yellow blade of rock detached from the wall. Climb the crack (IV+, officially the crux) and traverse for a pitch back L to the dièdre which is split by a narrow chimney. Climb the chimney direct for 110m. It is possible to avoid the last few m of the chimney through a small hole and up an icy cave, but more satisfying to finish up the chimney itself (mostly IV with two sections of IV+).

It is important to note that though one part of the chimney looks most repellent and a traverse on the R wall appears to offer an easy way round, this is a trap, despite pegs etc. left by retreating parties, the higher one gets the harder it is to get back to the chimney.

From the shoulder, the summit may be reached by the Ordinary Route.

SOUTH-WEST RIDGE (GRAFFER ROUTE)
Graffer, Miotto, 1934.

A strenuous free climb, continually interesting, to the shoulder from whence it is possible to descend via the Ordinary Route.

Base hut – Tosa or Brentei 30 or 45min to the start 500m 7hr

1.34 Start 40m to the L of 1.33.

VI+
V/A0

7
8

1 30m Go up just R of the ridge (III) to a scree terrace

2 35m Continue by a crack (III,IV) passing between two niches

3 20m Move R and climb an OH (III,IV+)

4 30m Continue slightly L (V,IV+)

5 30m Climb a bulge (VI- or A0) and continue (V,IV) to a good ledge

6 30m Climb sloping grey rock to near the foot of a yellow crack easily seen from the start (IV,IV+)

7 30m Climb the yellow crack passing an OH on its R (IV,V-)

8 20m Continue up the yellow crack (IV+,V) to a large stance

9 35m Move R 4m and climb a wall to below a yellow roof (V,V+), move L and climb a faint crack (VI+ or A0)

10   35m Continue by a yellow corner to a good stance (IV+,V)

11   35m Climb a yellow dièdre (IV+)

12   30m Take a grey chimney/dièdre (IV) to a good terrace

13   50m Go past a roof on its R (IV-,IV+) and move L to a ledge below final OHs

14   20m Climb up a few m and then move L 15m (IV+,IV) below the large roofs and finally up to a stance below a chimney almost on the ridge

15   20m Climb the chimney and the slabby arête above (IV,IV+)

16   40m Continue in the same line to the shoulder (IV,IV+).

DESCENT

1.35   There are large abseil rings fixed at convenient intervals, the first of
7   which is situated 22m from the summit on the NW edge. Abseil straight down the NW edge to the chimney descending to the 'Stradone Provinciale'. Abseil down chimneys of the Ordinary Route to the easy rocks above the 'Pooli Wall'. Traverse on to the stance at the top of the wall, then abseil to the small ledge and descend the easy chimney to the Bochetta (col). (2½hr)

Campanile Alto 2937m

WEST RIDGE
Hartman, Krauss, 1927.

This is an elegant and interesting route – one of the most popular in the area.

Base hut – Brentei 30min to the start 550m 5hr

1.36   Reach the start by following the path towards the B d Brenta until
IV+   below the face and then taking the scree to the L of the ridge.

    Climb up short walls and ledges for 50m to a prominent ledge 20m to the L of the ridge (cairn). Climb the difficult wall up a layback flake (10m,IV+) to reach, in 15m, via easier rock, a ledge on the R. Now follow the arête on good, grey rock for 40m (IV-). 20m up a chimney gully on the L leads to a wall (8m,IV) and a niche below an obvious black and yellow, cracked dièdre.

    Climb the crack (25m,IV+) then a chimney (30m,III) to the first shoulder. Move to the R of the ridge, climb a crack, traverse L
40   and climb the cracked arête, in an exposed position, on excellent

rock, to reach the second shoulder.

Continue first on the R of the ridge, then direct up steep rock, on good holds (IV) finally on the L to reach a third shoulder. Go round L and climb to the crest of the ridge and follow it to a deep gash. Abseil 20m and climb a crack in the opposite wall (10m,IV-) then continue up the crest to a steep chimney on the L leading to the saddle behind the prominent gendarme. Take a crack to the shoulder and traverse R across the face to a gap between the two summits. Climb the wall on the R to the top.

DESCENT BY NE CHIMNEY

1.37 From the summit, go E down easy rock till a traverse can be made to the gap between the summits. Descend the L-hand gully, which at first looks improbable. The gully opens out. Zig-zag down ledges, aiming for a ledge with a prominent block just to the R of the ridge (facing out). From this ledge go L to the B Bassa degli Sfulmini. Descend the gully on the R and the Bochette path is soon reached. (30min)

Torre di Brenta 3008m

NORTH FACE (ADANG CHIMNEY)
Adang, Keller, 1903.

A classic climb, interesting and often climbed, on good rock with plenty of holds which follows two successive chimneys up the centre of the N face.

Base hut – Brentei 1½hr to the start 300m 1½hr

1.38
III+
12
From the Vedretta degli Sfulmini, a deep, wet, black gully at the foot of the N face is visible. It starts at the highest point of the snow. 40m L is a chimney crack.

Start a few m on the L of the chimney/crack and climb for 20m to a peg, traverse 2m R and get into the chimney/crack which is followed to the scree terrace in the middle of the wall.

The upper wall has three columns separated by chimneys. The Adang Chimney takes the chimney on the L of the middle column. First climb an easy gully to reach a chimney. Continue by pleasant climbing up the whole chimney to reach an easy gully which leads to red rock on the ridge. Follow this to the summit. If the chimney is icy or wet it may be possible to climb its vertical side wall on good holds. Another alternative is to follow the Via Treptow which climbs the next break to the L entering it from the R also at III+. 41

SOUTH-WEST FACE
Detassis, Battistata, Giordani, Marimonti, 1934.

Base hut – Alimonta 30min to the start 400m 5hr

1.39
V
2
Cross the Vedretta degli Sfulmini and go S to the base of the huge NW ridge. Go R and up a snow filled gully then traverse L to the start of the route at the foot of a vertical black stripe between yellow walls. The approach is loose and liable to stonefall.

Start up a difficult OH (V) then go some m R on wet rock (V) to a crack under another OH which is climbed (V). From the niche move L and continue to a ledge. Continue direct in a kind of groove to a higher ledge (30m). Traverse 5m L up a short dièdre, then successive walls to a ledge which crosses all the wall (cairn). Move 10m R to the foot of a large black step, visible from below and dominated by a large OH. Climb a nice grey wall (35m) then traverse 3m R (IV) and go obliquely R for 20m to reach a hidden chimney which leads to the roof. Traverse 2m R (IV) under an OH, then direct for 15m. Traverse R again (16m,IV) to a terrace. Climb a corner for 30m to reach easy rock leading to the W ridge and so to the summit.

DESCENT
By the Ordinary Route Grade II

1.40
12
This route presents no difficulty except that of route-finding, in which numerous small cairns are of assistance. From the summit take the W ridge for a few m then descend L into quite a large cleft and continue down ledges and steps to a fork in the ridge. Go on to the N side down a steep cleft and leave it when it opens out on to the wall. Traverse R into a small notch topped by a block, beyond which a slanting cleft leads to a large rocky ledge. Follow this ledge to the W for about 85m and when a large cairn is reached, descend a small slanting cleft until it becomes vertical. Then leave it, going R (E) along a ledge which passes round the ridge, until, still traversing R, the snowy foot of the N wall is reached. (1hr)

Cima Brenta 3150m

EAST FACE (VIA VERONA)
Navasa, Dal Bosco, Baschera, 1964.

This route gives mixed free and artificial climbing. It takes the steep, red wall on the L side of the E face. Some pegging is to be expected and usually one bivouac.

The route is in three parts. A lower section of 200m up the grey spur below the wall (III,IV), the middle 250m of hard climbing which leads to the terrace of the ordinary route and the Via della Bochette path and then 200m of easy rock (I) to the summit.

Base hut – Tuckett and Sella 1½hr to the start 500m First ascent 40hr

1.41
V+/A3
11
Start from the Tuckett hut and follow the path from the hut to the B d Tuckett. Descend to reach the ORSI path and follow this S to the foot of the wall.

Start a little to the L of the middle of the wall at an obvious chimney. Climb this for 80m (III). Traverse R for 50m to a large terrace. Climb, by slabs and short chimneys, for a pitch to reach a grotto (bivouac). Climb up easy rock for 50m then move easily R (N) to a grey pillar. Climb the pillar for 25m (IV) to its top. The main difficulties start here.

Climb diagonally R to a terrace (V). From the extreme R-hand end of this climb diagonally R (V+,A2). Continue R to a weakness in the roof (V+,A2). Traverse 10m R to the roof's ridge (V,A3). Slant first to the L then return R to the big corner. Climb the corner (V,A3) to two small terraces. Continue on bolts to a large terrace. Move to the R along this to below a large, black-yellow corner. The corner is climbed for 20m (V,A2), then climb L on black rock (IV). Climb a rope-length straight up. The last 60m is loose in parts. Climb to a big terrace from which easy rock leads to the summit ridge.

DESCENT
1.42
11
From the summit descend NE on a path (cairns). Cross a short snow ridge and then descend a steep, rocky gully for about 80m. Go 20m R to reach a large scree ledge. Follow the Via della Bochette path to the Tuckett hut. (2hr)

Croz dell'Altissimo 2339m

This isolated peak lies above the Val delle Seghe near Molveno. Although not a high summit it has a very big SW face. In contrast the E face is an easy, rather tiring walk.

SOUTH-WEST DIEDRE (VIA ARMANI)
Armani, Fedrizzi, 1946.

This route lies on the R half of the face and is somewhat shorter than the routes which lead to the main summit. It follows the corner between the summit and the prominent SE shoulder and is considered the most attractive route on the wall.

Base – Molveno 1hr to the start 700m 8hr

1.43 From the chairlift out of Molveno or the track near Pradel follow the
VII   path round into the Valle delle Seghe to below the corner. A short
VI/A1 scramble up scree leads to the bottom of the corner. 50m of easy rock
9   leads to the start of the climbing.

1   50m Start easily (III) then a narrow section (V+) leads to a dièdre which is left after a few m for the R wall (V+) which leads to a stance

2   35m Climb the triangular slab first R then diagonally L (VI-)

3   35m Continue direct (VII or VI/A1,VI) and then move L by a plaque

4   40m Follow the corner (III), turn an OH on the R by a ledge and wall (IV) and return to the corner

5   50m Climb a loose crack (V/V+) and then a small chimney leads to a stance out R

6   50m Return to the dièdre and climb it (V) past a jammed block (IV) to the top of a pillar. Continue direct (III)

7   45m A cracked corner, first L (III) then direct (VI)

8   50m The corner above is hard (VI+ or VI/A0) then eases (V) and finally leads to a ramp out R (III).

9   50m Do not continue in the corner but climb the steep R wall (III), to a niche. Leave this (V) to reach a second niche and above it (V) a stance

10 50m Go R to a chimney/crack. Up this (IV-) and then slant L back towards the corner (IV,III)

11 55m Continue in the same line (III) to regain the corner and follow it easily

12 50m The steep crack with moves on the L wall (VI-,V)

13 50m Avoid the crack above on the R (IV) until an OH forces a return to the crack. Climb this (VI or V+/A0,V)

14 50m Continue direct (V) up grassy rock

15 45m Move up L (V-) then traverse across R (V+) and finish in the corner (III)

DESCENT

1.44 Head E from the ridge towards Passe di Comici and Prat del Monte then follow mule tracks down to Andalo or Molveno. (2hr)

Geografica 1:25000 Sheet 79

The Pala Group is in the S of the Dolomites and is made up of a chain of peaks to the W and a group of peaks to the E with Monte Agner rather separate to the NE of these.

Most of the group is readily accessible from the valley town of San Martino di Castrozza with a chairlift to Col Verde, although Monte Agner is reached from the Val di San Lucarno and the Pala del Rifugio from Fiera di Primiero.

There are many easy routes on these peaks of grade III and IV and there are some excellent harder routes grade V and VI on the steep faces of Saas Maor, Cima Canali and Campanile Alto dei Lastei, while Monte Agner, whose rock emerges direct from the valley, provides 1600m of the longest VI in the Dolomites.

It is possible to do some routes from the valley in the day but there are huts in the mountains and it is possible to camp near the Pedrotti hut.

HUTS

Mulaz Hut 2571m. Approaches– i)from Falcade, path 722 (4hr), ii)from San Martino di Castrozza drive N and before the top of the P Rolle turn R, go up to Campigolo della Vezzana and park near start of path 710 (1½hr)

Pedrotti alla Rosetta Hut 2581m. Approaches– i)from San Martino di Castrozza by chairlift and cablecar then 10min on 701, ii)from San Martino di Castrozza by path 701 (3hr), iii)from Gares - path 704 (4hr)

Pradidali Hut 2278m. Approaches– i)from San Martino di Castrozza paths 702, 715 via P d Ball (3hr), ii)from Fiera di Primiero drive to Cant del Gal hut then path 709 (3hr), iii)from Pedrotti hut path 708 (2hr)

Treviso Hut 1631m. Approach– i)from Fiera di Primiero drive to Cant del Gal hut then path 707 (1½hr)

Madonna Hut 2358m. Approaches– i)from San Martino di Castrozza by paths 724,713,(3½hr), ii)from Malga Sopra by path 713 (2hr)

Bivouac Fiamme Gialle 3005m. On Cimone della Pala.

Bivouac de Pala or Guide Alpine 2982m. On Pala di San Martino

Bivouac Minazio 2250m. On a plateau dominating the Vallon delle Lede below the rocks of the Cima del Conte, S of Cima di Fradusta (on path 711)

HUT LINKS

Mulaz to: Pedrotti (703) via P d Farangole 2814m 4hr←4hr

Pedrotti to: Pradidali (708) via P Pradidali Basso 2658m 3hr←4hr OR (702,715) via P d Ball 2443m 2hr←2½hr, Treviso (709,708,707) via P Canali 4hr←4hr OR (711) via P Pradidali 2443m, P d Lede 2777m, Biv Minazio 2250m 5hr←6hr, Biv Fiamme Gialle via P Bettega 2650m 2½hr←2hr

Pradidali to: Treviso (709,711) via F Sedole 5hr←5hr OR (711) via P d Lede 2777m & Biv Minazio 5hr←5hr, Madonna (739) Via Ferrata del Velo 3hr←3hr

Campanile Alto dei Lastei 2813m

WEST FACE
Pfeffer, Kamp, 1929.

This route lies on the highest of the three Lastei towers and is seen from the Mulaz hut as a great dièdre cutting the upper half of the steep W face. It gives excellent free climbing.

Base hut – Mulaz 45min to the start 400m 6hr

2.01 Start up snow in the steep gully below the face to reach a little corner
VI opposite a rognon at 2500m.

1   15m Climb the vertical corner (IV)

2   30m Easily L by scree covered slabs to below a steep wall (II)

3   20m Climb the wall R then L to a grass band (IV-,IV)

4   30m Move 10m L and climb the wall above direct (7m,V) then go L to a yellow niche

5   30m Leave the niche on the L then obliquely R for 30m (IV)

6   80m Traverse horizontally R for two pitches (II)

7 35m Climb directly up the Lward sloping ledges above (IV,III)

8 35m Climb a groove L to a leaning pillar (IV+,III)

9 30m Move back R to the foot of the dièdre via a short crack and a smooth slab (IV)

10 80m Three pitches up the dièdre (V-,IV,IV+,V+,III) to a large cave

11 20m Move up the L wall, then traverse 5m L and climb a smooth slab for 5m, finally move R (easier) for 10m to a stance (crux) (VI)

12 60m Climb the chimney to the top (IV,II)

The summit is up to the R.

DESCENT

2.02 This is rather complex and getting advice at the hut may help. First go down on the N face by the obvious Oberwalder Chimney (II) to reach a saddle between the Cima Mezzo and Cima Alto. Next descend a couloir E to reach a col S of Punta del Mar (P Lucan) below the E face of the towers and cross this to descend to the path (752) leading back to the Mulaz hut. (2hr – 1hr descent and 1hr walk)

Cima della Vezzana 3192m

SOUTH-SOUTH-EAST FACE
Freshfield, Tucker, 1872.

An easy scramble up the highest peak in the group giving excellent summit views.

Base hut – Pedrotti 1½hr to the start 270m 45min

2.03 From the hut follow the normal route for Cimone della Pala (well
I   marked) over the Bettega Pass and the Val dei Cantoni. Finally over snow to the Travignola Pass. From here scramble R up scree and snow to a shoulder and follow the wide ridge to the top.

WEST FACE DIRECT
Langes, Zagonel, Rossi, Castiglioni, 1926.

Popular free climb, one of the best in the area. The route takes a direct line up the W face to the summit.

48 *Start from road 2hr to the start 600m 4hr*

2.04
IV
19
From near the Rolle Pass cross to the Travignolo glacier. Climb this to reach the L-hand of two snow gullies below the face. Move up and R to reach a wide terrace. Zig-zag up on easy ledges to reach a second terrace. Above the wall steepens.

Go R along the terrace and then up steep slabs. The climbing is exposed on good rock. Continue zig-zagging up the wall and chimney on good holds. In the upper section of the wall the climb follows a deep chimney which leads to a notch in the ridge 30m from the summit.

DESCENT

2.05 Descend the SSE Face route described above. The ice gully on the R of the W face is not recommended. 2hr to Pedrotti hut (40min descent + 1¼hr walk)

Cimon della Pala 3184m

NORTH-WEST RIDGE
Melzi, Zecchini, 1893.

This is a fine classic route. Normally the lower part of the ridge, which is not very interesting, is avoided by traversing across the lower of the two slanting terraces which cut across the SW face.

Start from Rolle Pass or Col Verde 1½hr to the start 600m 4½hr

2.06
III
19
From the Rolle Pass traverse across to the foot of the ridge or from Col Verde traverse across under the SW face to the start of the terrace. Small cairns mark the route.

Traverse across the terrace, keeping to the L, then climb up broken rocks and rubbishy ledges to the very end of the terrace, on the NW ridge (1hr). The ridge starts as a large rocky depression, which ends in a vertical wall and leads up to a narrow section. Follow the ridge, along a horizontal section then on the NE side past a tower to an obvious col keeping on the E side. Continue on the SW side and descend a broken ledge under a yellow wall, after which a gully leads back towards the ridge. Climb a chimney on the R of the dièdre, which is at the top of the gully and traverse L to regain the ridge at another col. From here continue up the ridge, which is very narrow and steep, to below a large, yellow wall (Becco del Cimone). Traverse diagonally L below the OHing wall, to a gully (some ice), which leads to a col overlooking the small glacier on the W side.

49

Continue up a slanting crack on the L for 40m or so below the ridge. Traverse across a small gully and turn a small tower (the first on the S of the Becco del Cimone) by a short crack on the N side. Descend several m on easy rocks, to a steep crack which leads to a gap on the summit ridge to the SE of the tower just passed. A short vertical wall leads to the horizontal ridge which leads pleasantly to the summit.

(If the N face is in poor condition it is possible to climb direct over the yellow, loose OHs (IV+) after 20m of traverse, by a steep crack and to continue up the wall above (exposed) to reach a small col. Then climb the ridge for 12m until forced obliquely L. Continue steeply to reach the end of the original route (130m in all, 1hr).

VIA FERRATA BOLVER LUGLI (HIGUSI – ORDINARY ROUTE)
Darmstadter etc. 1889.

This scramble follows a Via Ferrata as far as the Biv Fiamme Gialle and then takes the E face to the summit. It is the usual descent route but it can be quite difficult in a poor season due to ice and snow on the N side of the ridge.

Start at Col Verde 1hr to the start 900m 3½hr

2.07 From the Col Verde follow 706 across scree and grass to the foot of the
II wall (memorial sign). Follow a rock spur (red spots) and then various wire ropes etc up the middle of the wall. A 50m wall and a 30m chimney give interest and lead to a col from where the bivouac hut can be reached up scree.

From the hut follow a path round the L side of the first tower and continue L up a short gully to a col. Descend 10m, move R and go through 'Il Bus del Gat'(a cave). Next move up and follow an easy gully to a col and then metal ropes up a vertical wall to a terrace (30m). Go 10m L up a chimney and then a gully. Continue L up a gully (snow?) to a deep gap in the ridge and continue for a pitch to easy ground and the summit.

DESCENT
2.08 Follow the main ridge SE for 60m and descend to the gap. Climb 60m down a gully to the W and then follow fixed ropes L to a snow gully. If icy, abseil from mid-way along the fixed ropes, otherwise descend 30m to a large cave. Traverse 35m horizontally L to another cave and abseil 9m down a wall. Scramble up L on easy rock to a col and down

a path to the bivouac hut – 1h from summit depending on conditions. Now either descend 706 to Col Verde (1hr) or go E to join the descent from Cima della Vezzana and reach the Pedrotti hut via Bettega Pass. 2½hr to Pedrotti hut (1hr descent in good conditions + 1½hr walk)

Croda Paola 2770m

NORTH-EAST FACE (VIA MINUCCI)
Franceschini, Ferrario, 1958.

This small face on a spur of Croda della Pala gives short training climbs, ideal for introducing climbers to the style of Dolomite climbing or for short days in unsettled weather.

Base hut – Pedrotti 50min to the start 150m 1¾hr

2.09
IV+
Reach the face by following the path over Bettega Pass and then NE directly below the face. Three routes are possible, first the E Dièdre (III), a grey corner, then E Face Direct (IV and V) and finally, 60m further, the NE Face.

The route starts just below the gully which marks the R-hand end of the face. Climb for two pitches, first direct and then L to reach an obvious yellow niche (IV+,30m). Leave the niche on the L and reach a vertical dièdre. Climb this for 60m and reach an exposed stance on the L. Finally climb a yellowish wall and finish L direct to the ridge and the summit.

An easy descent along the S ridge leads to the Bettega Pass. (20min to Bettega Pass)

Dente del Cimone 2680m

This is a subsidiary peak directly between Col Verde and the Bettega pass.

WEST RIDGE
Langes, 1919.

A classic and popular climb on a low peak suitable for training or poor weather.

Start at Col Verde 1¼hr to the start 350m 2½hr

2.10
IV
Follow 701 towards Pedrotti hut until below the face. Head for the

gully on its R and then traverse L across steep grass to the ridge.

Start up an easy gully to the R, then short walls to a large terrace which rises to the R. Follow this to the edge of the SW face. Then climb direct to a cave, leave this on the R and continue by a gully to reach a ledge. Take another chimney to the next ledge and go L to reach the foot of a corner (this corner gives a direct variation, grade V). Climb up to the R and then take the wall above which leads to the ridge and so easily to a large terrace sloping R. Descend this a little, climb a difficult chimney, go through a hole, then obliquely L on easy rock to the summit.

DESCENT
2.11 By easy NE ridge (20min to Bettega Pass)

Pala di San Martino 2982m

SOUTH-WEST PILLAR (GRAN PILASTRO)
Langes, Merlet, 1920.

This is a fine route, exposed and interesting. The descent is complicated in poor visibility. Bivouac hut on summit.

Base hut – Pedrotti 1hr to the start 600m 4hr

2.12 From the cablecar station or the hut follow path 702 down to below
IV–   the Pillar. Start about 45m L of the couloir between the Pala and Cima
▢17   Immink. This point can be reached from San Martino di Castrozza by climbing up path 702 in 2hr. Easy rocks lead to a niche (30m,III), then a traverse is made to the L for 18m (III).

Climb obliquely R (IV–) towards the large hollow at the foot of the chimney which separates the large lower tower and the main pillar. Avoid the steep section below the chimney on the R (IV–), to the hollow. Then follow the chimney for 140m (IV–,III,IV–) to reach a ridge near two pinnacles.

The pillar has three long parallel cracks. Climb the central crack for 110m (III) to a shoulder on the pillar and traverse L (25m,I) to the edge of the pillar. Continue up the W side of the pillar to below the yellowish crack, visible from below, which leads with difficulty (IV–) to another hollow. Climb out of this (IV–,III,II) to the L to reach the final ridge which leads, in 80m (II) via a little gap, to the summit.

DESCENT

2.13   Descend following a good track to the NE. Steeper rocks (two abseils from pegs) lead to a gap high above the Pala glacier. Do not descend to this. Traverse to the N round a series of large fingers aiming for the easy rounded summit to the N. From this summit the N Ridge leads down to path 708 and the Pedrotti hut. (II,2hr)

Cima di Val di Roda 2791m

NORTH-WEST FACE (VIA LANGES)
Langes, Reinstaller, Lorenz, 1920.

This is a long, classic route on an impressive 700m wall. The rock is mainly good, views superb and descent easy.

Base – San Martino di Castrozza 2hr to the start 750m 5hr

2.14   The start is reached from path 702 by a traverse from the Val di Roda
III   across grassy slopes to reach the large hollow at the foot of the NW
 face directly below the summit. In the centre of the face is a noticable hollow with a black water drain coming down from it, nearly to the screes. It is more obvious from San Martino di Castrozza than from the foot of the face. Start near this point about 40m L of a steep and large chimney which goes obliquely L to R. Climb rock covered with holds first R then direct for 3 pitches to reach a vast scree terrace. From the L side of this traverse L for some m (peg) to reach the start of a very narrow chimney. Climb this for a pitch (III-) to a hollow then two pitches R (rock not too sound). After another hollow climb L and then vertically (bulge at 20m) and then take a series of pitches (III-) up a 50m chimney to reach a large terrace near the middle of the wall at the summit of a kind of pillar. Climb direct for a pitch, then take an awkward traverse R across a chimney (often wet) and continue up R to reach a higher terrace with a niche. From the L of the terrace go direct and then slightly R to reach the arête between the W and NW faces at a large hollow. Follow the edge for 2 or 3 pitches then leave the ridge R and continue by chimneys (jammed block) and slabs to arrive finally near the summit.

DESCENT

2.15   The ordinary route leads very easily down between the Cima di Val di Roda and the Cima di Ball to the path which leads back into the Val di Roda. (1hr)

Cima della Madonna 2752m

NORTH-WEST RIDGE (SPIGOLO DEL VELO)
Langes, Merlet, 1920.

*One of the classic routes of the Dolomites traditionally known as the Scarf
Ridge, interesting and on superb rock.*

Base hut – Madonna 20min to the start 450m 4hr

2.16 Reach the foot of the ridge by traversing L for several hundred m.
V This is the start of the Via Ferrata del Velo to the Pradidali hut. Climb
10 steeply on the extreme L of the ridge, overlooking a gully, then easily
up slabs and the crest of the ridge for 150m till the rocks steepen on
the R. The Via Ferrata goes off L in this section. Climb a crack,
slanting to the R, and continue R across a steep wall (III), past a niche
to easier angled rocks above. Continue up the crest for several pitches,
across a gully and up a steep crack till one is overlooking a large,
slabby terrace on the SW face.

A direct variation (60m,V+) goes straight up the wall ahead to
the top of the tower, but the usual route moves R round the arête to
reach a chimney line with moves on the R wall leading to the top of
the same tower (IV+).

Beyond, the ridge is steeper and is climbed on good holds for
30m. Then a short traverse L is made to avoid an OH (IV+).
Continue up easier rock to the top of a pinnacle. Stride across the gap
on to the steep wall, move L and go up a crack (V). Climb several
more pitches up chimneys, or the wall on their R, to the top. (IV,III)

DESCENT
2.17 By the Winkler Chimney. Walk along the summit ridge towards Saas
Maor to a deep chimney cutting across the ridge. Scramble
horizontally L, where there is a large, cemented abseil point. Make
one 45m or two shorter abseils on fixed pegs. Move R and scramble
down for 60m to the col (one final, short abseil) between Cima della
Madonna and Saas Maor. Easy chimneys lead down to the path on the
S side. From the col scramble down 100m to a large chockstone and
then take the R-hand fork and follow cairns forking L lower down to
a last short abseil. Descend scree to the Madonna hut. (1½hr)

Sass Maor 2814m

EAST FACE
Solleder, Kummer, 1926.

One of Solleder's three great classic climbs in the Dolomites. An excellent climb on very compact rock, with few pegs. The direct start reaches the great dièdre from low down on the R but is not described.

Base hut – Madonna 1hr to the start 1000m 10hr

2.18
VI
14

From the hut follow the path over Cima Stanga and then descend path 742 to a grassy saddle and continue to a big, obvious gully. 200m after the gully is a grassy shoulder. Start here up fairly easy rock (II/III) up the obvious Rwards break for 4 pitches. This leads to a narrow ledge below a steep wall and the great dièdre. The corner has been climbed direct (VI) but the original route takes two traverses which are the crux of the climb.

1 40m Climb up to a crack (IV) and up a short dièdre to a stance on the R (V)

2 35m Continue up a yellow dièdre (V-) to a narrow ledge, traverse R (10m,V) along it (stance?), past a shallow groove and then slant diagonally R up a yellow wall for 30m (V-,V) to a spike on the rib

3 30m Climb up a scoop (V+ or A0) and a steep crack to a black OH which is turned (V) on the R and continue above (V-) to a stance

4 40m Continue more obliquely and then nearly horizontally to the L (IV+,V) across the shallow groove crossed lower down

5 15m A semi-hand-traverse for 12m (V) leads to a big niche near the great corner.

The route now continues up the corner by a crack on its L wall (VI or A0). It continues for two pitches up dièdres (V) to a terrace. Finally move R and climb a chimney (V-) exiting through a hole (V-,IV). Easier climbing up the L wall leads to a ramp sloping up L (III-). This leads to a broken gully and so to the summit.

SOUTH-EAST RIDGE
Castiglioni, Detassis, 1934.

A fine, exposed, free climb on good rock with magnificent situations. The route follows the SE ridge of Sass Maor, starting from the gully which separates the Sass Maor from the Cima della Stanga. This is the first

gully to the L of the great introductory buttress of the E face of Sass Maor.

Base hut – Madonna 1hr to the start 700m 7hr

2.19 The start is common with 2.18 and shares the same approaches.
VI–   Follow the original Solleder Route for 100m to the first grassy shoulder. Then traverse to the L along grass covered ledges towards the gully (or climb the gully direct). Scramble up to where it is almost blocked by a small yellow tower under the L of which is a narrow gully, filled with snow and blocks. Climb to the R of this gully to beneath a black wall which rises at its head. This point is 400m above the start (1½hr). The wall is split by a long OHing crack which is followed, first up an OH then up a narrow section (VI-) which is best overcome by bridging. Continue slightly more easily for another 30m to a scree-covered terrace, above which the ridge rises steeply.

From the top L-hand end of the terrace climb for 10m to the L to reach a partly undercut, OHing crack (V). This leads to a grassy niche on the edge of the ridge. Continue straight up to a red niche, climb its OH (V-) and go 2m L to another niche. Climb its OH to reach a narrow ledge. Follow the ledge until it ends on a smooth wall (V). Traverse 3m to the R to reach a stance (V). Climb up the vertical wall on improving holds for 30m to reach a chimney which is climbed. This is followed by a gully which leads to the notch in the ridge beneath the final bastion of the wall. There is a cairn at this point.

Above is a grey wall, split by a shallow corner. Climb a vertical chimney to the L of the ridge to a niche (IV). Leave the niche on the L-hand side and climb by chimneys and cracks, which are narrow at the start, to the second notch. This notch lies above the upper Val Pradidali. It is followed by a black, vertical section with an OHing chimney higher up. Climb the yellow corner, then the wall (V-) to beneath the great OH. From here slant L to reach a small niche (V+) and continue Lwards to a small cave at the start of the final chimneys. Ascend these (IV) and then climb 3 pitches of easier rock to the summit.

SOUTH-EAST FACE DIRECT
Biasin, Scalet, 1964.

This is a modern, serious climb. Originally climbed with sections of aid climbing it is now apparently climbed free. It takes a bold line up the centre of the vertical and partly OHing tower of the SE face.

Base hut – Madonna 1hr to the start 600m 2 days for 1st ascent

2.20 Start as for 2.18 then go direct. The first 300m are continuously grade
VIII   IV then nearly 300m of very hard free or artificial climbing – beware
VI/A2 of false lines leading L in the hard section.

14

DESCENT
2.21 Follow the ridge N for 40m and then descend onto the NE face. A
10 40m abseil leads to a scree terrace. Walk round to the W above the col
between Sass Maor and Cima della Madonna and scramble down loose
rocks to the col. The gully is descended easily with one abseil at the
bottom if one has chosen the harder of the lower exits. The path leads
easily to the Madonna hut. (1½hr)

Campanile di Pradidali 2791m

NORTH-EAST CHIMNEY
Langes, Merlet, 1920.

*The route follows the prominent chimney on the NE side of the Campanile.
Very interesting climbing with one very difficult section.*

Base hut – Pradidali 20min to the start 350m 3hr

2.22 Traverse easily from the P Ball to the start of the series of chimneys.
V   The huge entrance OH is bypassed on the R by traversing round an
15 OHing, yellow corner of rock. Continue up with difficulty to the
second OH which should be bypassed to the L up the wall (V) –
difficult moves but on good rock. Re-enter the chimney which proves
to be easier the higher one climbs. Continue to the summit which is
decorated with a small bell cage and a fine, clear sounding bell.

NORTH-EAST FACE
Castiglione, Detassis, 1932.

Base hut – Pradidali 20min to the start 350m 2½hr

2.23 Traverse easily from the Ball pass as for the previous route and
IV   continue L to below the OH which marks the start of the route
15 proper. (Also reachable from the screes directly below).
Move a few m to the R, then climb straight up the vertical wall
which is exposed but has good holds and shallow cracks. After about
50m bear over to the L. The wall climbing continues by means of thin

57

cracks to beneath the yellow OHs. Traverse below these to the L, over a rib and into a big gully with numerous little OHs. Where the gully bends to the L climb a steep rock wall on the L-hand edge. Climb the following gully to the ridge from which the summit is soon reached.

DESCENT

2.24 Take particular care not to dislodge loose stones and take heed of parties above.

Descend to the col between the two summits. Go down to the W (cairn) in the direction of Cima di Val di Roda. Traverse round a large chockstone to the L. Halfway down cross over to the L and continue to a series of gullies. Descend these. The gully opens out into a chimney. After 130m, where it branches, take the L-hand fork towards the cwm which slopes away between the Campanile Pradidali and Cima di Val di Roda. Descend a series of short walls and grooves until one abseil of 20m leads to the scree below the face. (1½hr to Pradidali hut)

Cima Canali 2900m

NORTH FACE

Zecchini, Brodie, 1894.

With the normal descent route, this provides one of the most varied and interesting traverses in the group.

Base hut – Pradidali 30min to the start 600m 3hr

2.25 From the Pradidali hut, walk across to the foot of the face. The start
III lies up a slanting, shallow gully, which is almost a crack on the NW
16 ' face. Follow this for about half of its length and break off towards the large gap between the Cima Canali and a subsidiary tower the Campanile Canali. Keep to the L up broken slabs and up the deepest gully above these, which leads to the gap.

Above the gap the wall is very steep. Climb up for a pitch near an arête to the bottom of a chimney. Continue up this chimney (40m,III) to reach the base of a pinnacle which one turns on the L. Now go obliquely R to a large niche, then straight up on good holds and in three pitches reach the summit ridge. This leads quickly to the summit.

ORDINARY ROUTE
Tucker, Bettega, 1879.

This is fairly interesting, much better in descent, with some stonefall danger in the couloir. Many cairns but not easy to follow down in mist.

Base hut – Pradidali 15min to the start 700m 2½hr

2.26
III

The route follows the R bank of the gully which slants R across the lower face below a prominent yellow tower, the Torre Giallo. In the upper reaches take the L-hand branch reached by a chimney and continue to the R to the col.

Next by chimney and walls reach a large scree slope which leads to the base of a cracked chimney. Climb the chimney (15m,III) and continue R to a little col. A gully leads to the crest which is followed, keeping just below it with a view of the N and E faces. Rejoin the ridge and so the summit.

WEST FACE
Simon, Wiessner, 1927.

This and the following route climb the main W face taking respectively the central gully and the crack directly up the wall to its R.

Base hut – Pradidali 15min to the start 700m 2½hr

2.27
V

From the hut walk round to the L end of the big terrace cutting the lower face and follow it to its R end.
      Start up a long and narrow crack with a big OH (difficult), which leads to steep slabs. These lead L, under big yellow OHs. A tension traverse is made to the L to a small pillar, which leads up in an exposed position. Move R to a chimney and over a yellow OH. Continue up the chimney and then up a crack on the R for about 40m, until it is possible to traverse L (difficult) to a couloir, leading to a huge roof. This is turned on the L by a steep wall and a crack which lead to a ledge on the arête bounding the couloir. Continue up the arête to the hollow under the summit ridge and then L to the summit.

WEST FACE (BUHL ROUTE)
Buhl, Herweg, 1950.

Base hut – Pradidali 30min to the start 600m 7hr

2.28
VI–

The long obvious crack of the Buhl Route can either be reached direct from the traverse under the yellow wall by a very hard pitch

(40m, VI-), or by following the Simon, Wiessner Route (2.27) for two more pitches until it is possible to traverse R and down to reach the crack where it becomes a chimney. Keep to the crack and chimney on very sound rock and over several OHs, for a few rope lengths, until the chimney ends below a steep wall. Continue up an impressive and exposed arête and then a ridge which leads easily to the summit.

DESCENT

2.29
16
By the Ordinary Route (often crowded). Start down the S ridge to the F Canali between the Cima Canali and a subsidiary peak, the Figlia della Canali, to the S. Scramble down to the top of the chimney and abseil to the scree below. Now follow cairns to the top of the couloir, and with one more abseil reach its far bank and descend this to the valley. (2hr)

Torre Gialla

WEST FACE
Solda, Martin, Sida, 1951.

The Torre Gialla is the obvious great yellow pinnacle on the R of the main summit of the Cima Canali viewed from the Pradidali hut. The route runs up the L face of the pinnacle following, at the start, the crack slanting L. The line is straight up the middle of that face. The route is comparable to the Yellow Edge (17.07) in length, exposure and difficulty. It is a classic of the area.

Base hut – Pradidali 40min to the start 440m 5hr

2.30
VI−
16
Start up the normal way down from the Cima Canali (2.29) and climb to the foot of the tower either up the gully or the easy ridge on its R. From above a large jammed block, traverse in L and go up to a stance (24m, V). Climb easy cracks to a cave (35m). Climb up past the L of the cave towards the bottom of a crack (40m, V-, V). Continue up the dièdre and reach easy ground in the crack (45m). Follow the chimney/crack past a terrace to the foot of a steep wall (70m). Climb up the steep wall until it is possible to swing across R into a groove and ascend to a ledge in 20m (VI-). Go up the next 10m wall, either on the L if dry (V-), or straight up with tiny threads (VI-). Climb up the chimney from the ledge to a sort of cave then go L round a corner and

up the arête to the yellow OHing dièdre (about 30m,V). Climb this
dièdre for 10m to the yellow roof and then make a long and very
exposed traverse R out of the dièdre, round the corner for 10m and up
to a poor stance in the crack (30m,V+). Climb straight up above the
belay, straight over the OH to another poor stance (20m,V+). Climb
up behind the stance on poor rock to the OH and surmount it with
great care (25m,V+). It is better to avoid the hard section R by
traversing L below the yellow roof and then diagonally L (V) to avoid
the upper OH. Scramble more easily for 70m to the top (III,IV).

DESCENT

2.31   The descent to the col above the main descent gully can be seen
from the top of the Torre.

From the end of the sharp summit ridge facing the main mass of
the mountain (E), abseil 20m down the ridge from a small knob
towards the gap. Scramble 20m down on the ridge until about 10m
above the gap and abseil into it. From the gap slightly up and R on the
opposite side to a cairn. From the cairn, traverse into an obvious
chimney and abseil 20m down this to a scree amphitheatre where the
normal route of descent from the Cima Canali (2.29) is joined. (2hr to
the Pradidali hut

Pala del Rifugio 2394m

NORTH-WEST RIDGE
Castiglione, Detassis, 1934.

*This route is on good rock with exposed climbing of a high quality. It
follows as nearly as possible the line of the ridge.*

Base hut – Treviso 20min to the start 700m 6hr

2.32   From the hut follow path 707 to below the ridge.
V   Scramble up grass and scree on the R of the ridge for 60m then
take slabs on the L to reach the ridge at an obvious col, 120m from the
start. Follow the ridge to the base of the first step. Climb a chimney in
this to reach a stance below an OH. Climb the OH (2m,V) on the L
and a 30m chimney to a small grass stance on the ridge. Now move
into a smooth, steep chimney crack on the N face and climb this (V)
for 60m to the top of the first shoulder.

After some easier rock climb R past a black OH (IV-). Next take
a wide chimney exiting L. Cross steep slabs to a gully which is

followed until it is possible to climb smooth rock to a large niche. Traverse R to regain the ridge at the second shoulder. (The Frisch Route on the NW face (V) joins the ridge here.)

Climb at first on the R (40m) then on the edge and finally on the L. Now climb good holds on the vertical L wall (IV+) to a niche and continue for 80m to a scree covered terrace below final OHs.

Go along the terrace R for a few m and climb boldly on superb rock for 80m (very exposed, IV, IV+) to a final shoulder. A short chimney leads to the summit.

DESCENT

2.33
III
Continue along the ridge E towards the Sasso d'Ortiga, climbing en route the subsidiary summit of the Punta del Rifugio, and descend the E ridge of this to its lowest point at a great jammed block. (From here it rises again to become the W Ridge of the Sasso d'Ortiga, 2.34)

Descend to the R (1 abseil) to the upper cwm leading to the F d'Ortiga. Follow the marked path (720) to the Treviso hut. (1¾hr)

Sasso d'Ortiga 2634m

WEST RIDGE
Kees, Wiessner, 1928.

This is a fine climb, one of the best in the group. The ridge is that which leads from the Punta del Rifugio to the Sasso d'Ortiga. The climbing is on good rock and gives fine situations. If the climb is linked with the NW Ridge of the Pala del Rifugio, a combined route of over 900m is possible. All free climbing.

Base hut – Treviso 1¼hr to the start 250m 3hr

2.34
V
From the Treviso hut follow the path, which is marked with paint, towards the F d'Ortiga. Leave it in the upper cwm. On the L, at the lowest point of the ridge, is a massive, yellow pinnacle. To the R of this is a deep gully ending in a smooth, vertical chimney. Climb the chimney for 60m and continue in the same line by gullies and chimneys to reach a notch in the crest of the ridge at a great jammed block (one section of IV). Climb up the ridge, first over a pinnacle and then to a small notch. Follow the almost vertical arête for 200m, which gives superb climbing on good rock (IV) until the top of a yellow pillar is reached. Between the pillar and the ridge is a jammed block which can be seen from the valley. Move along a rounded ledge

and climb the chimney/crack and wall onto the jammed block (V), then climb a difficult section to continue up the steep wall above (IV,V). Finally climb 15m up a corner. A further easy rope length leads to the summit.

DESCENT

2.35 Scramble down the S Ridge over grass and scree to a steeper step which is breached by an easy chimney to the foot of the ridge. Scramble down to the F d'Ortiga. From the col return to the Treviso hut via the marked path (720). (2hr)

Monte Agner 2872m

NORTH FACE

Andreoletti, Zanutti, Jori, 1921.

The route takes the highest wall in the Dolomites, giving a magnificent climb. However the main chimney takes a lot of water in bad weather and the N ridge is much more popular. There is a bivouac hut at the foot of the face.

Base – Val di San Lucarno 1½hr to the start 1500m 12hr

2.36
V+
21
From the Val di San Lucarno (from Taibon) the approach is marked by a sign 'Via Monte Agner' about 3-5km from Taibon on the L-hand side of the road. The path orienteers through the woods, crosses a river, and follows a 'dry' stream bed. Cross the col below the N ridge to the Van de Mez valley and over screes to the foot of the climb. In general the route lies to the L of the big chimney system with occasional excursions into it to avoid serious difficulties.

Two rope lengths in the chimney lead up to an OH. Continue by a series of cracks for 2 or 3 rope lengths, first to break out R and then to regain the chimney bed above the OH. Next, scramble up on the L and climb the main chimney for 4 or 5 pitches where it splits the steeper walls of the face (smooth chimney climbing, IV and V, mainly wet). Break out L for one pitch and climb the steep wall above, which is split by an obvious groove (V). Turn the loose OH above either on the L or R (V). Traverse L and return R above the steep wall on to easy ground. Easy ribs to the L of the main chimney are followed for about 200m to vertical rock. Move R into the chimney which is climbed for 45m. Now move out L and climb a series of steep cracks and chimneys for about 4 pitches (IV+). These lead to a scree terrace on the L. Move L round to the back of the obvious detached pinnacle.

Climb straight up slabby walls for 3-4 pitches (mainly IV, but VI at the top). The last pitch may be avoided by climbing the chimney immediately to the R.

The obvious steep chimney crack is climbed for several pitches (V, V+) until easy ledges break out L. Slant up L for about 75m under steep walls until a narrow traverse leads for one pitch to the bottom of the exit gully. This is entered by a short, wet slab (V) and followed for 4 pitches (V) to easy rocks close to the summit.

NORTH RIDGE
Gilberti, Soravito, 1932.

A long, serious free climb on a magnificent natural line up the highest face in the Dolomites. The rock is mostly very good, stances and bivouac sites excellent. The climb is in four sections. First, the lower buttress covered with scrub thicket and leading to a large shoulder. Then a steeper section to the second shoulder, also vegetated. Next a series of chimneys to the R of the ridge leading to the top of a tower. Finally a steep 200m step including some of the hardest climbing on the route.

Base – Val di San di Lucarno 1¼hr to the start 1700m 12hr

2.37
V+
21

Approach as for N face until at the foot of the N ridge. From the saddle, which is reached by a traverse L on loose rock from the gully, climb a 25m corner in the edge of the ridge, which is wide at this point (V-). Climb straight up the ridge, sometimes on the L, sometimes on the R, for 200m, to a large shoulder covered with dwarf pines (IV/ V). Climb over the vegetation to where the ridge steepens again. Climb the ridge in the direction of the second shoulder (IV in places with a final pitch of V+). This point needs to be reached in four hours from the start of climbing to avoid a bivouac.

Over this second shoulder the ridge now becomes OHing and is by-passed by a large chimney and gully line on the R. Climb diagonally to the R and up the chimney and gully system, for 110m (II). At its end, climb back up and L to the ridge. Climb the L-hand side of a small, leaning pillar on the ridge. Make a wide stride from its top to reach the wall of the ridge and traverse 25m to the R, first horizontally and then ascending (V), to reach a crack system. Climb this for 80m to a step in the ridge (from where it is possible to see the last steep step of 200m). Continue up the ridge. A further pillar is climbed on its L (good bivouac site), to the foot of the last steep section (IV and V up to here). Now climb a crack, OHing in part, for 60m (V) to reach a wide ledge (bivouac possibilities). From here traverse 10m down and to the R to reach an OHing crack. Climb this for 20m (V). Then a few m down and to the R to reach another OHing crack, which is climbed for 30m (first section VI-, the crux, then V+) to a stance. From the stance, climb 6m to the L and then 25m up over a slabby wall (very exposed,V). Continue up the slabby wall to a small crack then higher to a ledge (80m,V). Now zig-zag up the closing wall. Then move to the L and up the ridge (V+). From here, without difficulty, climb up to reach the big terrace which lies to the N of the summit. (From here it is possible to traverse R and reach the descent route). Straight up and over easy rock to the summit (I,II).

DESCENT

2.38 This is well marked. Follow the W ridge to the F d Pizon – bivouac box (30min). There are three via ferrata routes from this bivouac. All lead to the Scarpa hut. The most direct goes S to the L down a gully to a grass ridge 300m below, steeply down to a parallel gully to the L then across Malga Losch to the Scarpa hut (1742m). Then to the valley at Frassene by path 771. (3-4hr)

Geografica 1:25000 sheet 7

The Catinaccio (Rosengarten) is situated E of Bol⁄ano and being
fairly low with few N face routes it comes into condition early in the
season. Many of the routes are short and of an amenable standard and
it is a good area for a first visit to the Dolomites. Access is easy and
most routes are possible in a day from a hut or camp site. Classic
routes like the Steger and those on the Vajolet Towers can get
crowded in good weather.

HUTS

Ciampedie Hut 1998m Approaches– i) from Vigo di Fassa by path 544
(1½hr), ii) from Vigo di Fassa by cablecar, iii) from Pera by path 543
(2hr)

Gardeccia Hut 1949m This hut and the neighbouring Stella Alpina hut
are both private and have a big parking area. It is an ideal base for
many of the routes in the area. Easy access to the Crepa di Socorda
and all the Catinaccio E face routes. Approach by foot (2hr) or car
from Mazzin (6.5km). Note that the road is closed at 8am, after which
there is a taxi service

Catinaccio Hut 1900m Private. 10min walk S from the Gardeccia Hut

Vajolet Hut 2243m Good access to Vajolet Towers and Punta Emma.
For approach see Hut Links below

Alberto Hut 2600m (Gartl Hut) Stands at the summit of the scree shoot
of the Gartl. Easy access to Vajolet Towers. For approach see Hut
Links below

Passo Santner Hut 2741m Small, private

Fronza Huts 2339m (A Fronza alle Coronelle, Coronelle or
Rosengarten hut). For routes on Roda di Vael and La Sforcella and
easy routes on the Catinaccio W Face. Approaches– i) from road near
Passo Nigra by cablecar, ii) from Costalunga Pass by path 552 then
549 (2½)

Paolina Hut 2125m Private. Open all year. For Roda di Vael routes.
Approaches– i) from W of Costalunga Pass by chairlift, ii) from

Costalunga Pass by path 552 (1hr), iii) from Roda di Vael hut

Roda di Vael Hut 2280m For Cima dei Mugoni routes. Approach from Costalunga Pass by path 548 (1¾hr)

Bergamo Hut 2134m (Valbona, Grassleiten hut). For Cima Val Bona routes. Approach from San Cipriano by path 3 then 3a (3½hr)

Antermoia Hut 2496m Approach from Campitello by paths 577,580 (4hr)

Principe Hut 2601m (Passo Principe hut). Very small private bar/hut

HUT LINKS

Gardeccia to: Vajolet (546) 1hr←45min, Fronza (550 via P d Coronelle 2630m) 2½hr←2hr, Roda di Vael (541 via P Cigolade 2561m) 2½hr←1½hr, Antermoia (583) 3½hr←3hr

Catinaccio to: Ciampedie (540) 45min←45min

Ciampedie to: Roda di Vael (545) 1½hr←1hr

Roda di Vael to: Paolina (549,539) 45min←45min, Fronza (549) 1½hr←1½hr, Fronza (541,549 via P d Vaiolon 2550m) 2½hr←2½hr

Paolina to: Fronza (552,549) 1hr←1hr

Fronza to: Alberto (550,542) S via P Santner 2741m). Steep ice gully! 2hr←1½hr

Vajolet to: Alberto (542) 1hr←1hr, Principe (584) 1¼hr←45min

Principe to: Antermoia (584) 1hr←1¼hr, Antermoia by via ferrata over Catinaccio d'Antermoia 3004m 3hr←3½hr, Bergamo (554, 3A) 30min←45min

Roda di Vael 2806m

SOUTH-WEST FACE
Dibona, Verzi, Broome, Corning, 1908.

This is the only relatively easy route on the impressive 'Rotwand'. The climb is pleasant and on reasonably good rock. It reaches the broken corner on the R of the face by a grey pillar and follows a chimney system to the S ridge only a short walk from the summit.

Base hut – Paolina 15min to the start 400m 4hr

3.01 Reach the face by following path 549 and then heading up the screes.
IV Start at the R end of the wall below easy, scree covered grey slabs.
23 Climb these and the sound, grey, slabby ramp above (120m,II,III).
Above take the middle of three cracks (IV+) for 40m to a platform.
Traverse 4m L and climb a white/yellow, loose wall (20m,IV) to a
stance. Climb a narrow chimney (30m) to a detached slab. Up this
(IV) and a narrower chimney to a wide ledge (IV-). Move R 10m and
climb the grey wall to reach the ridge by the pillar. Follow a zig-zag
crack over a block and so in two pitches (IV,II) to the S ridge.

WEST FACE (BUHLWEG)
Brandler, Hasse, 1958.

*The famous 'Rotwand' has at least five routes, all but 3.01 are hard, often
with some aid climbing but have now been climbed free or nearly free. This
is the best of the five giving excellent free and/or some artificial climbing. It
takes the challenge of the main wall but has a dangerous poised flake in the
lower wall.*

Base hut – Paolina 45min to the start 350m 10hr

3.02 Start at the foot of the chimney to the R of the obvious grey pedestal at
VIII the foot of the face.
VI/A1
23 1 40m Climb the chimney (II) and the wall on the L (IV-) to the top
of the pedestal

2 35m Step across the gap to the obvious thin crack. Climb this (VII
or A1/V+) to a stance on the R

3 35m Easily R (III) to a steeper move (IV+) and stance

4 35m Go direct up the wall (V) then either climb a corner or the
wall on its L (V+)

5 30m Move up into a white corner (V) and then go R to a flake (VI)

6 15m Continue to a precarious stance at the top of the dangerously
poised flake (V+)

7 25m Climb the crack above direct (VI+ or A1/V+)

8 25m Continue diagonally R up the vertical wall (VIII or A1) to a
stance on a ledge near a niche

9 30m Step R and climb an exposed wall (VII or A1)

10 25m Continue in the same line moving L at the end (VII or A1) to
a stance near a slight ledge

11 25m Move up to a crack (VII or A1), climb this (VI+ or A1), step L 2m to a resting place then easier up R (V)

12 20m Turn the bulge above on the L (VI- or A0) to reach easier climbing diagonally L (IV/V)

13 25m Climb a slanting corner, step R then direct to a stance (IV)

14 30m Move up R (IV) to reach a ledge leading easily R (route book)

15 40m Move up a ramp L to reach an awkward crack (VII- or V/A1) and continue (VI or A1) R to the ridge

40m easy walk L to the summit cairn.

WEST FACE (MAESTRI)
Maestri, Baldessari, 1960.

This route takes the dièdre on the L of the face. Mostly artificial. Just to its R is the Direct, a purely aid route straight up the wall (Via del Concilio, Franceschi, 1962).

Base hut – Paolina 45min to the start 400m 10hr

3.03 Start up the large dièdre below the black roof. Climb it (V/A1,100m).
V/A2 Traverse R just below the roof to reach a second dièdre. Climb this
23 (A2,80m) to a ledge. Continue by a steep crack (A1) and leading to the black water streaks. Continue to a small stance between these steaks and some others further L. Traverse 25m L up to a gully and the end of the difficulties.

WEST FACE (SCHROTT-ABRAM)
Schrott, Abram, 1967.

The route follows the big dièdre on the L of the Maestri Route. It goes through the black overhangs on the R, traverses back L above them and finishes up the Eisenstecken Route.

Base hut – Paolina 45min to the start 350m 10hr

3.04 Start 100m L of the Maestri Route and climb the dièdre, of which the
V/A3 first 60m are loose, for about 150m (V,VI). From here climb up to the
23 OH and traverse R to the crack in the roof. Climb this and the corner above, to an obvious overhanging rake. Follow this into an easy-angled gully (A2,A3). Climb the gully for 45m to a black OH (IV). Climb up to the R of this and then up steep slabs above trending R (40m,V,V+). There is very little protection. Finally continue on the L (IV) to the top as for 3.05.

WEST FACE (EISENSTECKEN)
Eisenstecken, Rabanser, Oberrauch, 1947.

This is a popular free climb up the L-hand side of the 'Rotwand'. It is dangerous in rain but stances are mainly good and most of the poor rock has been cleaned off.

Base hut – Paolina 45min to the start 350m 5hr

3.05
VI

Start on the L side of the face at a vertical chimney which leads to a black roof.

1 20m Climb the chimney (IV,V)

2 30m Continue past a bulge (V)

3 30m Reach a yellow corner on the R. Climb this (V-)

4 40m The steep chimney/crack above leads to a stance by a jammed block (V/VI)

5 40m Move up to and round the roof above on the L (VI-,VI or A1,V-)

6 35m Climb the black chimney (V,VI-)

7 30m Traverse R across a slab (IV-) then direct by a crack (IV+) to a ledge

8 35m Take the dièdre on the R (IV) and then move L (V+) to reach a slabby area

9 50m Poorly protected climbing up the slabs R (V)

10 40m Continue direct (V-,IV)

11 60m Move L round the edge and follow a gully (IV) past a bulge to the top.

DESCENT
3.06 An easy path leads N down the slope to the P Vaiolon from where path 511 leads back to the hut. (30min)

Cima Sud dei Mugoni 2734m

SOUTH-EAST FACE (ZENI-GROSS)
Zeni, Gross, 1963.

The SE face is an impressive vertical yellow wall facing the Roda di Vael hut. It dries quickly and is ideal early or late in the season or after bad weather. Bivouacs are possible under the boulders at the foot of the face.
    The main face has four hard routes, three following obvious weaknesses, the fourth taking the arête on the R of the face. The L edge of the face is also climbable at III (exposed) starting up two long black chimneys whilst the Vinatzer route (V+) climbs the SW wall to the R via a long dièdre.
    This route takes the corner and groove line on the L part of the wall.

Base hut – Roda di Vael 30min to the start 350m 6-9hr

3.07
V+/A2
24
Start a few m to the R of an obvious niche with a peg belay. Climb up R over grass-covered rock to a corner. Traverse 3m L to reach a crack. Climb up this and then move R to a short chimney which is followed to a pedestal. Traverse a little to the L on loose rock then climb a crack to the R. Continue L to a ledge, traverse 5m R and go straight up to a large niche. The major difficulties start here.
    Traverse 5m L and move up R on pegs (poor rock) to a second niche. This is followed by three strenuous pitches of artificial climbing with good stances ending in a niche. Traverse R to a ramp and follow it to its end. Climb to the R by short walls to the foot of an impressive, OHing corner. Climb the corner with a hanging stance at mid-height and leave it by moving R on very poor rock, climbing first by a crack and then by an OHing chimney. Follow easy rock to the ridge. From here climb easily to the summit.

SOUTH-EAST FACE (EISENSTECKEN)
Eisenstecken, Pircher, Rabanser, 1946.

This fine route takes a diagonal line up the lower part of the face and then breaks R through the final OHing section. It has been climbed free except for the final traverse which was avoided.

Base hut – Roda di Vael 30min to the start 300m 6hr

3.08
V+/A1
24
Start at the large boulder bridging the path near the start of the Grand Dièdre.

1 40m Climb to the top of the boulder from the L (IV+)

2 30m Follow a chimney leading L (IV,V-)

3   40m Continue up a chimney to an OH (IV+). Pass this (A1/V) and continue on poor rock (V)

4   40m Continue via a chimney (V-)

5   40m Another chimney in places narrowing to a crack (V+/A0)

6   50m Climb a steep slab to a good grassy ledge (IV)

7   25m Ignore an exit R from the ledge and instead climb a corner crack to a pulpit (V) and then continue to a black niche on the R (V+)

8   40m Move out R from the niche across a smooth slab (A1) for 15m then direct up a crack (A1) to a jammed block

9   25m Easily up loose rock (III) to the ridge.

SOUTH-EAST FACE (GRAND DIEDRE)
De Franceschi, Innerkoffler, 1955.

This route follows the corner just R of the great arch. It may now go free.

Base hut – Roda di Vael 30min to the start 350m 6hr

3.09
V+/A1
24
Climb the corner to the first roof. Climb this (V+) and continue to a second OH and cave stance. Turn this, first direct and then diagonally R (A1) to a loose stance. Regain the corner and continue to a dark OH. Climb the groove for 50m (A1) to a poor stance in a niche. Traverse L on grassy, grey, rock, then up and R to above the final OH. Easier grey rock up a gully leads to the summit ridge.

SOUTH-EAST PILLAR
Aste, Stenico, 1961.

Base hut – Roda di Vael 30min to the start 300m

3.10
VI/A2
24
This hard route starts 50m R of the Grand Dièdre and follows the arête for two thirds of its height. The first section is free but with loose rock. Then a section on poor pegs and bolts. Finally it breaks L to join the final pitches of the Grand Dièdre.

NORTH-EAST FACE
Haupt, 1910.

A fine exposed route in a good position.

Base hut – Roda di Vael 1¼hr to the start 200m 3hr

3.11 From the hut go up towards P Cigolade under the NE face, to the end
II+ of the gully coming down from the col between the E and S summits,
where a free-standing buttress rises out of the scree. To the L, behind
this buttress, there is another, higher rock tooth with several towers.
Its S face is split by a crack. Start the NE face of the S summit
opposite this tooth. A 40m chimney is avoided by a diagonal crack.
Above climb a steep groove for 60m; 2m from the edge of the E
buttress make a very delicate traverse R and up. Then go back easily
L towards the E buttress to a thin crack. Climb this for about 25m to
the buttress. Now climb first on the buttress, then take a broad gully
to the SE Face and continue for 60m to the top.

DESCENT
3.12 Go down easy-angled, scree covered rock to the NW to a cairn. Then
I descend easy chimneys and terraces to the upper cwm. Descend the
cwm to a path on the R which leads to the hut. (1hr)

La Sforcella (Tscheiner Spitze) 2791m

EAST FACE
Liefmann, 1910.

A varied and interesting route.

Base hut – Roda di Vael 1½hr to the start 180m 3hr

3.13 From the hut start up the path to the P Cigolade (241), but fork L to
III+ reach the big hollow between Cima Mugoni and La Sforcella – the
Gran Busa di Vael. Head up L to the foot of the steep E face which has
an obvious white patch near the centre. Close to the white patch is a
wide, snow filled gully, which descends from the large tower on the
ridge between the E and N faces.
From the foot of the face keep to the L at first, then traverse over
steep crags to the R to the mouth of the gully and up this into the
mountain. Climb the gully up to a gap on the L. Descend 2m on the
other side, climb up to a ledge under an OH and follow this to the R
(N) to a crack. The crack is formed by an immense slab leaning
against the wall. Climb up the crack, with a chockstone, to the top of
a slab, and straight up the wall on good holds to the ridge. Climb the
groove on the other side of the ridge which leads to the E summit,
then N into the gap and on to the main peak.

WEST FACE
Langes, Merlet, 1921.

One of the classic climbs of the area on good rock.

Base hut – Fronza 45min to the start 300m 4hr

3.14 Follow the higher path (549) until below the face. The R-hand side of
IV+ the yellow wall is cut by a gully slanting up to the L. Start up grey
rocks on the L for 50m to a large ledge and traverse 20m across this to
the R. Follow the gully for 10m to a tower and then for another 10m.
Traverse 6m L under the grey wall. Climb straight up the wall for
50m to a small yellow niche then up the broken gully until it finishes.
Continue straight up for 30m to a ledge and follow this to its end.
Climb straight up again for 40m to another narrow ledge and continue
up broken rocks to the large terrace under the final summit walls.
First climb 6m straight up then diagonally L for 20m to a crack which
goes up the yellow summit walls. Climb the crack for three pitches to
the summit.

DESCENT
3.15 By Ordinary Route. From the main summit descend easy rocks into
II the gully which descends from the gap between the two summits.
Climb down the gully, keeping to the L (one short difficult section),
and then cross the gully to the R. Descend an icy groove, then
traverse back across the gully and up to a gap in the ridge on the L of
the gully. Continue down the L-hand side of the gully, branch off
down a subsidiary gully to the L and down this to the foot of the NW
face. Join the path leading back to the Roda di Vael Hut. (2hr)

Catinaccio 2981m

*The Catinaccio peak itself is basically a north-south ridge with a
magnificent E face towering above the Vajolettal. From its S peak (2731m)
it rises to the highest Central summit, continues to the N peak (2911m) and
finishes with the much lower Punta Emma which overlooks the Gartl and
faces the Vajolet Towers. Whilst the major routes are on the E face and
Punta Emma the descents and easy routes are found on the much shorter W
face above the P Santner. All the routes on the E face are described from
the Gardeccia hut, but the Vajolet hut could also be used as a base. For the
W face routes the Alberto hut is the best base.*

SOUTH-EAST FACE OF SOUTH PEAK
Hepperger, Mayrgundter, 1926.

Pleasant free climbing by a good natural line. Of a lower standard of difficulty than the other E face routes. The climb is at the L-hand end of the E face. It can easily be identified by a massive pinnacle formed by two converging groove lines which meet 180m below the summit. The climb follows the L-hand line.

Base hut – Gardeccia 1hr to the start 500m 5hr

3.16 Start from the L of the groove on the L of the giant pinnacle.
IV Continue up grooves and chimneys on good rock to the summit of the
20 pinnacle. From the top the route ascends the final wall by a series of grooves and chimneys. The way is obvious and the route is easy to follow. Continue to the summit.

EAST FACE DIRECT OF SOUTH PEAK
Haider, Machl, 1965.

A fine climb on good rock similar to the Steger (3.19) but not quite so sustained. The rock is good. The climb takes a direct line up the steep E face to the S summit.

Base hut – Gardeccia 1hr to the start 600m 6hr

3.17 Start under the S summit and a little to the L. Climb a gully system
V (III and IV) upwards for 5 pitches to a yellow overlap which crosses
20 the wall. Surmount the overlap and hand-traverse to a corner crack (V). Climb up this for 25m. Continue R to a short chimney. After climbing it go diagonally L to a rib. Climb up this to an OH which is overcome from L to R. Now follow a short chimney with a jammed block and continue further to a small ramp. Follow it for 30m to the R. Climb up for 8m to a yellow cave. Climb L to a prominent pillar and further to a black corner. Now climb R up walls to a L-sloping ramp. Slant R for 15m. Climb an OH (pegs). Continue straight up over slabs, crossing a small terrace, to reach a black trough. Leave it on the L and climb to reach a ledge (approx 50m under the summit). Climb a yellow chimney/crack for 10m and then over slabs tending to the R emerging on the ridge, which is followed for 30m to the summit.

DESCENT FROM SOUTH PEAK
3.18 Either descend easily (II and III) down the S ridge (1hr) OR from the S summit scramble along the ridge N to the central summit and descend by the Ordinary Route. (1½hr)   75

EAST FACE DIRECT OF CENTRAL PEAK (STEGER)
Steger, Weisinger, Masi, Dari, Lechner, 1929.

One of the really great routes of the area. Very popular, usually climbed with the aid of an occasional peg on the early crux and the final two pitches. An early start is essential to avoid queues in good weather. The route follows the obvious crack in the lower part of the face, then the more clearly defined chimney in the middle and finally a diagonal slab, a steep wall and a chimney to the ridge near the summit. The moves to the R after the first section are easily missed due to misleading pegs.

Base hut – Gardeccia 1hr to the start 600m 6hr

3.19
V+
20.
Start by climbing easily from the L to the foot of the obvious grooves which split the centre of the face. Climb 40m (III) to the foot of the L-hand grey/black dièdre. (A dièdre further R is the much harder Vinatzer variation). Climb this easily at first then at 30m pass a protruding yellow block and a yellow OH (V). 6m above the OH traverse L to the edge of the dièdre (easily missed) and climb this to a stance. Move straight up to a black crack, and follow this over an initial bulge and then two more OHing sections to a stance under a large yellow OH (40m, V+, V). Avoid this roof by a traverse R into the next crack, up to a cave then back L to the original crack (IV+). This bulges (V) and is climbed to easier ground.

Continue for 70m to a stance below three cracks (IV). The L one is black, the centre one a steep chimney/crack in a dièdre and the R-hand one is a loose yellow crack slanting R. Climb the R-hand one for 6m, step R to a black dièdre/crack which is followed for 60m (V) to a long chimney in the middle of the face.

Follow the chimney for 230m. First climb a long smooth chimney (V), next pass under a large chockstone to an easier section (III), finally a steep corner (IV,V). Escape is possible L from here (II,III,IV- then easy).

Move Rwards below the final yellow walls, go over an awkward bulge (V-) and traverse R to a stance. Continue Rwards for two pitches (50m,IV) above the large yellow OHs, to a small stance directly below the yellow summit chimney. Climb the steep wall (30m,V) to the chimney and climb this (wide bridging) (40m,V+) to the ridge. Follow this easily to the summit.

DESCENT FROM CENTRAL PEAK
3.20
By N ridge and W face. Scramble along the ridge N past a small col to a prominent col above a gully descending W. Go down this for 12m,

step out into the true R (N) bank, bear R for a short distance until easy ground leads back L to a chimney near its foot. Descend snow to the Santner Pass (small bar!). From here follow paths N to the Alberto hut then path 542 and 546 to the Gardeccia hut. (1hr to Santner Pass)

OTHER ROUTES ON CENTRAL PEAK

On the east face of the central peak various lines cover the face to the L of the Steger. Some long traverses are possible, whilst the Livanos Route climbs a parallel line to the L of the Steger at around V+, finishing directly at the summit, and the Barbacetta Route (Via CAI A A) takes a hard line up the arête to the R. A little further R the Deye/Peters Route (V) climbs cracks and chimneys up the big water streaked wall to the large scree hollow above (often wet).

SOUTH-EAST DIEDRE OF NORTH PEAK

This dièdre is the prominent corner on the R of the wet wall below theN summit. It gives pleasant free climbing.

Base hut – Gardeccia 1hr to the start 400m 5hr

3.21
V+/A1
22
Start by traversing across an easy ramp to reach the foot of a thin groove on the L of the main one. Go up this to a small ledge (V,V+). Climb the slab above and traverse into the main dièdre (V+). Follow the main dièdre for two pitches to a poor stance below a large and very loose roof (IV,V). Move diagonally L up steep grey compact slabs and then back R over the OH into a niche (V+). Go up the crack on the L to a ledge (IV,V) and up the corner above for one pitch to another ledge (V,V+). From the top of the yellow pedestal, traverse R across a wall (V+/A1) and then climb up two steep grey cracks (V+) to a stance on the main face. Traverse R along the ledge and climb up a groove to the top of a large pedestal (III). Climb diagonally R to reach the summit ridge (II,III).

EAST FACE DIRECT OF NORTH PEAK (VIA OLYMPIA)
Di Francheschi, Romanin, 1960.

An exposed climb, mainly artificial on bolts on the lower part, which climbs the steep wall between the SE Dièdre and the icy gully next to the Punta Emma. It is becoming a popular route and may include much more free climbing.

Base hut – Gardeccia 45min to the start 600m with only 250m of hard climbing 5-8hr

3.22 From the hut reach the grassy rake which runs below the yellow face
V+/A2 beneath the N summit. Scramble up to the well-defined dièdre facing
22 L. Climb this (IV and V) to a higher terrace almost in the centre of the
face. Climb a steep, loose crack directly above (45m,V+,crux) to a
large ledge with a bolt belay. Directly above is the yellow wall with the
obvious line of bolts starting 6m R of the belay. Climb these for 40m
to above the initial OHs, to a hanging stance on the vertical section.
Ascend a further 25m to a small stance and bolt belay.

Above, pass a yellow flake, then follow the line of bolts R, with
finally 12m free to a large stance. Now go up to the L to below a black
OH, which is surmounted to the L on bolts. Continue at first to the
L, then back R finishing at a niche below the crest. This is the end of
the serious difficulty.

From the crest, head diagonally across the basin (II) and gain
the N ridge of the Catinaccio fairly high up.

DESCENT FROM NORTH PEAK
3.23 From the summit follow the S ridge to join the normal route, or from
the N ridge climb down the rake (II) which starts about 50m above
(N) of the Forcella Punta Emma. (1hr to Santner Pass or Alberto Hut)

Catinaccio West Face

*Various climbs are possible up the walls R and L of the descent route. All
can be reached from the Alberto Hut or the Santner Pass in about 15min.*

NORMAL ROUTE
150m 1½hr

3.24 Start up the gully above the Santner Pass then take the L bank.
III Return to the gully for the last 12m. Follow the ridge N to the
summit.

PEDERIVA ROUTE
150m 1½hr

3.25 Climb the face a few metres R of the Normal Route. Take the N ridge
IV+ to the summit.

PIAZ-DELAGO ROUTE
150m 2hr

3.26
IV+
A good route directly up to the summit. Start up a chimney and continue by a groove which finishes just L of the summit.

DULFER ROUTE
150m 2hr

3.27
IV−
Takes the wall further R, just L of an icy gully and finishing near the summit.

VIA ANNA MARIA
150m 2hr

3.28
IV+
Start as for the Dulfer but traverse the ice gully to the buttress on its R and climb this direct.

NORTH-WEST FACE
Vinatzer, Peristi, 1935.

This is a short hard training climb up the big face well to the L of the descent route, above the Alberto hut.

Base hut – Alberto 15min to the start 300m 3hr

3.29
VI
V/A1
Climb the obvious chimney which splits the face, becoming a narrow crack higher up, for 140m to the foot of a yellow face (II,III,IV) (It is possible to escape by an easier route from here (IV-) up the rocks to the R of the yellow wall). Climb the thin crack (V,IV) for 15m to red/yellow rocks, then 30m on red rock up the cracked corner to a niche (VI or A1,V/A1).

Climb the OH above on the R (A1) and continue by a crack for 25m (VI- or A1/V) to a second niche. Climb the OH above for 10m to grey rock (V), then take the wall near the crack for 70m (V-,IV) until the difficulty decreases (III) and the crest of the ridge is reached just below the N summit.

Punta Emma 2617m

SOUTH-EAST FACE
Masè Dari, Bernard, 1929.

A free climb which climbs the R wall of the gully which falls S from the Forcella Punta Emma.

Base hut – Vajolet 30min to the start 400m 4hr

3.30
V–

From the Vajolet Hut traverse easily on to the ledge which runs completely round the foot of the Punta Emma. Start directly below the F Punta Emma. Go up either chimney to a large ledge below the mouth of the Forcella (30m). Step R into a prominent corner above which is a steep crack. Climb this to a large ledge (30m). From here an obvious wide crack ascends obliquely R. Follow this easily for 60m until out on the centre of the face. Go straight up 15m to a small pinnacle, with a peg in the wall just above it (the L-hand of several pinnacles). Now go 3m L, then up 7m to another small pinnacle. Traverse R round a bulge, then immediately back L to follow a rising traverse L to an OHing black wall (spike, peg belay). Now climb the crack to the L, traverse 3m R past a yellow bulge, then up obliquely L over a yellow OH to a stance. Climb the black groove above past an OH to a large black chimney. Go up this 60m to easy ground. 100m or so of scrambling remain to the summit.

EAST FACE (STEGER)
Steger, Weisinger, 1929.

A popular free climb offering a good alternative to the Piaz route (3.25).

Base hut – Vajolet 30min to the start 300m 3hr

3.31
V

Start directly on the path below the Piaz Crack at the foot of a Lward sloping ramp.

1 180m Follow the ramp L (II,III) to a stance below and R of a leaning pillar

2 25m Climb a corner (IV) stepping L to a stance

3 20m Do not continue up the corner but move L again to a stance near the top of the pillar. (The Aste Route (V) goes L up exposed walls and chimneys)

4 25m Diagonally R across a smooth slab (IV/V) and up a little to a stance below a corner

5   20m Climb the corner (IV+) and move R over a bulge to a stance further R

6   35m Go direct to a niche, step R and climb a wall (V-) and a Lward leaning crack (V) to a col

7   40m Either climb the dièdre above (IV+,V) or move L and take the black crack (IV)

8   100m Easy climbing (II) to the summit.

NORTH-EAST FACE (PIAZ CRACK)
Piaz, 1900.

This is a strenuous free climb up the prominent crack which goes up the centre of the face when viewed from the Vajolet hut. Not recommended in wet weather.

Base hut – Vajolet 30min to the start 250m 3hr

3.32 Start by scrambling up L and traversing to near the foot of the crack. Thread belay

V/A0
25

1   35m Climb up easily L (III,I) to the start of the main crack

2   35m Climb the corner crack (III) past an OH to the R at 25m (V or IV/A0)

3   35m Continue up the crack (V or IV/A0) and a narrow chimney with a bulge (IV) to a scree ledge

4   35m Continue slightly L (III) by a ramp then on the L wall (III+) and finally back to the corner (III)

5   20m Move up to a thread, step L and then direct to a hollow above (III)

6   100m Easier climbing to the summit (I,III-).

NORTH FACE (EISENSTECKEN)
Eisenstecken, Sepp, 1946.

This attractive hard route takes the wall to the R of the Piaz Crack (3.26) up extremely compact rock.

Base hut – Vajolet 30min to the start 200m 3hr

3.33 Start on easy ground as for 3.26 until below the smooth N face slabs

V/A0
25

1   30m Move up L and climb a chimney (IV)

2 80m Continue R along a great detached flake (II/III) to a stance by a pinnacle

3 40m Move R to a dièdre. Up this and over a roof on the R (VI/A0) then by a slab to a stance on the L below a crack

4 40m Climb the crack on the R of some pinnacles (IV), step L, back R (V) and then direct up a smooth slab (V+). Now traverse down L and finally up L to a ledge. All this pitch is below the fina impending OH

5 40m Move L again up a smooth slab (V) and finally over a roof (VI) to easy ground.

DESCENT

3.34 Scramble down the NW ridge. After 30m a notch in the ridge is reached and descent is possible towards the F Punta Emma. At the end of the ledge leading L for 10m a large abseil ring will be found in the wall. Make a 25m abseil to the gap then descend easily N down the gully. (1hr)

Vajolet Towers

Above the Alberto hut to the N rise the famous towers: from L to R, the Delago, Stabeler and Winkler with the smaller Piaz in the foreground.

Base hut – Alberto 10–30min to the start

Torre Delago 2790m

SOUTH-WEST RIDGE

Piaz, Jori, Glaser, 1911.

An exposed and exciting climb.

120m 2hr

3.35 From below the S face scramble up and L via a terrace to the foot of
IV   the ridge (15min). Climb directly up the ridge passing a difficult whit
26   slab to reach a small stance on a flake of rock in a spectacular position
      (40m,IV). Continue up the ridge climbing on the L and then moving
      R to reach a good ledge. The yellow OH above is turned on

the R and then the ridge climbed direct until it widens to form two vertical corners. Either is climbable to another ledge. A few metres L a crack leads to the summit.

SOUTH FACE (PREUSS CHIMNEY and PIAZ FINISH)
Preuss, Relly, Piaz, 1911.

A good combination. Direct and sustained, this route splits the S face about 10m L of the Delago Chimney (3.37), joins that route for its middle pitches and then finishes direct up the wall above R.

120m 2-3hr

3.36 Start up a short OH chimney and follow the crack for 60m to a shelf
V– (IV). Move L and climb the R-hand polished chimney above (IV+, as
26 for 3.37) over a chockstone to a belay on the L (25m). The Piaz crack, rotten and OHing at the start, lies directly above and is avoided on the L. Climb by layback (5m,V) to reach shallow chimneys on the L, traverse R to a thin crack and climb it to a peg (V). Traverse R to a chimney which leads to the top.

SOUTH FACE (DELAGO CHIMNEY)
Delago, 1895.

A classic route taking the chimney between the Delago and Stabeler Towers then the easiest line up the upper half of the S face.

120m 2hr

3.37 Start on the line of the chimneys up an initial OHing chimney (12m)
V and then follow the line of weakness for 50m (two variations are
26 possible on the R wall). Now move L onto the broad shelf which cuts the S face and climb a polished chimney with a chockstone (IV+). Exit L at the top and take the corner crack on the L (IV) to the ridge just below the summit. Continue on the L (III) to the top.

DESCENT
3.38 By abseils on the Stabeler face (35m) and then on the R wall of the gully (fixed rings). (1hr)

Torre Stabeler 2805m

SOUTH FACE
Fehrmann, Perry-Smith, 1908.

This recommended route follows cracks and chimneys up the centre of the steep S face.

120m 2hr

3.39 Scramble up to the foot of the central crack. It is smooth and tiring
IV with an OH at 10m. Continue to a small terrace below a red roof
26 (III,IV-). Move L and continue up a steep dièdre (IV). Continue to a
ledge below a prominent OHing crack (IV-). Avoid this by a traverse
then climb the wall by a groove, moving back L to a col. Continue by
the Ordinary Route to the summit.

Variations include a harder start just R of the normal, or a
scramble up well L followed by a traverse and a direct route up the
OHing crack.

DESCENT
3.40 Abseil 35m down the gully on the N side of the tower to a ledge.
Follow this round to the col between the Delago and Stabeler Towers
Abseil down the gully. (1hr)

Torre Winkler 2800m

SOUTH-EAST CRACK (WINKLER CRACK)
Winkler, 1887.

150m 1½hr

3.41 The route starts on the S face at the foot of the gully between the
IV Winkler and Stabeler Towers. Climb a rib to the R for 40m to the
26 second ledge which traverses across the S face. Follow this to its
R-hand end and climb a narrow chimney (Winkler Crack, IV) or the
easier wall to its R (III). Continue up chimneys above (III) to a
shoulder on the E face. Climb a series of grooves and cracks in the L
edge or the big loose looking corner on the R for 20m to the summit.

SOUTH FACE DIRECT
Steger, Weisinger, Masè Dari, Paluselli, 1929.

A fine climb following the prominent crack on the L of the S face. It is well protected with pegs and threadable wedges or big chocks.

110m 3hr

3.42 Start from the second ledge of the Winkler Crack (3.41, 40m). Climb
V+ 30m to a good stance below a yellow OH. Climb the OH and go R
26 over a second OH to a small stance (10m). Climb the steep crack
above for 20m and then traverse L to a large stance below a large OH.
Climb the crack to the L of the OH in two pitches to the top. Beware
old wedges!

EAST RIDGE
Piaz, Del Torso, Maraini, 1935.

*This exposed route on good rock is reached from the Winkler Crack (3.41)
traverse.*

100m 3hr

3.43 Continue the traverse of the Winkler Crack descending slightly to the
V scree shoulder below the SE ridge. Descend a chimney for 15m onto
the NE face and traverse R 10m to the centre of a terrace. Climb up
into a L facing corner and use a crack on its L wall, stepping R at the
top. Continue R to a stance in a cave (25m). Move L and go up to
another shallow cave (10m). A few m L is a thin crack. Climb this to a
ledge in the ridge and follow this in the R-hand side to a good ledge.
Step L and climb a thin crack (peg) to a large ledge and pinnacle belay
(40m). Continue easily to the shoulder on the Ordinary Route and
follow this for 30m to the summit.

NORTH-EAST FACE
Del Torso, Maraini, Piaz, 1932.

*This hard and strenuous free climb starts from the F Winkler – the col to the
E of the Winkler Tower.*

Base hut– Alberto 45min to the start 150m 4hr

3.44 Scramble up to the obvious OHing yellow chimney. Climb the first
V+ short, loose, gently OHing chimney to a small ledge, and continue
with difficulty over the roof above to more chimneys and a good
stance on the L. Move L to a second OHing dièdre. Climb this (crux,
40m), and continue direct to a shoulder (120m from the start). From
here either traverse well to the R (N) to reach a large dièdre and follow
this to the gap between the summits, or, after a 10m traverse R, finish
by the E Ridge Route (3.43) which is much more appropriate.

DESCENT

3.45 Abseil down to the shoulder on the SE ridge (20m). Follow the ledge round to the R (N) descending slightly to reach a ledge facing the Stabeler Tower. Abseil down to the gap between the towers and then down the gully to reach the second ledge on the Ordinary Route and descend this. (1hr)

TRAVERSE OF THE VAJOLET TOWERS
Winkler, Stabeler, Delago

A justifiably famous expedition – prior knowledge of the Towers is an advantage.   5hr

3.46
IV
Take the Winkler Crack (IV) to the summit of the Winkler Tower. Abseil 20m to the shoulder on the SE ridge, and follow a ledge round to the R (N) to a ledge facing the Stabeler Tower. Abseil 35m into the gap and make a stride onto a small ledge on the Stabeler. Climb straight up a chimney/crack to a belay on a horizontal shoulder (30m). A second pitch in the same line leads to a belay on the true shoulder. Cross onto the main tower and traverse L behind a large block. One pitch to the summit. Descend by same route to the true shoulder and follow a ledge to the W to a stance between the Towers, or abseil from a notch on the summit down the N side to a ledge which leads to the same place. One pitch on the Delago side leads to the Pichl Crack. Either climb the crack (IV) or the less strenuous wall on the immediate R and so to the summit. Two abseils back down the same route and more abseils down the S face chimney.

Torre Piaz 2670m

Various short routes are found on this small peak.

SOUTH-WEST RIDGE
Interesting climbing on good rock.   60m

3.47
IV
Climb the ridge facing the hut.
Other routes are the NW Face (90m,V+) & the N Crack (40m,IV)

26

DESCENT
3.48 By abseil down E face.

26

Torre Est 2813m

SOUTH-EAST FACE
Piaz, Kronstein, Muller, 1907.

This climb on the tower to the E of the main Vajolet towers takes the obvious cleft, the Piaz Crack, well seen from the Vajolet Hut, in the lower cliff to the Torre Est, reached from the highest point of the scree. Escape is possible at the first terrace.

Base hut – Vajolet 30min to the start 450m 6hr

3.49 Climb the natural break to a grotto at the foot of the chimney (45m).
V Go over an initial OH into a deep cleft. The crack above overhangs a long way and is loose and strenuous. Above follow the loose gully to exit R on top of a yellow pillar. Continue up the L-hand side of the cleft, over two small OHs into a deep chimney. Climb up the L wall diagonally to a steep crack which runs up to the large roof above. Climb this to a good peg belay below the roof (extemely loose). The crux now follows. By an exposed traverse follow the roof round into the easy groove above. Climb this to the first terrace.

Cross the terrace Rwards and gain the second terrace by an easy groove. From this terrace, the deep chimney almost directly above is followed. If the top half is iced or wet an easier exit can be made by traversing L, at half-height, to the L ridge which is climbed to the third terrace. From here traverse R round the summit buttress and climb any of several easy cracks to the top.

DESCENT
3.50 Descend to the W on loose rock to the F Est and then down screes to the path. (50min)

Croda di Re Laurino 2813m

WEST FACE DIRECT
Rizzi, Rizzi, Munk, 1897.

This route lies on the wall below and to the W of the Vajolet Towers on the NW side. It is a good climb comparable to but easier than the classic S Face Route on Marmolada (7.06).

Base hut – Fronza 1hr to the start 500m 6hr

3.51 The route is reached by a long traverse N across the screes from
IV– the hut. It starts from the L end of the lower great terrace below

the face, directly below the gully which falls from the col S of the summit. It climbs the L side of the main face.

Start over slabs of white rock, then by dièdres go up and L to a rounded ridge. Then by scree ledges keeping L to a small col. Climb a difficult wall for about 50 or 60m then delicately R to a shoulder and along the crest. Abseil into the gully then climb up towards a big ledge, next take a smooth chimney and finally a wide, OHing, difficult chimney. Move R onto a ledge and from its middle go up to a small niche. Continue for 30m and then traverse for 40m to less difficult climbing leading to the SW summit. The main summit can be reached from the top of the difficult chimney by climbing up L.

DESCENT

3.52 Edwards down easy, loose rocks from the main summit. To descend to
II the Fronza hut from here via the P Santner follow the Via Ferrata (542). Beware the ice gully a little way down!

Cima Orientale di Val Bona 2705m

NORTH-WEST RIDGE
Dulfer, Schaarschmidt, Schroffenegger, 1912.

This fine route climbs the obvious ridge opposite the Bergamo Hut.

Base hut – Bergamo 20min to the start 450m 4hr

3.53 From the hut follow the steep path up the valley, cross the stream on
V the R and scramble up to easy slabs on the L of the ridge.

Start easily up the slabs to reach the ridge. Move R and up close to the ridge to the foot of a 20m wall. Climb this (V-) on the R to a yellow niche, and then traverse L round the ridge on small holds and go up a series of short cracks to a small stance. Continue up close to the ridge to a scree ledge, then L to a second yellow niche. Move L and climb the OH (IV+), then go straight up a crack with another OH to a large scree-covered slab, topped by an OH. Climb this and the wall above (V), and continue up the ridge, or on the L of it, to reach the higher W summit.

DESCENT

3.54 Traverse round the E summit and descend S to a chimney leading to a
II col. Descend the chimney, moving out R down broken walls to the col. Descend a gully to the E keeping R (S) of a rib in the lower part. (2hr)

Crepa di Socorda 2440m

SOUTH-WEST FACE DIRECT
Bernard, Tosco, Soraruf, 1933.

This fine free climb has given problems in the past due to wrong marking on guide book diagrams.

Base hut – Gardeccia 20min to the start 600m 7hr

3.55
V+
27
The Crepa di Socorda is a subsidiary peak in the Larsec group to the R (E) of the main valley. It is easily reached from the hut. Follow the path (583) round the valley until the rocks come down to it.

Start beside a square niche just R of the centre of the face. The large crack above, well seen from below, is the line of the route. Avoid the initial OHing chimney by slabs on the R, going diagonally from the niche for 25m. Now climb direct for 5m on undercuts (VI) and continue for 27m of very exposed climbing to a stance and spike belay. Above the crack becomes a corner with a yellow R wall and a grey/black wall on the L. Climb on the L for 20m (VI-) to a higher ledge. Move L 2m (VI) and climb for 40m up the crack in the OHing wall (VI- where the crack peters out.). Go directly up a groove for 22m to below an obvious OHing roof. An exposed 10m traverse L (VI) leads to a large cave. Follow a ledge diagonally R to a hollow above the OHing part of the face (end of main difficulties). 180m to here.

Follow easy rocks L for 150m over two large grassy terraces. Contour round the main face to the start of the crack which leads to the summit. Start in an earthy corner below a triangular block. The crack is followed completely, often with difficult but interesting climbing. At a large yellow scree-covered cave, climb the R wall and move back into the groove above. One more pitch on the L of the chimney leads to the summit ridge and another to the top.

DESCENT
3.56
I
Descend to the gap where the crack meets the ridge. Descend 10m towards a col and then traverse R on easy ledges. Descend towards the col and then follow the SE gully to the bottom R-hand side of the face. (1hr)

Geografica 1:25000 sheet 7

This group provides some of the longest routes in the Dolomites. The Sassolungo itself is a massive impressive rock peak dominating the scenery and rising steeply from the valley. The N face provides some 1000m rock routes and these are obviously a serious undertaking. On the S and W side of the group the mountains provide routes of varied lengths from the short routes of 200-350m on the Punta della Cinque Dita to longer routes up to 600m on Sasso Levante. Some of the routes on the Punta della Cinque Dita are short and provide a good introduction to the Dolomites for the less experienced climbers, particularly as they are within easy reach of the road. The Sella Pass is an ideal base with the Sella group on the E and Sassolungo group on the W.

HUTS

Sella Pass Hut 2183m. Open all year. Large, busy hut/hotel at top of Sella Pass giving easy access to Sella and Sassolungo groups. Booking essential. Camping possible in areas near hut. Many private huts etc nearby.

Demetz Hut 2681m. Small private hut on the F d Sassolungo. Popular bar. Approach from Sella hut by path 525 (1½hr) or gondola lift.

Vicenza (Langkofel) Hut 2253m. A popular busy hut with a bar. Booking advisable. Approaches– i)from Santa Cristina via Monte Pana by 525 (2½hr), ii)from Selva via Monte Pana by 525 (3hr) iii)from Sella hut via Demetz hut by 525 (2½hr)

Comici Hut 2153m. Small private hut with bar below N face of Sassolungo. Approach from Sella Pass by 526 (1hr)

Bivacco Guiliani 3096m. Bivouac hut with room for 5 SE of principal summit of Sassolungo. Stay here if no more than three hours of daylight left!

Sassolungo (Langkofel) 3179m

This is a big and complex mountain with various subsidiary summits providing peaks in their own right. It runs from SE to NW with first the Spallone del Sassolungo overlooking the Demetz hut, then a col and a high ridge, next a second col with the prominent bivouac hut near it and then the main summit. This has an East Tower and a North Tower each supported by pillars. Further NW is the West Tower and pillar and below the West Tower the Gran Campanile. Il Salame is NW of this peak. The NW face of the mountain is 1.5km long and over 1000m high. To the SW the Ordinary Route is long and complicated with possible snow or ice in places. In descent after one of the harder routes it can be difficult to follow and it is certainly advisable to spend a day on the easier routes getting to know the mountain and so avoid a later bivouac.

SOUTH-WEST FACE (ORDINARY ROUTE)
Grohmann and party, 1869.

A long and serious route with difficult route finding.

Base hut – Vicenza 30min to the start 800m 7hr

4.01 ORDINARY START
II+   From the Vicenza Hut head up the screes to 100m L of the line
30 of the outflow of the big corrie which fills the SW face of the
mountain. Climb up R on yellow rock to reach a long, exposed
horizontal traverse then continue on good holds to reach a rib.
Continue up this keeping the glacier stream to the R until a flattening
below steeper walls. It is possible to go R here and join the Fassani
Ledge start and continue up the Canalone Basso, but this can be
dangerous with stonefall. The rock route moves up L via a gully with
a large jammed block (Canalone Alta) leading towards the col behind
the Gran Campanile. Follow this gully (red marking) to a fork, L
would lead to the Gran Campanile col, ahead up a steep ice gully
(Canalone Grohmann) whilst a traverse R below steep OHing walls is
the correct way and leads to the Amphitheatre - a large scree or snow
covered terrace (3-4hr)

FASSANI LEDGE START
    From the Demetz Hut descend 60m from the col to the start of
the Fassani Ledge which traverses horizontally from E to W across
the face. Traverse the ledge L for 100m then climb slabs until it is
possible to continue easily L again to reach a ridge. Climb this until
the glacier is reachable by a traverse L. Climb a steep icy gully leading
L from near the foot of the glacier (Canalone Basso), (stonefall

danger), to reach the col above. A short descent leads to the Amphitheatre (3-4hr).

From the middle of the Amphitheatre climb a deep gully, then short chimneys and finally zig-zag up steps to reach a gap behind a tower with a large chockstone forming a window. Continue on poor rock to reach a col and the bivouac hut. Climb NW up a steep wall and then move E along the summit ridge, sometimes on the S side to reach the S summit. Descend to a gap and climb a ridge NE over a subsidiary summit and another gap to reach the main summit.

NORTH FACE – EAST TOWER

Haupt, 1911. Plaichinger, Teifel, 1907.

There are many routes and variations on this face. A large terrace cuts right across the NE Face for over 600m. Above and to the R of it is an obvious amphitheatre. This combination reaches the amphitheatre direct (IV) and then climbs the dièdre (III+) between the E pillar and the NE face to reach the crest leading to the summit. It is little affected by its N aspect with little ice or water and stonefall danger only on the first section. It is classic and one of the best routes on the mountain.

Base hut – Sella 1¼hr to the start 900m 8hr

4.02
IV
33

From the Sella Pass follow the path until below the amphitheatre L of the E pillar. Start up a snowy gully on the L of a 40m pillar. From the grassy top of the pillar, climb to a niche on the R at the foot of the face proper. Keep to the L up slabs on small holds for one pitch, then continue up a wet gully on the R to a small scree ledge at the foot of a long black crack, parallel to a similar crack on the L. Climb the former crack on poor and sometimes OHing rock to a ledge, then leave the crack to the L, and climb straight up over rocky steps to a scree terrace leading to the hollow below the massive NE dièdre (2hr from start; to avoid any danger from stonefall it maybe better to solo this first section). This point can also be reached by the long (600m) traverse from the L.

From the back of the hollow a long gully leads up to the col between the E pillar and the OHing E tower. A chimney with large chockstones and jammed blocks leads up to the gully, which is easily followed to the col (ice early in the season). From the col climb to the R at first, then for 30m up the crest of the ridge to an OH. Traverse 6m L and follow an exposed ledge to a poor sloping stance. A pleasant 30m chimney leads back to the crest of the ridge to a second col below a yellow/brown OH.

Now move L and up to a pulpit (poor red rock), the back of which falls away to the bottom of a gully. Cross over the ridge (hard), then climb a groove cut by several OHs (hard) to a gully behind the large OH of the pillar which leads to a col on the ridge. Follow the ridge for another 140m, passing several pinnacles, to the summit.

NORTH RIDGE
Pichl, Waizer, 1918.

This classic route follows the large depression between the E and N pillars, slanting from L to R to meet the N pillar above the nose. In normal conditions there is little snow or ice but there may be water falling from the summit snow patches.

Base hut – Sella 1¹/₂hr to the start   1000m 6-8hr

4.03
IV

31
33

From the Sella pass follow path 526 below the NE face. Start directly below the E pillar, above large boulders, where a short chimney leads up to grassy ledges on the R. Go up these for 25m to a gully, climb this and then a short chimney to the top of a tower. From here continue up between the vertical walls on the L and the slabs on the R. There is no particular difficulty at first till a half moon shaped bulge in the slabs is reached. Either climb this direct, or avoid it on the R more easily, to a small col. Continue on the slab beneath the black bulging wall (waterfall), traversing R past a steep step above some white slabs and then up for 20m on steeper rock in a groove which is not obvious at first. This is hard but well protected. Continue more easily in a gully and a chimney and finally up cracked slabs to the col between the N pillar and the final ridge leading to the N Tower. The summit of the N pillar is an excellent viewpoint and can be reached in a few minutes.

From the col climb up to the L at first above a large block to reach the N ridge and up the ridge for 25m until it gets really difficult then move L to a slab above a yellowish niche. Climb back to the ridge and then go horizontally L to below a large steep wall in the form of a square, with a wet yellow chimney in it. Climb the chimney for a pitch then go up an icy couloir with a large jammed block to arrive below a step in the N ridge, from which rise some long chimneys. Climb the chimneys until easier rocks can be used to avoid the third and last chimney on the L. These lead to a cave and a little higher is a long gully leading to a col formed by a secondary summit. Follow the main ridge to a large hollow and from the col at its head keep to the R up the ice couloir to easy rocks leading to the main summit.

NORTH FACE DIRECT
Bertoldi, Solda, 1936.

This and the next route are hard climbs, rarely done, up the N nose area. Original descriptions are given but seem difficult to follow! Messner has soloed this one. A direct and impressive route. There is a committing diagonal abseil at the start of the main difficulties. The line follows the rocks on the R of the famous nose of the N pillar, finishing up the OHing grey/yellow/black dièdre which leads to the N summit. In a poor season there can be a lot of ice and water and possibly stonefall.

Base hut – Sella or Vicenza 1¹/₂hr or 1hr to the start 1100m 15-20hr

4.04
VI
31

Start at the foot of the E gully which comes down between the N and W pillars. From the top of the snow or scree cone climb over rubble for 60m to a prominent crack in the L wall of the gully. Climb the crack (VI) for 50m and then a short wall which ends on a huge sloping grass ledge. Walk to the top of this where it meets the rock wall. There is a groove to the R of the OHs, overlooking the great gully on the R. Climb over a bulge (V) on to a small ledge (wood wedge). From the R-hand end of this climb a crack (IV+) which leads to another ledge. A short pitch diagonally R leads to easy rock. Climb without difficulty for 120m over shattered steps always tending slightly R and ending on a narrow broken ledge which overlooks the big gully. From this ledge ascend a short, steep loose chimney and wall (VI) to reach a traverse line leading R. Follow this traverse line without much difficulty until, at about 20m from the gully, it peters out. (Peg). Descend from the peg down and to the R over smooth grey rock for 6m to a second peg. Tension R into the gully bed and climb a few m over smooth rock (hard) to where the gully eases (VI). Climb easily up the gully for 20m to where it is possible to leave it. Climb a slab on the R to a peg and small stance (IV+). From here climb a groove (two pegs) for 50m (VI). Belay in slings.

Go up a continuation crack and groove for a rope length (VI) to a scree ledge. From behind this ledge climb cracks and grooves on the L (IV+,V+,VI-, very loose for 120m). Eventually the way is barred by OHs (30m higher than the col of the Pichl Route 4.03). Traverse to the L (free, pegs, loose, VI-) to reach easier grooves and chimneys (loose, IV and IV+) leading to the N ridge and follow this to the summit.

NORTH PILLAR
Esposito, Butta, 1940.

This is more difficult than the N Face Direct Route (4.04) but with less objective danger. It takes the famous nose of Sassolungo, ending at the col on the Pichl Route (4.03), which is followed to the top. At one time there was doubt that this route had been climbed.

Base hut – Sella or Vicenza 1½hr or 1hr to the start 1100m 20hr

4.05
VI
31
Start at the foot of a ridge about 20m L of the mouth of the E gully. Start up a sort of crack for 40m followed by a delicate section (V+) to a good stance. Continue straight up for two pitches, climbing several short walls (IV+) to a large grassy terrace. Keep straight up again for another 100m to the foot of the long black walls where the serious difficulty starts. It is possible to walk on or off here by grass ledges on the L. Climb straight up these walls for about 200m (VI, mainly because of the difficulty of planting good pegs for protection or belays), finishing below a large OHing red wall at a reasonable stance. From here traverse 50m to the R (V+) to a crack between the red wall and some slabs. Climb the crack over several large OHs (VI) for 80m to a large ledge. Continue straight on above the red wall, up a 15m slab (V) to a small niche. Climb the OHing wall above (VI, pegs) for 25m to a 1m roof and climb this direct (VI) to the smooth slab above (crux). Continue slightly L across three smooth slabs separated by small OHs (VI, pegs) to a large ledge at the top of the OHing rocks of the nose.
    Continue for 60m up easier rocks to a vertical step. Climb straight up it by a ridge (V+) for 70m to the summit of the N pillar. Now descend to the col of the Pichl Route (4.03) and follow this route to the summit or descend it.

NORTH PILLAR (DEMETZ ROUTE)
Demetz, Wehse, 1935.

This avoids the hard climbing on the nose by taking the steep slabs on the L between the nose and 4.03.

Base hut – Sella or Vicenza 1½hr or 1hr to the start 650m 5hr

4.06
IV+
33
Start about 200m R of 4.03 and climb grey rock on the E flank of the nose for 200m to reach yellow OHing walls. Traverse R for 15m on difficult rock (IV+) and then continue on easier rock, still with awkward moves, to the top of the tower and the junction with 4.03.

DESCENT BY ORDINARY ROUTE
This is route 4.01 in reverse.

4.07
II
From the main peak the bivouac shelter can be seen clearly on a col, towards the SSE. Descend to a ridge below the main summit on the WSW and climb up to a subsidiary summit. Traverse a second gap to the R to reach the S peak (3160m). Follow the summit ridge, keeping on the S side in an E direction until almost over the small col with the bivouac shelter. A 10m abseil leads to the col (1hr).

From here descend towards the tower which is below and in the direction of the Sassolungo Glacier. Descend broken rocks to the gap before the tower, which has a large chockstone forming a window. Turn off to the R (NW) and zig-zag down over steps and down short chimneys to the deep gully which leads down to the Amphitheatre (1hr).

Traverse across to the R under steep and OHing walls to the junction of the Canalone Grohmann and the Canalone Alta. The Canalone Grohmann is invisible from the Amphitheatre but the Canalone Alta comes down towards you from the Forcella Alta. Cross over the junction (usually snow) to the rocks on the SE ridge of the Gran Campanile and on the other side of the gully which descends from the junction (red markers). Climb up a few m to a narrow gap on the ridge and descend to the NW along an easy inclined crack with steep red walls on the L, to broken rocks and more red markings. Climb down to the S over broken rocks to boulders and scree. Bear L, back towards the gully crossed previously and climb a broken chimney across its retaining rib to reach the gully under a large black chockstone. Continue down the gully, keeping near the water, then keep to the R and leave the gully across broken rocks on the R. Descend for a long way towards the S until one can see the hollow of the Sassolungo Glacier and then continue down a boulder slope towards the SE to near the junction of the gully which has been followed and the one coming down from the glacier (2hr).

Continue to the SW down an easy ridge and then down an easy gully to the W. From the foot of the gully follow a narrow shelf to the S and continue in the same direction down a chimney near the stream coming down from the glacier. From the foot of the chimney go down over smooth rocks and a grassy crag to the W, descending to the foot of a large concave recess. Climb up a few m and down again on more difficult rocks to the L which lead to the yellow rocks at the bottom (1½hr).

VARIATIONS TO THE DESCENT

a   From the 'window' col descend the gully down towards the
    Sassolungo Glacier and then back R down the lower gully to reach
    the ordinary descent lower down. This is probably easier than the
    described route but more likely to have snow and ice and can be
    dangerous with stonefall.

b   From the lower part of the descent it is possible to break across to
    the L and traverse the rocks of the Campanile Venere by the
    Fassani Ledge to reach the F d Sassolungo and Demetz Hut (II,
    1hr more).

    Total descent time will normally be above 5hr whichever route is
    taken.

Gran Campanile del Sassolungo 3077m

NORTH-WEST RIDGE
Amodea, Osnaghi, 1940.

*A fairly short route giving some fine, sustained climbing. It follows the ridge
closely from the F d Salame to the summit.*

Base hut – Vicenza 1¼hr to the start 300m 5hr

4.08
IV+
30

From the hut reach the F d Salame up screes to the L of the start of
4.01 and then via a gully. The ridge OHs at first and the start is up a
chimney on the L (N) side of the ridge. Climb up for 40m past a large
block to a shallow gully near the ridge and OHing the first chimney.
Climb the gully past a difficult wet OH until a rising traverse across
the R wall leads to the ridge about 70m above the start.
      Continue straight up for 70m on good rock, passing two small
OHs to a small tower separated from the main ridge by a 40m gap.
Climb down to the L for 10m from where an 18m abseil leads on to
the chockstone filling the gap. Traverse 12m L to an OHing chimney,
and climb it for 20m to a small ledge (IV+). Continue diagonally to
the R and keep close to the ridge to a large flake of broken rock.
Follow the ridge for 60m to another pinnacle with a gap behind it.
Traverse down to the R for 10m to reach the gap and then climb up to
the L to a point about 30m away (exposed). Continue up the ridge
towards another pinnacle, first up a smooth wall with an OH on the L
then a traverse R descending slightly to above a third gap on the ridge

(hard). Descend another 3m in a crack to the gap then climb up a
narrow crack in the other wall. Follow the ridge until a 7m descent
leads to the foot of the last step (40m). Climb this to the summit.

DESCENT BY WEST GULLY

4.09 Follow easy rocks down from the summit to the top of the gully which
leads down to the easy rocks near the F d Salame. (2hr)

Il Salame 2836m

NORTH FACE
Comici, Casara, 1940.

*An impressive route similar to the N Face of the Cima Grande (17.13) but
not as long or as sustained.*

Base hut – Sella or Vicenza 2¹/₂hr or 2hr to the start 400m 6hr

4.10 Approach by path 526 & scramble 200m on snow & scree up the gully
VI which divides the tower from the main peak to reach the foot of the
V+/A1 face. On the L of the face is a rib with a loose black gully on its R. Climb
31 the rib for 30m and traverse into the gully at a massive jammed block.

1 30m Traverse diagonally R (V) to a small ledge. Continue R and
down slightly on a steep wall on good holds for 12m then climb
direct to a pinnacle (IV+)

2 35m Move R again for 6m on a black wall, then climb a crack (V)
to below a roof which is obvious from below and climb this (V+ or
A0),and continue straight up the crack to below another roof

3 35m Either climb the roof and crack above direct (V+/A0,V) or
move L and climb the steep wall (V+,V-)

4 40m A diagonal crack in a black dièdre leads L for 10m (V) and is
followed by a thin crack up the wall (V-) trending L to a stance at
the end of the grey walls. Above the rock is yellow and the crack
disappears at a roof between two black holes

5 30m Climb 20m up the yellow rock (V+) to below the roof and
climb it first on the R, then L (VI+ or A1) to a small stance

6 25m Follow a long OHing crack (V+) until it disappears into a
compact black wall

7 20m Move L along a narrow ledge for 9m (III) and then get up

into a small black niche (IV-, route book) where the wall starts to overhang

8   15m Climb L or R of the niche (V) to reach a horizontal traverse R for 10m on yellow rock

9   30m Continue traversing (IV) on black rock, climb a bulge for 3m, move R 3m and climb a final black bulge (V+) to reach final yellow walls (cairn)

10 40m Climb up to the R then back L in a chimney to a pinnacle (IV)

11 100m Traverse horizontally R along an overhung ledge to another loose chimney. Climb this (IV-) and a higher chimney for 60m (III) leading to a ridge and reach the summit via a little col.

DESCENT BY SOUTH-WEST FACE

4.11   This is the ordinary route (III+). From the summit descend the SE ridge. Abseil to the col then abseil from near a cairn on a ridge to a large scree ledge which leads easily to the F d Salame. Keep L to reach screes and the Vicenza hut. (2hr)

Spallone del Sassolungo (Langkofeleck) 3069m

This is the attractive, broken looking peak seen from the Sella Pass. Some parties find the routes and descent quite long! A 30m high statue of the Madonna hangs in a niche in the centre of the main face.

SOUTH-EAST FACE
Schietzold, Delago, Schmitt, Mayr, 1907.

This is a fine route. The route finding is rather complicated: after a long traverse across the lower buttress of the Torre del Spallone the route crosses the foot of the massive yellow triangle of rock then ascends the large dièdre on its R to finish with another traverse to the summit.

Base hut – Sella 1hr to the start 800m 6hr

4.12   From the Sella Pass follow path 525 towards the F d Sassolungo,
III   branching off R to the foot of the rocks of the lower buttress. Climb
28   easy rocks and ledges onto the buttress and make towards the N for 40m to the deep icy gully between the Torre del Spallone and the triangular tower. Climb a short way up the gully (stonefall), then up the other wall by a short gully and ledges to reach the L-hand end of

the rubbishy lower buttress below the triangular tower.

Follow the long ledge to the R for 100m to join the Ramp Route (4.13). Now climb a hidden chimney on the L for 40m to a scree terrace below the large dièdre between the triangular tower and the wall on its R. Continue up to the R across loose gullies, passing a tower on the L by a red chimney, to a crack with a massive jammed block at 7m. Climb up past this, then go up a shallow gully and over a short step to the base of the gully, from which the obvious black water streaks on the SE face go down the wall to the upper part of the ramp. Climb the gully without much difficulty by any of the various channels in its bed to a large scree terrace at the foot of a triangular tower. Climb up to a col between this tower and another, and traverse round the N side of the first tower and round the back (W) of a second. A short steep step leads to a crenellated ridge which is followed for 60m to the foot of the final step. Climb this by an OHing chimney (the Camino Delago), and finish out on the R to the summit.

SOUTH-EAST FACE (RAMP ROUTE)
Forcher-Mayer, Haupt, Oertel,1907. Redlich, Stephansky, 1911.

This route takes the obvious line slanting up from R to L which forms the R-hand side of the triangular tower. The Ramp is about 300m. The original finish was in common with 4.12 but the Direct Finish is described here.

Base hut – Sella   1hr to the start   800m   6hr

4.13
IV
28

From the Sella Pass follow path 525 towards the F d Sassolungo and traverse under the foot of the face below the Ramp. Two parallel chimneys lead up to its foot. Follow the R-hand one for 80m to a massive block on the large scree terrace at the foot of the Ramp, which is 30m wide at its base. Climb the Ramp by short gullies and small steps to a break where the massive black water streaks come down the wall above from 4.12. Traverse L and up a crack which leads back to the Ramp. A smooth and difficult 12m wall (III) leads to the scree ledge where 4.13 traverses across.

Continue up the dièdre between the triangular pillar and the wall on the R, in a deep and wet chimney with several difficult pitches (IV). The chimney finishes on the crest of the ridge behind the triangular tower. Follow the ridge towards the NW to another tower on the E side of the large icy gully. The ridge is broken and there is a window between two pinnacles giving access to between the second tower and the final walls. Climb steep chimneys to a scree terrace and so to the final pinnacled ridge leading to the summit.

DESCENT BY WEST RIDGE

4.14 Any descent is complicated and errors will lead to epics. Descent (a) is safer but longer and passes the bivouac hut.

a If the summit ridge is reached in good time and if the weather is good enough, by far the best thing to do is to traverse the whole of the principal ridge to the main summit of the Sassolungo, descending by the Ordinary Route of SW face of Sassolungo (4.07). From the Spallone to the main summit the route finding is complicated round the numerous pinnacles with one abseil near the bivouac hut and can take any time from 2-5hr. The Ordinary Route descent can take 5 further hours!

b None of the gullies leading directly down from the Spallone is safe from stonefall. The only reasonable descent is to follow the main ridge to the W to its lowest point, the Sella di Spallone, then turn S and descend the broken rocks on the R to the F d Ghiacciao. Descend to the R (W) down to the Sassolungo Glacier and down the glacier to join the descent from the main summit. The quickest way back to the F d Sassolungo is then along the Fassani Ledge (see 4.07). (4-5hr)

Punta delle Cinque Dita (Funffingerspitze) 2998m

SOUTH-WEST RIDGE
Boegle, Niedermayer, 1906.

This is a very popular climb which traverses round all the pinnacles to the main summit. It is a fine route with some exciting and unique positions.

Base hut – Sella 1½hr to the start 250m 4hr

4.15
IV
29
Reach the F d Cinque Dita up a snowy couloir on the Sella side. Climb straight up for 30m and move R to a belay. Follow the large dièdre above and, where it becomes difficult, traverse R to climb a large flake on good holds. Traverse horizontally L to rejoin the dièdre above the first belay and go up on the L to easier rocks. Follow these to a secondary ridge and traverse the easy rocks in the W side to reach the col between this ridge and the Little Finger (all III, easier alternatives R).

From the col climb on to a little pinnacle and make an enormous stride on to the wall of the Little Finger. Traverse slightly R and go up a crack leading to a sloping slab on the E side. Traverse

101

almost horizontally across the wall to the R, descend a few m and traverse to an enormous block on the next col.

Start up the Ring Finger by a ramp sloping up to the L (III) to a little col. Then traverse round the W side to reach the next col.

The wall of the Middle Finger is split by a crack which becomes a dièdre (the Schuster Crack). Climb it to a resting place on a loose block (III) and then continue up the dièdre (IV, hard to start) which leads to easy rocks and a path to the summit.

SOUTH FACE (SCHMITT CHIMNEYS)
Schmitt, Santer, 1890.

This is one of the famous and classic chimney climbs of the Dolomites. It follows the line of chimneys on the SE face, leading to the col between the Middle Finger and First Finger. In a poor season the chimneys may hold a lot of ice.

Base hut – Demetz 15min to the start 300m 4hr

4.16
IV
29

From the Demetz hut descend and traverse to the ramp at the foot of the chimneys. Climb the ramp (loose) and the slabs on the R for several hundred m. (II and III, solo) to a scree ledge at the foot of a steep chimney. Climb this chimney to a terrace at the foot of the Schmitt Chimneys proper. Scramble into the chimneys, and climb a narrow crack with a chockstone to a large, black, wet cave. Climb up the back of the cave and traverse through its roof (exposed) to the chimney above. Climb straight up for two pitches (IV,IV) then two more pitches on the L (IV, IV-, the second with two chockstones) to a scree ledge at the same height as a large, sloping terrace on the Middle Finger.

Leave the chimney to the L, below where it is blocked by a roof, and climb an exposed 25m wall keeping to the L to reach a sort of ridge. Then move back R along grassy ledges to a ledge in the chimney, separated from the L wall. Descend 2m into the chimney where a large crack leads up the opposite wall of the chimney. Continue up a difficult wall (IV) and traverse R to a ridge (descent route 4.19 goes R) which leads easily up to the col between the First and Middle Fingers. Climb the wall for 20m first by a chimney and bulge, then R up a narrow, smooth crack (III-) to easy rocks and the summit. The chimney can be climbed direct all the way (IV+).

SOUTH FACE (DIAGONAL CRACK)
Kiene, Haupt, 1912.

This route starts from the foot of the Schmitt Chimneys proper and follows the prominent crack across the face of the Middle Finger to reach the summit by the Schuster Crack (see 4.15). It is a fine and exposed route with interesting technique.

Base hut – Demetz 15min to the start 300m 4hr

4.17
IV+
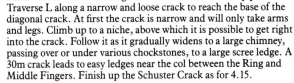
29
Follow 4.16 to the scree ledge at the foot of the first steep pitch. Traverse L along a narrow and loose crack to reach the base of the diagonal crack. At first the crack is narrow and will only take arms and legs. Climb up to a niche, above which it is possible to get right into the crack. Follow it as it gradually widens to a large chimney, passing over or under various chockstones, to a large scree ledge. A 30m crack leads to easy ledges near the col between the Ring and Middle Fingers. Finish up the Schuster Crack as for 4.15.

THE THUMB BY THE NORTH RIDGE
On the N side of the Thumb is a prominent, pinnacled ridge which makes an ideal climb for a short day.

Base hut – Demetz 5min to the start 250m 2hr

4.18
IV−
Walk behind the Demetz hut and cross a snow patch to reach a short,steep wall on the L of the ridge. Climb this for 20m to reach a ledge which leads R to the ridge at a col behind a subsidiary pinnacle (III,III+) and a higher pinnacle. Go round this on the R and continue up the ridge to the knife-edged summit. The pitches are 35m long with cemented belay pegs and small stances (mainly III, some IV-).

To descend traverse along the ridge W for 40m to reach the first abseil anchor. Two or three abseils lead to the col between the Thumb and First Finger (F d Indice). From here continue as for the normal descent (4.19).

DESCENT BY ORDINARY ROUTE
4.19
III
29
This route added to 4.15 completes the classic traverse of the Cinque Dita. From the summit climb down on the Sella side (E) to a ring peg on the shoulder overlooking the col at the top of the Schmitt Chimneys (4.16). Abseil 20m to the sometimes icy col between the summit and the First Finger. From here descend easily for 30m on the Sella side SE to a peg. From here make an easy but exposed traverse 15m to the R round the First Finger and to an abseil peg

above the F d Indice. To reach this col between the First Finger and the Thumb make three easy abseils of 20m from good abseil rings. Descend the gully S until a traverse leads out L round onto the Thumb. Abseil (or climb) 60m down the slabs. Then follow an easy horizontal traverse round to the rocks overlooking the F d Sassolungo above the Demetz hut. From a peg on top of this shoulder DO NOT abseil but descend for 5m and traverse 6m N to reach a big ring peg. Three 20m abseils from good anchors lead to the Forcella and the hut.

Sasso Levante (Grohmann Spitze) 3114m

SOUTH FACE AND SOUTH RIDGE
Dimai, Summermatter, Eötvös, Eötvös, 1908.

This is a fine route without excessive difficulty but with interesting route finding.

Base hut – Sella 1½hr to the start 600m 4hr

4.20
IV
32

Walk up the screes to the shoulder below the S ridge. The lower part is well defined. Climb up easy rocks on the L of the ridge for about 150m to a large scree terrace. Traverse L below the OHing step to the foot of a smooth gully with running water, parallel to the S ridge. (I,II)

Follow the gully keeping to the L (II), then move L by dièdres (III,III+) to a good ledge below the red and grey walls which block the route (300m from start).

Climb straight up a crack up a yellow wall for 30m (III+) to a narrow ledge and move R 5m to a stance. Follow the ledge R for 10m round an arête (III+, exposed) and then go straight up again to another ledge above the first. Follow this over a short step and a grey slab (III) to the foot of a smooth, narrow crack about 20m L of the main gully. Climb the crack with difficulty (III) to some wet OHs. Avoid these by a semi-hand-traverse up to the R for 15m (III). Climb a narrow ramp rising back L to the crack (IV) and continue up itfor 10m (crux pitch known as the Mantrap). Climb a gully for 20m, then L along a narrow ledge for 20m and then back R again (exposed) to the black crack (IV-). Continue more easily for 75m to a deep chimney (III) which leads to the final block (III) and the summit plateau.

SOUTH FACE DIRECT
Wallenfaels, Harrer, 1936.

This is a fine route if you can find all of it, reputed to be one of the best in the area. It really follows the SW ridge and is not on the S face.

Base hut – Sella 1½hr to the start 600m 7hr

4.21
V
32

Start about 50m R of the mouth of the gully dropping to the W of the face.

Climb the wall on the R of the gully for 150m finishing at the first of two bands of OHs which cross the wall diagonally. Now climb first L then R on friable rock to below a yellow OH. Climb this obliquely R, then traverse 3m R and reach less steep rock above the OH. Now traverse R past a rock window for 35m to easy ground (from which it may be possible to escape to 4.20). Trend L until the rock of the great tower steepens. Continue by a dièdre/chimney until a small yellow wall is reached. Here the climbing again becomes harder. Climb the little corner at the junction of the yellow wall and the grey rock, then traverse L to a peg (belay). Go up a very steep wall trending slightly L to the foot of a 70m crack. Climb the exposed crack (V) to its end and move L to a good ledge. Follow this ledge round a ridge to the final walls. Continue up on the L of the ridge, and then follow it to the final ridge which leads to the summit.

EAST-NORTH-EAST RIDGE
Enzensperger, Chelminski, 1895.

This is a classic route which also serves as the descent. From the F d Cinque Dita it traverses a series of towers to finish up the ENE ridge to the summit.

4.22
IV–
29

Reach the Forcella as for 4.15 and climb L across broken rocks (sometimes ice) to the foot of the first tower. This is the L-hand of the two prominent yellow towers. Climb up to the L between the first tower and a subsidiary of the S tower. On the L is a chimney leading to the col between the S tower and the second tower. Climb the chimney for 25m and before reaching the col move R across rubbishy ledges to a narrow crack which leads with difficulty (12m, IV-) to the col between the first and second towers. Abseil this pitch in descent.

Continue up a crack to the summit of the second tower, which is divided from the third tower by a narrow 60m gap. Step across the gap and continue up the ridge to the summit of the third tower. Descend to the next col and climb up the fourth tower which is slightly OHing but not difficult. Descend to the next col and climb a slightly OHing chimney to the main ridge. Follow this easily to the summit.

Punta Pian de Sass (Innerkofler Turm) 3098m

SOUTH FACE (**RIZZI CHIMNEY**)
Rizzi, Davarda, Mayer, Mayer, 1908.

This is one of the most famous chimney climbs in the Dolomites. It is very strenuous and is climbed almost entirely by classical chimneying techniques. At times the climbing is so deep in the chimney that it is difficult to see the holds. It is best climbed during a spell of good weather in high summer. It is slow to clear of ice and is dirty when wet. A retreat in bad weather would be most unpleasant. The route is the longest and most easterly of the three chimneys which cleave the smooth S wall. The line is classically direct.

Base hut – Sella 2hr to the start 500m 8hr

4.23   Approach as for 4.21 and go round beneath the impressive S face of
V   the tower. Traverse into the chimney from the R. Climb the chimney

32   for 400m mostly by chimneying technique and bridging. (Dark work). The chimney is blocked by two OHs, the first of which is climbed on the L, the second on the R. 50m beyond the second OH traverse R to reach a ridge and continue up this until easy climbing leads to the summit.

SOUTH PILLAR
Hasse, Schrott, 1959.

This and the next route are hard, artificial and free climbs up big walls. Descriptions are based on translations of original ascents. On the first ascent almost 200 pegs and 20 wooden wedges were used. The wooden wedges and about half the pegs were left in. Difficulties are not as great as those on the Brandler Hasse Route (17.14) on the Cima Grande N face.

Base hut – Sella 2hr to the start 500m First ascent – 4 days

4.24   From the foot of the S pillar go up over easy rock directly below the
VI/A3   obvious leaning corner. The crack ahead (V) leads to a steep yellow

32   wall, whose lower part is cut by the obvious OHing corner that runs out to the R (the start of the chief difficulties). Follow the roof formed by this corner for two long pitches almost to the end of the corner (A2 and A3). Traverse out L to the ridge of the corner (belay in étriers). Make a further short traverse L, then climb diagonally up L and finally vertically up a shallow groove running up to the R. Leave this over the OH on the R. Shortly after this a narrow sloping band is reached (belay). Climb 25m over a series of walls and scoops to a bulging fork in the rock. Follow the shallow semblance of a groove up to the L. Belay beneath an unusual umbrella-shaped roof. Climb it on the R, traverse L above it and go up L for 27m (belay). Traverse L over a smooth, steep slab to the start of a shallow, gently OHing groove. The groove soon leads to free climbing and a sloping ledge beneath a yellow crack (belay). From the start of the crack traverse L out of the groove, round the ridge and so to steep grey rock with good holds. (The chief difficulties are now over). Climb over easier rock beside the large chimney that cuts the upper part of the tower (IV) to a small rock nose above a slab (belay and route book). Follow the chimney (III and IV) and exit through a hole in the rock and so reach the top of the pillar. Cross over to the chief summit without difficulty.

SOUTH-EAST WALL (GRAN DIEDRO)
Loss, Destfoni, Bonveccio, 1966.

A steep, modern route up the obvious dièdre. 150 pegs, 2 bolts and 20wedges used on first ascent.

Base hut – Sella 2hr to the start 500m First ascent – 23hr

4.25
VI/A2
32

1 30m Scramble up black slabs with one awkward move (III) to a stance below a small, dark OH

2 40m Climb a loose crack to a small turf covered ledge (IV)

3 40m Bear slightly R to a yellow niche (V)

4 10m Continue direct (V+)

5 35m Climb a crack and traverse L to a stance (V)

6 30m Climb a 10m yellow wall to a large roof. Turn this on the L (A2) and continue to a stance

7 20m Follow a crack on wedges to the top of a pillar (A2)

8 25m Climb 15m L to reach a black dièdre (A1). Then get over a 4m roof (A3) to a stance

9   40m Climb a second dièdre over a small roof for 30m, traverse L for 3m and climb for 10m direct

10   40m Continue in same line (V)

11   20m Climb the chimney/crack above (IV)

12   150m 5 pitches (III/IV) to the summit (or traverse R to reach and descend 4.26.

SOUTH-EAST RIDGE
Dibona, Rizzi, Mayer, Mayer, 1910.

A good, ice-free route on firm rock.

Base hut – Sella 2hr to the start 450m 4hr

4.26 Start below the L-hand gully falling from the F d Sasso Levante.
IV Climb up easily (snow?) to reach the foot of the steep rocks of the SE
32 ridge.
      Climb the R-hand of two steep cracks over two bulges then on the L to reach a small col. Traverse L for 30m by a narrow, sloping ledge and then move up near the SE arête to a series of chimneys which mark the edge of the SE face. Follow these with good climbing for 130m to reach a noticeable col between a subsidiary ridge and the main wall. Climb the wall by a sloping slab, go up L for 30m (IV, crux) finally R over a narrow slab. Climb a little rib, a chimney on the R and a friable gully to reach the final crest and follow this to the summit.

DESCENT
4.27 This is not perhaps the fastest way down but it is the best descent.
III Climb from the summit across the E face to the gully falling from the F d Sasso Levante, the col between this peak and Sasso Levante (45min). Now descend to the N parallel to the ridge down on to the Sasso Levante glacier (easily crossable in summer). Continue down the glacier following either the direct route leading to the track to the Vicenza hut or turning off earlier and climbing down at random over ice and rock beneath spurs of the Sasso Levante and Cinque Dita peaks to join the same track at a slightly higher point. Continue down to the Vicenza hut or, via path 525 up to the Demetz hut. (3hr)
      It is also possible to descend via the SE Ridge (4.26). Climb down from the summit to the S to a ledge which leads down to the SE ridge. Abseil down the ridge and climb down to the foot of the gully. (2hr)

Geografica 1:25000 sheets 5 and 7

The S face of this group has numerous short routes of all standards, nearly all on good rock. Many of the routes are shown on the photograph and only brief details are given as they are quite well worn. Peaks can be connected to make a traverse. The ridge has 8 peaks, 6 with good S face routes and then Sass Rigais and Furchetta. The S face climbs can be reached by cablecar from Ortisei (St Ulrich) to Seceda or from the Firenze Hut in 45min.

Furchetta with its famous N Face is reached from the Val di Funes (Villnoss Tal).

NOTE: the above maps seem to have changed the names of many of the peaks around Furchetta. All other sources show Furchetta (3025m) to be the peak marked as Furchetta Piccola (3030m) so the general consensus has been adopted here.

HUT

Firenze (Geisler) Hut 2039m Good base for S face routes. Approach from San Cristina (1½hr)

Piccola Fermeda (Kleine Fermeda) 2814m

WEST RIDGE (NORMAL ROUTE)
Santner, 1884.

A short, pleasant route, used as the descent from the other routes.

300m 1½hr

5.01
I
Follow the W ridge from the col behind a subsidiary pinnacle following grooves near the crest and a final 10m chimney.

SOUTH-WEST GULLY
Trenker, 1917.

A pleasant route.

300m 2hr

5.02
III
Climb the open gully parallel to the W ridge, starting at the same

place as 5.01, with a traverse R and joining the ridge near the top.

SOUTH FACE
Jahn, Huter, 1917.

A very pleasant climb.

400m 2hr

5.03
III
35
Below the yellow OHing S face is a grass shoulder. Get onto this from the L, then take a steep crack on the L with a jammed block and continue until easier rock leads R and the SW ridge leads to the S summit. Continue N to the main peak.

SOUTH FACE – DIRECT START
Vinatzer.

Rarely repeated.

90m 1hr

5.04
VI
35
Climb the steep crack to the R of 5.03. Start from the grass shoulder and finish by 5.03.

SOUTH-EAST RIDGE – DIRECT START
Vinatzer

Rarely repeated.

100m 1hr

5.05
VI
35
From the R-hand side of the grassy shoulder below the S face climb diagonally R across the yellow OHing wall to join the SE Ridge (5.06).

SOUTH-EAST RIDGE
Leuchs, 1904.

A popular route.

400m 2¹/₂hr

5.06
III
35
Start at the W Fermeda gully between Piccola and Gran Fermeda and after 100m, at a jammed block, move out onto the ridge and follow this to the S peak.

WEST FACE AND SOUTH-WEST RIDGE
Leuchs, 1904.

A link in the traverse of the peaks.

200m 2hr

5.07
III
35
From the top of the W Fermeda gully climb a chimney and then reach and climb the SW ridge.

SOUTH-WEST FACE (YELLOW CHIMNEY)
Leuchs, Euringer, 1904.

150m 1hr

5.08
III
35
On the R of the W Fermeda gully is a detached tower, the top of which can be reached by 5.09, or by a traverse from 5.11, or direct by 5.10. This obvious chimney cuts the wall above and L of this tower and then joins 5.11 to reach the summit.

WEST FERMEDA GULLY CONNECTION
100m 30min

5.09
III
35
Traverse out R to below the Yellow Chimney (5.08) from the stance above the jammed block on 5.06.

SOUTH-WEST FACE – DIRECT START
150m 1hr

5.10
III
35
A steep gully leads up from the middle of the face to the top of the subsidiary buttress. Climb this and then either move L for 5.08 or descend a little R to reach the first chimney of 5.11.

SOUTH-WEST FACE (ORDINARY ROUTE)
Bettega, Schulz, Compton, Martin, 1887.

An exposed and popular route also used for descent with two or three abseils.

400m 2hr

5.11
III+
35
Start near the foot of the gully on the R-hand side of the face (E Fermeda gully).

Follow easy rocks to reach the lower end of a long slanting gully which leads from R to L across the lower face. Follow this up grassy rocks past a pinnacle below a steep crack until the angle of the rocks above eases. (A continuation of this weakness would lead to the top of 5.10 and a little further to 5.08). Climb a steep 20m chimney (III) leading to a gully, follow this to another chimney and climb this (III). Continue up a gully and chimney (III,II) to reach a traversing line leading L along a well marked ledge indicated in places by red marked rock. At the end climb up by a little pillar (II) to a col above which is a Madonna.

Climb up easy rocks trending L to a steep slab with good holds (III) and continue up a steep wall (III+). Above this section easier rock leads L then R to a gully which leads to a col between a fore-peak and the main summit.

SOUTH-EAST RIDGE
Berger, Muroder, 1897.

A very good route on firm rock.

400m 3hr

5.12
III

Start at the foot of the ridge and climb easy rocks to reach an obvious niche. The route continues near the ridge up steep walls, a dièdre and well marked rocks, passing a little OH on the R, until easier climbing leads to the top of 5.13 and the summit.

NORTH-EAST FACE
Lorenz, Wessely, 1894.

An excellent route up the steep face above the E Fermeda gully. One of the best routes in the group.

400m 3½hr

5.13
IV+

Start at the foot of the E Fermeda gully and climb this for 200m (I,II). Move L for 40m into a hidden gully and climb this (II) for 70m to a stance below obvious pinnacles on the R wall.

1 40m Climb the wall trending L past the pinnacles (III) to a smooth slab. Cross the slab and climb a short corner (IV) which leads to a scree hollow

2 40m Climb a slab and crack on the L (IV)

3 40m Climb a chimney (IV+), move 3m L and climb a higher chimney (IV)

4 30m Climb a steep OHing crack for 5m (IV+)and continue up a

chimney to easy rock. (Possibly an easier variation to the R)

5   60m Traverse easily L to reach an easy gully

6   40m Climb to the R-hand chimney and climb it (IV,III) to a little col

7   40m An easy gully leads to the SE ridge (III)

Follow the ridge easily to the summit (II).

Campanile di Funes (Villnosser Turm) 2840m

SOUTH FACE (DELAGO CHIMNEY)
Delago, Forcher-Mayer, 1895.

A classic, interesting climb.

400m 2hr

5.14
V
35
Start as for 5.13 and follow the gully until below the obvious chimney up the red R wall of the gully. Climb the chimney, with excursions out onto the walls beside it, to the summit. Descend on the N side and then the SW face until the col at the top of the E Fermeda gully can be reached. Descend the gully to the bottom.

Odle di Cisles 2780m

SOUTH-WEST FACE – DIRECT ROUTE
Dibona, Eller, 1917.

An elegant route.

400m 2hr

5.15
V
35
Start on the R of the face and climb easily up a gully slanting L behind pinnacles to reach a shoulder below the steep SW face. Climb this R over walls and ledges until a traverse L leads to below two yellow OHs. Finally climb the walls above (IV) for about five pitches to the summit.

SOUTH FACE (DULFER CRACK)
Dulfer, Berth, Franz, Wolff, 1914.

A difficult and exposed route.

400m 3hr

5.16
V

From near the start of 5.15 climb direct up chimneys to the crack, which lies next to a deep chimney (Teufel Kamin) and leads to the SE ridge. Climb the crack and continue up the SE Ridge (5.18) to the summit.

SOUTH FACE VARIATION
Livanos, 1966.

A harder variation to 5.16.

400m 3hr

5.17
V+

Above the chimney of 15.16 climb diagonally L across the steep wall to reach a very steep crack. Climb this direct up the OH wall for 90m to join the SE Ridge (5.18) and follow this route to the summit.

SOUTH-EAST RIDGE
Ofner, Laviat, Sharmer, 1908.

A very enjoyable ridge climb with various alternatives which may vary the standard, which was originally thought to be only III.

500m 3½hr

5.18
V−

Start near the gully on the R of the face and scramble up for 100m to a shoulder on the L of the ridge proper.

1 40m From a stance near a block climb up to a peg and then take a yellow corner (IV) and continue towards the ridge by a gully (III)

2 150m Either: climb 5m up to a little hollow and a crack (IV), a chimney (IV), a harder crack (V-), an open gully and the arête for 4 pitches or: from the little hollow take a ramp R and climb gullies on the R of the ridge (mostly III with a move of IV near the end up a steeper wall) to the same place

3 210m Continue up near the ridge for 5 or 6 pitches (mainly III) with one awkward section above a cave (IV+) to reach a subsidiary summit

4 60m Continue to the main summit over various pinnacles (II,III).

114

NORMAL ROUTE FROM EAST
Hartmann, Fistill, 1887.

An uninteresting and complicated route, usually used for descent.

500m 2hr

.19
I
Climb the gully between this peak and Sass Mesdi moving L to the col between Odla di Cisles and Gran Odla. Continue up slabs and ledges to a col between Odla di Cisles and a subsidiary tower and climb steeper rocks to the N summit. In descent make 5 abseils of 20m from pegs and slings – beware old slings!

Gran Odla 2832m

SOUTH-EAST RIDGE
Klose, Reifschneider, 1934.

500m 4hr

.20
/
Climb 5.19 to the col behind the Odla di Cisles and then climb the steep SE ridge.

Sass de Mesdi 2762m

SOUTH-WEST RIDGE
Dibona, Huter, Jahn, Eller, 1917.

The best route on this face. Exposed and on generally good rock. Escape possible L to a gully at mid-height.

400m 4hr

.21
/ –
35
Start on the R of the main gully on the L of the face, up a short gully leading R until ledges R lead to the foot of another gully which narrows to a chimney (also reachable from the R).

1   35m Up the gully to the chimney and climb this (IV) to a stance on jammed blocks

2   30m Continue up the chimney and then move R (III)

3   25m Move L to a gully. Up this (II) to a stance below the ridge

4   40m Climb up for 4m and then traverse L round the edge to reach

a narrow ramp (III). Climb the ramp L (IV-)

5   35m Continue up the ramp (IV)

6   35m Climb a crack (III-) then 20m L to a shallow chimney. Up this (IV-)

7   40m Move up to a ledge (III). Traverse R and take a short wall (IV-)

8   10m Easily R to below a black wall

9   40m Move up 6m L then traverse diagonally R past a loose OH (IV+) to reach a grey crack. Climb this on good holds to a stance near a scree ledge

10 40m Slant R to a higher scree ledge. (Escape L and 5.22 start here)

11 15m Easily R to a little col

12 40m Climb R on red rock to a narrow chimney (IV+). Climb this by bridging and then on the R wall (V-) to reach a stance on the L of a narrow gully

13 100m Easily up the gully and ridge above to the summit (II).

Descend down the SE ridge (II) to the foot of the gully on the R of the S face.

WEST FACE
Huter, Jahn, Merlet, 1917.

Really a variation to 5.21. There is also a Solleder finish near here at V.

150m 1hr

5.22 From the stance after pitch 10 of 5.21 traverse L, go round the edge
IV   and take a grassy gully to its end (III). Move 3m R, climb a wet
35   chimney (IV) and continue to the summit (III,II)

SOUTH FACE (HANNEMANN CRACK)
Hannemann, Holzhammer, 1912.

A difficult route with some loose rock.

250m 2½hr

5.23 The route climbs the dièdre cutting the centre of the S face. Start as
V   for 5.21 and traverse R to the foot of the yellow corner. Climb the
       loose dièdre to exit onto the gentle SE ridge giving an easy descent.

SOUTH FACE PILLAR
Huter, Jahn, Merlet, Muller, Richter, 1917.

A good exposed route up the slabs to the R of 5.23.   *250m 3hr*

5.24
IV
Start as for 5.23 but move R from the foot of the dièdre to a grey slab forming the L face of a pillar. Climb the slab and cracks above keeping about 30m R of 5.23 until forced R near the top round the edge. Finally climb a wall on good holds and a crack.

SOUTH FACE CRACKS
Unknown c. 1908 or Vinatzer.

The R-hand part of the S face is short and cut by at least three climbable cracks.

100m 1-2hr

5.25
V
Each crack gives a good short climbs with an easy descent. The R-hand one is recommended. Below the face a prominent pinnacle, Deint de Mesdi (Kassnapoff Turm), 2437m gives an excellent little route (V-,80m) with a 40m abseil descent.

Sass Rigais 3025m

SOUTH FACE (NORMAL ROUTE)
Chamois hunters or Bernard, Bernard, Wagner, Niglutsch, 1878.

This route gives an easy approach to an excellent view point.   *600m*
3hr

5.26
I
Follow path 13 until it is possible to turn R and follow red markers up the large hollow in the SW face (Mittags Schlucht). From here red marks and wires lead up the S face to the summit.

EAST RIDGE
Hess, Schulz, Schmitt, 1888.

This route can be combined with 5.26 to give a delightful traverse.

150m 1hr

5.27
I
Head for the col between Furchetta and Sass Rigais and climb a gully L to the foot of the rocks. A 10m step equipped with wires leads to the slabby scree-covered E flank which is followed without real difficulty to the summit.

Il Pulpiti (Kanzeln) 2787m

WEST FACE
These small crags lie NE of the Firenze hut above path 13.

5.27 This is an interesting practice area and ideal for introducing beginner
I to basic Dolomite rope technique.

Furchetta 3025m

WEST RIDGE (ORDINARY ROUTE)
Santner, 1880.

It is possible to combine this with the traverse of Sass Rigais.

400m 1hr

5.28 Easy rocks lead from the col between Sass Rigais and Furchetta
I (2696m) up the W ridge to the summit.

NORTH FACE
Solleder, Wiessner, 1925.

*One of Solleder's three great routes. The lower face is loose and unpleasant
but the final 200m is excellent. It is important to memorise the exact
position of the Pulpit on the way up to the wall as it is difficult to recognise
when on the wall itself.*

Base – Val di Funes (Villnoss Tal) road 1½to the start 600m 5hr

5.30 Start at the foot of the rock spur protruding from the N Face. Climb
V+/A0 the L(E) side of the spur to a small cwm which links the spur and the
wall (III,IV). Now climb through gullies in the direction of the large
scree-filled basin below the Dulfer Pulpit, taking care not to be forced
too far to the L on to the ridge (II,III). Cross the scree-filled cwm to
the R. The conspicuous yellow pillar rising to the L of the scree-filled
cwm is NOT the Dulfer Pulpit! The latter is located immediately
above the cwm. Bearing slightly to the R, climb some steeper sections
of wall (IV) until a point beneath the broad Dulfer Pulpit, which is
now clearly visible, is reached. This section can be soloed but is rather
loose. The Pulpit and the wall now form a short chimney.
  The Solleder finish starts below the Pulpit. Cross beneath the
Pulpit to the R for 10m until a hidden crack system is reached. Climb
the crack for 40m (V+) to a stance by a small knob. The crack now

continues slightly to the L to an OH. First bear to the R of the crack over slabs, then re-enter the crack and climb it (V+) to a stance beneath an OH. Climb over the bulge (V+) continuing for 20m to beneath the roof which is breached on the R by a narrow chimney. Make a horizontal traverse across slabs to directly below the chimney (V+). First climb straight up friable rock for 15m, then cross L (V+/A0) to a short crack (thread). Climb this crack, coming out under the roof which is cut by the exit chimney. The chimney is very narrow so the roof is climbed with a runner threaded round a chockstone. Squeeze into the chimney, in which there is a good stance (route book). Climb this chimney for one pitch to the W ridge and climb this to the highest point.

DESCENT

5.31 Take the track on the Furchetta S side, keeping somewhat to the W. This is easy going until you reach the gully between the Furchetta and the Sass Rigais. From this point either continue to the N side by abseiling into the gully from a large block (difficult to find) and descending it without difficulty, or take the safer walk down S to the Firenze hut. (2hr)

Geografica 1:25000 sheet 6

This large plateau has good rock climbing at various places round it. At the SW corner are the Sella Towers, popular peaks with many routes only 20 minutes from the road, while on the S side are found the big walls of Piz di Ciavazes and Sass Pordoi and the shorter routes above the Pordoi pass. To the NW are the Torre and Campanile del Murfreid whilst in the N facing Val de Mesdi there is the Daint de Mesdi (S face, IV).

HUTS

Sella Pass Hut 2183m. See Sassolungo Group

Boè Hut 2873m. Piz Boè (3151m) is an easy walk from here. Approaches– i)from Sella hut via Possnecker Via Ferrata and Piz Gralba by paths 649 and 666 (5½hr), ii)from Val Lasties by path 647 (3hr)

First Sella Tower 2533m

WEST RIDGE
Steger, Holzner, 1928.

Short but interesting, an often busy and well polished route.

Base hut – Sella 20min to the start 100m 2hr

6.01
IV+
38
Pass under the S side of the towers and get to the foot of the ridge proper, dodging a gendarme on the L (N); or climb direct from the S up an easy gully. Climb the easy rocks of the spur, keeping rather to the R, to the small gap with a little pinnacle. After dealing with a short but difficult wall (IV) or a chimney to the R (III), traverse about 20m R and return to the crest of the ridge by a crack (30m,IV). Continue to a platform on the ridge below the final steep section.

Move on to the crest and then R for a few m. Climb a difficult little dièdre (IV+). Easy rocks now leads to the top.

SOUTH FACE (TISSI ROUTE)
Tissi, Mariola, Gugliermina, Masè Dari, Aschieri, 1926.

To the R of the W ridge lies the W face then the SW ridge with a flake at the bottom and a roof near the top, then the steep S wall with cracks and a pillar to its R and finally the easy ground of the descent route (6.08). There are many routes in this popular area, rather in the style of a British crag and distinguishing between them has given problems for some parties. Six routes are described here. This route actually follows the SW ridge although it reaches it from, and finishes on the S face.

Base hut – Sella 20min to the start 170m 2hr

6.02
VI
V/A0

Start a little R of the yellow OHing ridge (Direct Start, De Franceschi) and scramble up a few m to the foot of a yellow vertical chimney/crack.

1   25m Climb the tiring, awkward chimney (IV+,V) and exit L to a stance

2   35m Climb a crack (V), traverse 2m L (VI or A0) to a chimney/corner which leads to a ledge near the top of the obvious pillar leaning against the SW ridge

3   35m Move a little L and climb a smooth slab on the L (III), return R and go up (V) to a good stance

4   18m Above is an obvious big black roof and an escape is possible L to join 6.01. However climb direct up a yellow dièdre (V-) and go round a roof on the L (VI or A0)

5   30m Climb a vertical black corner (V-) and the roof above (VI or A0), move R and continue up a pleasant yellow corner (IV-,IV) to reach a big ledge and to join 6.03

6   40m Go R along the ledge and climb a corner to a roof (III), move R (IV) and continue obliquely L on broken rock to the summit.

SOUTH FACE (ROSSI ROUTE)
Rossi, Chesi, De Marchi, 1943.

A good technical route, harder but not as strenuous as the Tissi Route (6.02). There is also a Schober, Kleisl route near here (V+/A0) but this is the most popular line.

Base hut – Sella 20min to the start 170m 2hr

6.03 Start at the middle of the wall between the Tissi (6.02) and Trenker
VI+ (6.04) Routes.
V+/A0
40

1 35m Climb up a shoulder of grey rock to a stance on a ramp
sloping R (III/IV)

2 35m Move up the ramp a little and then follow a descending
traverse L crossing a well-worn, smooth grey vertical wall (V+,VI
or A0) until moves lead up L (V+) to a stance also used by 6.02

3 35m Return to the R end of the ledge and climb an excellent grey
slab (V,V+) to a good stance on a yellow ledge

4 30m Take an easier ramp R (III,IV) to the foot of a grey pillar

5 20m Climb the pillar (IV+) and move L up a yellow corner (IV+)

6 35m Move R to a steep wall and climb it (VI+ or A0) until a grey
corner leads L (IV+) to a big ledge and a junction with 6.02

7 40m As for 6.02 to the summit.

SOUTH FACE (SOUTH-WEST CORNER)
Trenker, Pescosta, 1913.

*A well-polished route up the crack on the corner to the R of the S face
which, for its standard, requires some respect.*

Base hut – Sella 20min to the start 150m 1½hr

6.04 Start up easy rock for 30m to the foot of the crack proper (II).
V
40

1 30m Climb the corner crack (IV) to a small ledge

2 30m Continue up the crack (IV) to a smooth OHing section (V).
Climb this on the R to a small ledge. Continue up the crack to a
higher ledge

3 50m Continue up the crack for two pitches (IV,IV+) to a good
ledge

4 50m Ignore the steep parallel cracks above and walk R 20m and
move up to a chimney (III). Climb this steeply at first (III+), to an
exit onto the descent path (6.08).

SOUTH FACE (PILASTRINI ROUTE)
Gluck, Rezzera, 1935.

*A fine but polished route up cracks and grooves leading to the top of the
detached pillar.*

Base hut – Sella 20min to the start 100m 2hr

6.05 Start as for 6.04 but move well R just past a crack/chimney line (6.06)
V   to a ledge below a dièdre or the foot of a steep crack further R.

40

1   35m Climb a short corner, traverse R and move up to a stance
below a smooth grey slab (III+) or climb the steep crack direct (V)

2   20m Climb the slab from L to R (V) and continue up the crack
(IV) to a good stance

3   20m Continue up a vertical yellow corner (IV) to a stance below
OHs

4   40m Climb the OHing chimney (IV-) passing a bulge on the R
(III+) and continue direct (IV-)

5   35m Continue up and over the top of the pillar. Either bridge
across (!) or descend and re-ascend the far wall (III) and finish as
for 6.06.

SOUTH FACE (FIECHTL ROUTE)
Fiechtl, Katzer, 1924.

*A popular route, between the Trenker (6.04) and Pilastrini (6.05) Routes,
up the crack which cuts off the S pillar from the main face.*

Base hut – Sella 20min to the start 100m 1hr

6.06 Start as for 6.04 up easy rock to the foot of the crack (30m,II).
IV

40

1   40m Climb the crack (IV)

2   40m Climb the chimney until it forks (III). Take the L branch up
a corner passing a chockstone to a stance at a col (IV-). 6.07 comes
to here from the other side

3   40m Bridge up then climb the L wall for 15m (III), take easier
rock direct (II) to reach the descent route (6.08).

SOUTH FACE (SOUTH-EAST CHIMNEY)
Kostner, Gablonger, 1905.

A better route up the towers than the Ordinary (Descent) Route (6.08).

Base hut – Sella 20min to the start 120m 1½hr

6.07
III
40
Go round R from the main S face routes below the lower rocks of the S pillar until screes lead up into a corner below the obvious chimney which faces SE. Climb the chimney with quite spectacular climbing for the grade (II+) to join 6.04 and finish up this (III).

DESCENT BY ORDINARY ROUTE

6.08
40
Walk down a path E to the col between the First and Second Towers. An ascent from here by the SW face of the Second Tower (III) allows a traverse of the Towers to be continued. However, ascend a little and traverse some way across the S face of the Second Tower until descent is possible by steep but easy walls and ledges leading to grassy ledges and the foot of the S face.(30min)

Second Sella Tower 2597m

NORTH-WEST RIDGE
Gluck, Demetz, 1935.

Two routes climb the area of this ridge. This climb starts on the W face and moves onto the arête at half height where it joins 6.10 which starts on the N face. Both are excellent routes although route finding gives some problems on 6.10.

Base hut – Sella 20min to the start 250m 3hr

6.09
V/A0
37
Start near the centre of the W face to the R of the lower steep section of the ridge.

1 75m Climb easy rocks up the centre of the W face (II)

2 30m Continue direct then move L to a stance below a yellow/black bulge (III)

3 30m Climb diagonally L (IV) and then traverse horizontally L across a grey wall (IV+)

4 25m Take a steep black dièdre and pass a small OH on the L (V/A0) to a stance on the L

5 25m Continue on steep rock passing a prominent OH on the L (IV+)

6 25m Follow the same line near the arête (IV) to a stance on the shoulder halfway up the arête, and the junction with 6.10

7   25m Climb over a small OH (IV+) and then move L round the ridge on a narrow ledge. Climb a short crack (IV), move R back round the edge and climb a corner (IV) to a stance on the R

8   20m Climb a crack (IV+), move L round the arête and continue by another crack (IV-) to an exposed stance to the R of the edge

9   40m Climb direct to an OH, pass it on the L (V-) and continue R then direct up the edge in a shallow corner (IV-) to a scree ledge

10 40m Take the L-hand crack (III) to easy rock and a block stance

11 60m Continue up the edge to the summit (III,II).

NORTH FACE
Kasnapoff, Zelger, 1913.

A fine climb on good rock with considerable exposure. The traverse onto the NW ridge can be difficult to find.

Base hut – Sella   20min to the start   250m   3hr

6.10

V– ·
37

Start well to the L of the line of the NW ridge near a plaque.

1   35m Scramble across a ledge R and continue R for 10m until it is possible to go up (IV) to a stance

2   40m Climb a steep pitch on good holds (III,IV+)

3   40m Continue up a short chimney and then move R (III+) to climb a higher chimney leading to easier ground in a gully 10m L of the ridge

4   30m Follow the gully to a stance near a niche (III)

5   55m Either traverse out R for 10m on small polished holds to a stance on the edge (V-) and then climb up the edge over various bulges (V-,IV), or continue further up the gully line until an easier traverse R is possible (IV+) to reach the same shoulder on the ridge.

Continue as for 6.09, pitch 7.

NORTH-WEST FACE DIRECT
Messner, Messner, 1968.

A hard and serious route on very compact rock. Not a good route to be on when wet. Described by Messner in his book 'The Seventh Grade' the route takes a fairly direct line between the two obvious water stripes.

125

Base hut – Sella 20min to the start 200m 4hr

6.11
VI–
Start on the L side of the wall just L of a slightly OHing corner (small cairn).

1   40m Move up and into the corner past an OH (V+) and climb it on yellow rock (V) until a ramp leads R (IV+) to a stance

2   40m Continue R past a hole on black rock (V+) until moves up (VI-) and L lead to the L-hand water streak which is followed (IV+) to a stance in a cave

3   20m Leave the cave on the L and climb over an OH (V+) to an obvious corner leading to a stance on a flake (V+)

4   40m Move R onto the black wall for 15m (V+) and then go direct (VI-,V) to a stance below OHs

5   50m Climb direct to a yellow niche (V+) then move R over small OHs (V+) and finally up the wall moving gradually L below more roofs to a small stance

6   40m Climb up to the start of a ramp (V-) which leads R (IV) to a good ledge

7   50m Continue up a steep wall by a gully (IV) to the summit ledges.

DESCENT
6.12   Descend E by an easy chimney to the col between the tower and Piz di Ciavazes then either descend easy rocks S to join the descent (6.08) from the First Tower (1hr) or make abseils of 20m and 40m to join 6.13 and either go up this to continue a traverse of the towers or go down 6.15.

Third Sella Tower 2688m

SOUTH-WEST FACE
Jahn, Merlet, Dyrhenfurth, 1918.

A good alternative finish to the Ordinary Route (see Descent 6.15)

Base hut – Sella 20min to the start 350m 2½hr

6.13
III+
[34]
Either start as for the Ordinary Route (6.15) to reach the big spiral ledge or join the route at the end of the lower gully section by abseilling down from 6.12 as a continuation of the traverse of the towers.

Start about 5m R of the bed of the gully dividing the NW face of the Second and Third Towers. After 25m climb a chimney facing R (III). Higher up return to the bed of the gully which leads to a large ledge slanting up across the face to the L. Follow it for about 40m to the foot of a big dièdre facing the Second Tower.

Climb the dièdre for 75m (III) then traverse horizontally L for 25m (III+).Continue up two short steps to a scree-covered platform. Initially slant up L for 30m (III) then direct to the foot of a wide crack. Ignoring the easy chimney on the R climb a narrow crack on the L (III) which quickly opens out on to a good platform. Continue up the grey walls to the summit.

WEST FACE
Vinatzer, Peristi, 1935.

This is one of the harder routes on the towers. It takes a direct line up the centre of the face crossing the spiral descent ledge at half height.

Base hut – Sella 20min to the start 300m 4hr

6.14
VI–
V–/A0
[34]
Start almost in the middle of the wall at a gully-like weakness which trends slightly R.

1 30m Climb an obvious crack (IV)

2 40m Continue up a shallow corner slanting R (IV-)

3 30m Move up L towards a small niche below obvious roofs (thread belay)

4 40m Climb a crack on the L of the niche (IV+) and go round the roof on the R (V-)

5 40m Continue in the line of the crack (IV+,III)

6 20m Climb a delicate white slab to a niche below OHs (V-)

7 45m Traverse 15m L below roofs (III) and climb easier rocks to the spiral ledge. Walk a few m L to below a steep crack closed by OHs

8 30m Climb the crack (IV+) and pull round the roof on the R (VI- or A0) to reach a continuation crack

9   60m Continue up cracks and corners above (IV+)

10 30m Easier climbing leads R to a junction with 6.13, but ignore
    this and climb a delicate layback flake (V-) and the corner above
    (IV+)

11 30m Move round a bulge (IV+) and follow a crack (IV)

12 40m Easier climbing up grey slabs to the summit.

DESCENT BY ORDINARY ROUTE

6.15 Descend the N side of the Tower by an easy abseil from a ring peg.
34 Follow the easy spiral ledge which circles the Tower and leads to the
gully between the Second and Third Towers. This gully is the lower
part of the SW Face Route (6.13) and is descended with a final abseil
of 40m to the screes. (1hr)

Fourth Sella Tower 2605m

WEST FACE DIRECT
Not a popular route. Some loose rock.

Base hut – Sella 25min to the start 250m 2½hr

6.16 Start below the W wall of the Fourth Tower about 30m L of the start
V- of the gully between the Towers.
    Climb 25m to below rotten yellow rock, climb diagonally L for
20m and traverse L 10m. Climb straight up for 30m to a big OH.
Traverse 15m R to a block (V-) and slant L back above the OH. Keep
on up the wall for 25m followed by 30m of easy rock, to the foot of a
30m double crack. Climb the loose crack and traverse 25m R to a
shallower crack. Continue up the wall for 30m to a vegetated
platform. Above this a 60m chimney gives interesting climbing to the
N ridge leaving 30m of easy rock to the summit.

DESCENT BY ORDINARY ROUTE

6.17 Descend a loose chimney to the col between the Tower and the main
plateau. Follow the gully down between the Tower and the main face,
out on to the scree cone between the Third and Fourth Towers. (1hr)

Piz di Ciavazes 2836m

This peak projects from the Sella plateau in the shape of a wedge in a SW direction. It has no distinct summit but its massif is marked out both on the NE side (Piz Selva) and to the E (Piz Lasties) by deep gorges. To the S the massif is flanked by a 500m wall, which towers over the Canazei side of the Sella pass road.

NORMAL ROUTE AND DESCENT
Haupt, Mayr, 1907.

This route was originally IV but became one of the earliest via ferrata now known as Via Ferrata Mesules (Posneckerstieg). It gives a pleasant day out with superb views or provides an easy descent from routes reaching the summit.

Base hut – Sella 30min to the start 300m 1½hr or 1hr in descent

6.18 Follow path 649 for 500m beyond the N side of the Sella Towers to reach a chimney just R of an impressive black wall which is often wet.
    The route is obvious with iron rungs, cables and red paint. It first climbs a dark chimney to the top of a pillar and then a 100m wall to a traversing path L which leads to the saddle between Piz Selva and Piz di Ciavazes. From here the summit of Ciavazes is easily reached by its NE ridge or the scramble can be continued up a gully to the main Sella plateau.

SOUTH FACE
This face has at least twelve routes up it and most of them give excellent climbing. It is crossed by an obvious large terrace known as Cengia dei Camosci (Gamsband) which provides an easy traverse from the base of the Sella Towers on the W. Some routes finish at the terrace and very few parties climb the upper pitches of the three routes which do have top sections.
    The wall is divided into three sections by two great clefts. To the L of the L-hand cleft the SW dièdre (6.24) actually starts at the L-hand end of the terrace and climbs a dièdre in the upper wall. The first great cleft is climbed by the Solda Route which is hard (VI) and not often repeated whilst the arête on its L is taken by Via Italia (6.23), a spectacular aid climb. The grey wall to its R starting near the corner is climbed by the Rossi Route. This fine climb is IV with a short crack of V. It is marked with paint, has cemented pegs in place and finishes on the terrace.
    The South Face Direct Route (6.21) with the Buhl alternative to the terrace (6.22) climbs the centre of this face whilst the Schubert Route

(6.25) climbs its R edge. The second great cleft gives the line of South Chimney (V, Gluck, Demetz, Tutino) and the broken face to its R gives the Old Micheluzzi Route (IV+) This is a fine climb which starts below the cleft, goes R and then back L to reach the top of a prominent pillar after 100m and continues from the L going gradually R joining niches with steep wall pitches and finally passing between two yellow OHs to gain the terrace.

To the R an obvious ramp slopes from L to R across the face giving the line of 6.19. From the start of the ramp Via Irma goes direct up the wall (VI+ or V/A1) whilst the arête on the R-hand end of the face is climbed by the excellent SE Ridge Route (6.20).

Descent is possible from the R end of the Cengia dei Camosci (I) but is not obvious. It goes round the corner to reach the gully falling from between Piz di Ciavazes and Piz Lasties.

SOUTH FACE (RAMP ROUTE)
Del Torso, Lezuo, 1935.

A pleasant route useful early in the season but out of character with the other routes on the S face.

Base hut – Sella 15min to the start 300m 3hr (5hr to the summit)

6.19
IV
39
Scramble up to the foot of the obvious ramp and take the easiest line of grey rock tending R. After several pitches traverse L to reach a chimney which splits a steepening in the wall (IV). Continue up the rib until easier rock on the SE ridge leads to the terrace. Either walk off R from here, or go round the SE ridge and climb unpleasantly loose rock on the R (III) to the summit plateau.

SOUTH-EAST RIDGE
Abram, Gombocz, 1953.

A classic free climb with only one hard section.

Base hut – Sella 15min to the start from the road 170m 3½hr to the terrace

6.20
VII
V+/A1
39
Start 20m L of the ridge.

1   25m Climb direct (III) then R up red rock (IV-) to reach grassy ledges

2   35m Go straight up then slightly L (IV+) and finally diagonally R (IV) up yellow rock

3 40m Move up, bear L then R to reach a crack in a grey corner. Follow this over two bulges (V) to a good stance on the R

4 20m From the L of the stance climb a crack over a yellow OH (V+) and up a corner to an airy stance on a flake on the L

5 20m Return to the corner, climb it to its end and exit R below a roof (VII or A1,V)

6 40m Climb L up a slab on good rock (III+)

7 25m Climb a corner crack (IV+) and continue direct (V-)

8 40m Go past a bulge (IV+) and reach a stance at a col on the ridge

9 35m Climb a vertical crack (V-) on the R of the ridge

10 25m Bridge up a vertical crack very near the arête (V-)

11 100m Three easier pitches lead to the terrace (III,IV,III).

It is usual to finish here but the route does continue above the terrace starting slightly R moving from R to L near the upper arête for 100m (III,IV). Then move R to a very hard traverse (VI) and finally a wet black crack (VI) and chimneys which lead to the plateau.

SOUTH FACE DIRECT
Micheluzzi, Castiglioni, 1935.

A fine free climb probably the most attractive in the area and comparable with the Comici Route on the Cima Grande de Lavaredo (17.13) and the Steger Route on Catinaccio (3.19). The main difficulties are on the lower wall and the 90m traverse is quite spectacular. Some danger of stonefall early in the season. The route is well worn, very popular and there is an abseil escape from part way across the traverse.

Base hut – Sella 15min to the start from the road 300m to the terrace 5hr (7hr to the summit)

6.21
VI

Start at the centre of the wall at an arrow scratched into the face L of a yellow OH.

1 30m Move up the wall for 2m over smooth grey rock, then move 3m R and above a bulge (IV+), continue bearing slightly R for 25m (V-) to a turf-covered ledge

2 45m From the R-hand end of the ledge climb L over slabs (V) and then traverse L (VI-) to a rock knob. Continue 3m R to a dièdre

(V) which leads in 15m to a stance below a bulging OH

3   40m Move R and then back L over a series of slabs (V-) and reach a ledge leading to the foot of a loose yellow crack. Climb this (V-) for 8m to a good stance

4   40m Continue direct up a dièdre (V+) and then follow an easier gully (IV,III) for 20m to a ledge

5   20m Go R (III) to a ledge with a small pointed flake belay and ring peg

6   35m Now the traverse starts. Descend to a small rib and continue R (V+)

7   35m Continue horizontally and then descend slightly (V). Traverse 15m R and descend 2m to a turf ledge (V+) and a stance 5m R

8   30m Traverse slightly upwards, go 8m horizontally (V+), descend and make a hard move R (VI or rope move) and finally climb up 6m R to a good stance at the end of the traverse

9   35m Take a diagonal line R round the ridge passing an OH on the R (V+) and continue up a short crack to a good stance below easier slabs

10 45m Climb straight up for 30m first across a wall (V) then to the R of a small pillar (V) and finally up a short grassy crack (IV) to a rock knob. Go 15m slightly L to a stance

11 35m Continue slightly L (V)

12 80m Two pitches either direct (recommended), or slanting R, lead to the terrace (V,IV)

Most parties traverse off here but the route can be continued above. Go along the terrace 80m L to a spur. Climb grey rock, first up a 10m chimney then bearing L (III) for 120m to the L-hand upper end of the grey section. Stance in a deep niche below a big yellow OH. Go R on OHing rock (V+) and climb two easy traversing pitches R (III) to the bottom of a steep dièdre. Continue up this and a yellow buttress (V) and finally muddy cracks to the plateau.

SOUTH FACE DIRECT – SOUTH DIEDRE
Buhl, Streng, 1949.

This is really a direct variation to 6.21 although it is possible to reach the dièdre from below by a line parallel to the usual route. It climbs the big yellow dièdre in the higher part of the lower wall above the 90m traverse.

Base hut – Sella 15min to the start from the road 300m 7hr

6.22 Start as for 6.21 pitches 1–5 to reach the 90m traverse.

VI

39

6 40m Climb direct up a yellow dièdre (VI-) to a peg and sling. Descend 1m and move R (VI) and up to a small roof (V+). Move round this on the L and then return R to a higher dièdre which leads (V+) to a stance

7 40m Climb diagonally R across a steep yellow wall (V+,VI-,V+) to a corner just R of the line of the big yellow dièdre. Climb the corner (V) and step into the bottom of the dièdre

8 40m Climb the dièdre to a stance below an OH (V)

9 50m Go round the OH (VI) and continue up the corner (V+)

10 20m Go R past a niche and round a small roof (V+) to the terrace.

SOUTH FACE (VIA ITALIA)
Francheschi and party, 1961.

A good training or bad weather aid climb which takes the prominent yellow OHing ridge L of the gully and finishes on the terrace.

Base hut – Sella 15min to the start 250m 6hr

6.23 Scramble up the grass to the foot of the face proper (55-60m). Start

VI/A3 3m L of the ridge and climb grey rock, interspersed with grass,

39 trending towards the ridge (45m, V). Move R and climb a small corner to a ledge. Climb the OH to a better stance (two pegs) and belay in a small corner on the ridge.

The aid climbing starts here. Traverse 10m L from the belay (V) and climb the yellow, OHing wall to a good stance (25m, A1 and A2). Climb over a large flake on the L followed by a wall and OHs above to a stance in étriers below the 6m roof (25m, A2 and A3). Climb the wall to the roof (A1), then the roof itself on bolts (A3). Take a stance in étriers 3m above the lip of the OH. Climb the wall for 10m (A1), go L, then R (V+,VI, free and loose) to a traverse line to the R. Follow this for 10m (V) then climb up for 10m to a stance on the ridge. Climb up the ridge (loose) then the OHing dièdre above to a crack

133

branching out L (A1 and A2). Break out to the L and go straight up the wall above (A1), followed by a section of easier rock (IV) to the terrace.

SOUTH-WEST DIEDRE
Vinatzer, Riefesser, 1934.

This is an excellent route up the upper wall starting above the L-hand end of the terrace. With the descent by the Via Ferrata Mesules (6.18) and possibly preceded by a route on the S face of Ciavazes lower wall or S face of the First Sella Tower it gives a delightful day's climbing.

Base hut – Sella 30min to the start 250m 4hr

6.24 Reach the start by scrambling up the lower part of 6.08 to reach the
VI+ end of the terrace (Cengia dei Camosci). Start just R of the L-hand of
V+/A1 two clean cracks which meet in the prominent dièdre above.

1 35m Climb up grey slabs (III) to a stance below a roof

2 40m Turn the OH on the L (IV+) and continue up grey slabs near the L-hand crack (III,IV) to a stance in the crack

3 30m Climb the steep grey crack (V-) and go round an OH on the L to a good stance

4 40m Continue near the crack (IV) to a stance in the main dièdre

5 40m Climb the dièdre (V-) and a crack (V) to a cave stance

6 10m Move out onto the R wall round an OH (VI+ or A1) and up a short crack (V+) to an uncomfortable stance

7 30m Move back into the dièdre and follow cracks up it (V-,V)

8 40m A wall (IV+) and a final crack (V) lead to the plateau.

SOUTH FACE (SCHUBERT ROUTE)
Schubert, Mathies, 1967.

A good modern free route up the R-hand side of the central lower wall. The route follows the L edge of the deep chimney on excellent rock.

Base hut – Sella 15min to the start 220m 3hr

6.25 Start a few m L of the bottom of the chimneys at the foot of a yellow
VI dièdre.
VI-/A0
39 1 40m Climb the dièdre (V-), move L (V) and climb a grey slab

(IV+,VI-) until it is possible to move R into a crack. Stance
halfway up it

2   40m Continue up the crack (V), step R and climb to reach, and
climb, a higher crack (V,IV+)

3   40m Move up (V) and over a bulge (V+) and go R to reach a
dièdre (V). Climb it (VI-) to a good stance

4   40m Climb a yellow ramp R (V+) past a knob. Continue up a grey
slab (V)

5   40m Climb a difficult shallow corner R (V,VI or A0) and continue
direct up the steep wall (exposed, VI-). This pitch can be avoided
by an inferior but easier variant on the L (IV+,V). Both ways lead
to a good stance

6   40m Climb the steep grey wall first R then L (IV+) to reach a
dièdre (V) and then go L to a stance

7   40m Climb a smooth slab diagonally R (V+,IV+) and then go
more easily to a stance

8   25m Easily R to the terrace (III).

Sass Pordoi 2952m

*This summit is easily reached by cablecar or path from the Pordoi Pass.
Whilst the S face is short the NW and W faces are quite large. A scree
terrace which crosses these faces 200m from the top leads to easy ground in
either direction whilst if the top plateau is reached an easy walk R up the
line of a ski tow leads to the summit.*

NORTH-WEST FACE (FEDELE ROUTE)
Masè Dari, Bernard, 1929.

*The route is best seen from the Sella pass. On the L of the blunt ridge which
divides the W face and the NW face are two black water streaks. The route
zig-zags between these streaks as far as the big terrace. It gives some fine
wall and chimney climbing. It is not recommended in spring or wet
weather.*

*Base – Pian Schiaveneis 5km on Canazei side of Sella pass 30min to the
start 750m 6hr*

6.26
IV+
36

Start 100m L of the lowest point of the rocks. The first 60m are easy (II); then keep R up ever steepening shelves (30m,III) to where the wall becomes vertical.

Start from near the L-hand streak, climb a pitch up a crack in a dièdre (IV+) to a pulpit then traverse diagonally R across to the R-hand streak. Traverse across the streak and climb a difficult wall (IV+) to a good crack (IV+, crux) leading to the top of a small pillar (obvious from below). Now traverse diagonally L in a series of cracks and slabs for 60m (III+,IV+) to a second pillar on the L-hand streak. Climb a wet, vertical groove and return R along a ledge to climb a short dièdre (IV+) to a stance. Return L again up a steep ramp on good holds (III+) to a large groove near the top of the L-hand streak. After one pitch in the groove (IV+), it deepens into a chimney on the R of the streak (III). Move L and climb a deep yellow crack (IV+) in the L wall. Exit on the L by an exposed traverse on good holds to a deep, slanting chimney on the L. Climb it and a short wall to the main terrace near a huge block. Finish as for W Face (6.28) or walk R to finish up 6.27.

SOUTH PILLAR (PIAZ ARETE)
Piaz, Del Torso, Springorum, Piaz, 1933.

A good route on excellent rock climbing the arête between the SE and SW faces.

Base – Pordoi Pass 1hr to the start 250m 3hr

6.27
V+/A0

From the pass follow path 627 until it is possible to traverse R to the arête directly below the cablecar. Start just L of the arête by a triangular subsidiary pillar.

Climb 60m first up a groove (IV) to a ledge then go up onto the arête and up this to the top of the triangular pillar (IV+,III). Now go up to an OH and pass this (A0,V-) to reach a good ledge just R of the arête. Three pitches up the arête (V-,IV,IV) lead to the top of the S pillar. Descend to a col between the pillar and the main face and follow 6.31 to the summit.

WEST FACE
Dibona, Rizzi, Mayer, 1910.

A classic route up this great face similar to the NW Wall (6.26). It goes up to the R of the blunt ridge.

Base – Pian Schiaveneis 5km on Canazei side of Sella pass 30min to the start 800m 6hr

6.28
IV+
36
Start up easy rock 50m to the R of a black streak which falls from a large hollow in the middle of the face. Climb a subsidiary spur L over cracks and slabs to a short chimney on the L. Above this an exposed, sloping traverse over a great slab is followed by easier rock to the large hollow.

Follow a dièdre/gully at the back L-hand side of the hollow (a variant continues R) first climbing a few m L on a yellow wall. At the end of the dièdre climb L across a difficult slab (IV+) then over less difficult rock by cracks and chimneys to the great scree terrace. (Escape R).

Walk 80m L (N) to reach an immense block. Go L up a short wall over good rock to a ledge. Finally the 200m L to R sloping chimney gives interesting climbing to the summit plateau.

SOUTH-WEST FACE
Andreoli, Saggin, 1947.

A fine, free climb. Its S aspect means it is often dry when the NW wall is a waterfall.

Base – Pian Schiaveneis 5km on Canazei side of Sella pass 40min to the start 800m 7hr

6.29
V
36
Start 40m to the L of the prominent, preliminary rock step under the end of the S face and beneath a black section of wall between the Piccolo Pordoi and the W face of Sass Pordoi. Climb scree-covered rock (IV-) to where the wall becomes vertical. Climb a crack (IV+) to reach an amphitheatre four rope lengths above the start. Traverse across the amphitheatre R to the beginning of a crack. Climb the crack for two pitches and move L over a slab to an OH. Climb the OH on its R side. A few more m lead to a good stance. Climb up a crack from the stance (V+, crux). Climb diagonally R to a poorly defined ridge and climb half way up it to a good stance. Climb over easier rock for two pitches to reach a scree-covered ledge. One further rope length leads to a small amphitheatre. Follow the gully in its centre for several pitches to a black, detached slab, a few m to the R of which is a thin crack and a peg. Climb this crack and traverse R to reach a slab. Climb the slab on the R edge to a good stance under a small OH. One last short pitch leads to the great scree-covered terrace under the summit. There are routes up the wall above but the best option is to walk R and finish up 6.27.

SOUTH FACE (VIA DELLA GALLERIA)
Piaz, Scheibler, Seligman, 1930.

An interesting and enjoyable chimney climb up the wall below the cablecar station.

Base – Pordoi Pass 1hr to the start 250m 3hr

6.30
IV
41

Approach as for 6.27 but continue L for about 100m along the terrace which leads round to the W and N faces.

Start directly below a pinnacle (Ditone) visible high on the wall. Climb 60m up ledges and a chimney (III) to reach an obvious horizontal ledge. Do not follow pegs above but walk 40m R and climb up R (IV-) to the start of a ramp leading back L for 80m and finally up for 20m (III+) to a stance below the chimney on the R of the pinnacle. Climb a crack and the chimney (IV) for 40m and then move L behind the pinnacle (III) to reach a final chimney with jammed blocks which leads (IV,III) to the plateau.

SOUTH PILLAR (VIA MARIA)
Piaz, Dezuzian, 1932.

This pleasant but short route is one of the most popular from the Pordoi pass.

Base – Pordoi Pass 1hr to the start 250m 3af]hr

6.31
IV
41

Approach as for 6.30 but move R to a chimney on the R of the S pillar at the beginning of the SE face.

Climb the chimney between the S pillar and the main face, or a crack on its L for 40m (IV). Continue up the L wall past a small bulge to an obvious ledge (III,IV). Move 18m L on the ledge and climb a steep ramp R on good yellow rock until below a large yellow roof (IV). Move up a few m, traverse R round the edge and continue diagonally (III) to a col between the pillar and the main face. Bridge up and gain the main face and climb this R wards passing an awkward bulge to a stance in a niche (IV). Now continue, still R, over dirty poor rock for 40m (IV-) to reach a gully which leads to the summit in 50m (III).

Gran Campanile de Murfreid 2724m

NORTH EAST FACE
Pescosta, Trenker, 1912.

This is the more northerly of the two towers on the edge of the Sella plateau at the junction of the Gardena valley and the main valley. A fine climb on fairly sound rock.

Base – the road 3km below the P Gardena 45min to the start 450m 6hr

6.32
IV
Follow the broad ledge which cuts across the base of both towers to below the N Ridge of the Gran Campanile. Climb L up slabs for about 50m to a line of steep walls which bar the way. Move L round a small corner on the NE face and follow a series of easy chimneys to near their end, where a ledge cuts horizontally across the face. Traverse R to a small terrace and round the corner to a hidden 25m crack . Climb it to a good ledge, traverse along the ledge past a small red corner, and climb 35m up a wall of brittle rock to a comfortable ledge near the N ridge. From this point there is a long traverse leading L across to the SE ridge.

Follow a ledge leading up to the L for one pitch, then continue horizontally L for 40m on narrow shelves, finally slanting up to a grass stance below a stretch of grey slabs. Climb a narrow crack for 15m continuing to the L across slabs for 30m to where they become smoother. Here a crack is found, steepening towards its top. Climb it for 50m to a ledge on the SE ridge. Follow easier slabs for 20m to a pinnacle and climb a crack on the R to the foot of twin yellow cracks. Climb the exposed R-hand crack for 15m to a broad scree ledge below the final wall. Continue up a 30m chimney directly to the summit.

DESCENT BY ORDINARY ROUTE

6.33
Very loose but there are good abseil pegs. From the summit descend 35m easily to a col on the S side. On the R (W) is a short OHing chimney above a wide gully. Descend the chimney. Start down the gully without difficulty until it steepens, followed by two or three abseils with bits of scrambling in between, to the point where an obvious ledge leads out L (looking down).

Follow the ledge and go L down broken slabs to above an OHing wall with a chimney on the L. Abseil down the wall, from pegs, and continue down the gully bed towards the col between the W ridge and some smaller pinnacles. From a loose ledge about 30m above the col, abseil on to it and then descend the gully on the Sella side. Most of the gully is easy with short, awkward pitches at the top and one at the very bottom. The gully leads down into the hanging valley on the S side of the two towers.

Traverse across the valley towards the Sella pass and across the shoulder on a well marked path. The path contours round at the same level then descends to the road. (3hr)

Torre del Murfreid 2631m

NORTH FACE CHIMNEY
Covi, Hruschka, 1928.

This is the most prominent of the towers on the Sella side of the Gardena Pass. The N face is split by a diagonal chimney to give a hard, popular route.

Base – the road 3km below the P Gardena 45min to the start 400m 5hr

6.34 The route is in four sections. First a lower section up to the start of
V the chimney proper, next the chimney itself, then a hard section where it closes and finally easy rock to the summit.

Climb easily up to the bottom of a vertical chimney (60m). Climb this (V) for 35m to the foot of the main chimney, or take cracks & grooves on the R to a terrace & then traverse back L to the chimney.

Climb the chimney for 4 pitches (IV,V-) moving out L when necessary and passing several jammed blocks, a cave with a roof hole exit, a white slab, a wall, a 12m crack, more chockstones, and OHs usually turned on the L, to finally reach a small stance under a large OH level with the top of the chimney.

Climb diagonally L up a 12m OHing crack (V, crux) to a shallow niche. Traverse L across an exposed yellow slab to a crack and climb through the OHs above to reach a good ledge (V). Continue up an easier, pleasant crack. Continue more easily up to the R to the summit ridge for 100m and so reach the summit.

DESCENT BY ORDINARY ROUTE
6.35 Descend about 20m down a groove on the S side of the summit until a piton is reached on the R (looking out). From this abseil 25m to a ledge. Scramble down easy rocks, first R then L, to a deep gully. Cross this and traverse L along an obvious line until some abseil slings on a large bollard are reached. After a short abseil scramble over a subsidiary tower to reach the col. Take the gully on the E side of the tower away from the Sella pass. If the gully is full of snow go down rocks on the L and 45m from the bottom traverse back across the gully to easy ground. (1hr)

Geografica 1:25,000 sheet 6

This is the highest group in the Dolomites. The N side is a glacier partially used for summer skiing and served by a chairlift and cablecar whilst the S face is one of the greatest Dolomite walls. In recent years it has seen the change from peg and bolt to modern style free ascents.

The peaks can be approached from Canazei in the W or from Malga Ciapela to the E, and the walk over the Ombretta Pass, via the Contrin and Falier huts, gives a marvellous view of the wall, as does the easy ascent of Sasso Vernale.

There are three main summits. To the W is Marmolada di Penia, then Marmolada di Rocca and finally Marmolada d'Ombretta, a ridge rather than a summit, with a cablecar station at its W, higher, end.

HUTS

Contrin Hut 2016m. Approach from Canazei, path 602 (2hr) or drive from Alba, then path 602 (1½hr)

Marmolada E Castiglioni Hut 2054m. There are a number of other huts in this area. Approaches– i)from Malga Ciapela drive over the P Fedaia ii)drive from Canazei

O Falier Hut 2074m. Approach– from Malga Ciapela drive through the campsite and past a big farm on the R. Parking possible for next 500m; then walk up path 610 (1½hr)

Bivouac Marco del Bianco 2702m. On the Ombretta pass. Sleeps 9 and busy in good weather as it is a good base for many S face routes. Approaches– see HUT LINKS below

HUT LINKS

Contrin to: Falier (606,610) 2¾hr←3¼hr, Marmolada (606) 4½hr←4¾hr, Biv Marco del Bianco (606,610) 1½hr

Falier to: Biv Marco del Bianco (606,610) 1½hr

Biv Marco del Bianco to: Marmolada (606) 2½hr

Marmolada di Penia 3343m

NORMAL ROUTE - GLACIER
Grohman, Dimai, Dimai, 1864.

The route is tiring and perhaps even a little tedious. The chairlift can be taken from Fedaia to the edge of the glacier.

Base – Fedaia 700m 3½hr

7.01
PD
From the chairlift go up the glacier valley between the rocky N ridge of the Marmolada di Penia and the glaciated broad N ridge coming down from the Marmolada di Rocca. After a steep section the smaller glacial plain of the Pian dei Fiacchi is reached. Now bear slightly R up the valley following tracks. Before the steep wall up to the col between two summits, go R up easy steps and keep R to reach the broad snow ridge above the rocky N ridge. Keep on its R (W) flank and go up to the summit.

WEST RIDGE
Rizzi, Seyffert, Dittmann, 1898.

A much frequented route equipped with fixed ropes, ladders and spikes which remove all the difficulty. It is a very exposed route in fine position.

Base Hut – Contrin 450m 2hr

7.02
I
Start just below the F d Marmolada between the Gran Vernel and Marmolada di Penia. Climb the snow slope and go up a narrow gully with a ladder on its R wall to reach the col. From the col follow tracks on the N side to reach the ridge below a steep step. Now go up L (N) on fixed ropes and over a long, exposed series of steps to more gently angled slabs. Keep slightly L of the ridge on fixed ropes and climb a further step back to the ridge which is now not so steep. Follow tracks over easy rock to the upper snow-covered part of the ridge and so reach the highest point.

SOUTH-WEST FACE (SOLDA)
Solda, Conforto, 1936.

A classic climb with reasonable protection. One of the hardest pre-war routes taking 36hr on the first ascent. Rock generally good but a real danger of ice and water in the final chimneys and safer later in the season.

Base Hut – Contrin or Biv Marco del Bianco 1½ or 5min to the start 550m 8hr

7.03
VI
V+/A1
44

The start is below an obvious diagonal chimney on the L of the central nose and leads towards the R-hand end of an obvious terrace.

1   40m Take the gully (II) to the chimney (III) on the L

2   20m Climb a yellow friable wall (IV+), step 2m L to a ramp and climb this to a ledge

3   40m From the middle of the stance climb a smooth vertical crack (IV+), a ramp L(III) and another crack (V)

4   20m Continue up a ramp L (III) then scree-covered steps and ledges R

5   30m Continue to a higher stance

6   40m Zig-zag R up a smooth slab (IV+) and finally traverse R (IV+) to a good stance below ill-defined cracks L of a pillar

7   15m Climb a good flake crack (V-), step R and climb another crack (IV+)

8   40m Either step L and climb a vertical crack (V), or climb a crack direct (IV,V) and traverse L (A1). Continue up the crack (V-)

9   45m Climb a steep crack up the vertical wall (VI- or A1/A2). Continue (IV+,V-) to a narrow ledge on the L

10 20m Direct via a chimney (V-) to another small stance

11 30m Climb a friable dièdre for 12m (IV-), then an OH by a crack (V+ or A1) and continue to the half way terrace. Move L to below the great yellow dièdre which the route now follows

12 40m Climb a smooth slab (V) then an 8m chimney (IV) to reach two roofs. Take the first direct (V+ or A2) and the second on the R (V-,V+ or A1) to a stance in the corner below a chimney

13 20m Climb the chimney (IV+) then a roof (V+ or A2) to a little ledge

14 30m Step R and climb a yellow crack up an overhanging wall (V+ or A2) then easier R (IV)

15 40m Take an oblique crack R (V-), traverse a grey slab R (IV+) and finally a 9m dièdre (IV+)

16 20m Climb a dièdre (V) to a good ledge

17 40m Go R by a ramp (III) then a horizontal traverse R (IV) to reach a niche

18 30m Climb an overhanging crack up a black wet wall (VI or A2).
In bad weather this pitch is extremely difficult and retreat very
serious

19 70m Continue up the great chimney gully (IV+). In bad
conditions it may be easier to take to the wall on the L in this
upper section

20 35m Follow the gully on friable rock (IV+)

21 40m Loose slabs on the R (III) lead to the W ridge.

NEW SOUTH PILLAR
Kroll, Brandstatter, Iovane, Mariacher, 1979.

*This is a modern free route taking a direct line up the S pillar. It replaces
the S Pillar Direct of Scheffler and Uhner (VI/A3) with which it shares
some pitches. Not so badly affected by ice and water as the older chimney
and gully routes, with only two chimney pitches above the halfway terrace
suffering this problem. Very few pegs used but big chocks very useful and
50m double rope advisable. Some poor rock.*

*Three routes start near together at the foot of the pillar directly below
the summit. These are the Scheffler on the R, joining this route briefly at the
top of the great upper tower; the Micheluzzi (7.05) which climbs the
R-hand flank of the pillar finishing up the obvious groove near the top,
direct to the summit; and this route which keeps on the crest until its final
pitches which are on the R.*

*There is a little overhung bay at the base of the pillar. The Scheffler
takes the easy break a few m to the L, the Micheluzzi (7.05) starts from the
R-hand corner of the bay whilst this route goes direct from the L-hand
corner of the bay.*

*Base Hut – Contrin or Biv Marco del Bianco 1½ or 5min to the start
550m 8hr*

7.04
VI+

1 45m Climb an OH and crack (V+) on the R of a little tower, step
R and continue direct (V) to a stance

2 45m Take a smooth crack (V,V+) and then continue R (II) to the
first terrace

3 40m Climb the corner, then diagonally L up a loose chimney/crack
below a bulge and back R to a stance (V) below a dièdre

4 35m Climb the dièdre (IV) and then go R and up a little groove
(III) to a tiny stance

5 50m Climb a crack (IV+) on the L of the edge and then go diagonally R (III) to a ledge. Step R and climb a crack on the R of the edge

6 50m Climb a wall (IV,V), move R and climb a steep crack (V+) and a slanting slab (III) to a stance on the L

7 40m Climb a loose chimney/crack past an OH (VI-), then R to the second terrace at the foot of a chimney behind a great detached tower

8 40m Start up the R wall (V) then take the chimney (IV)

9 40m Continue up the chimney (III) to a stance in a col behind the tower

The next two pitches are in common with the Scheffler route.

10 30m Climb the wall above (VI+) to a bad stance (slings?)

11 30m Continue slightly L (VI) to another bad stance. The Scheffler route escapes from here up the Micheluzzi route a few m R in the corner chimney – still hard!

12 25m Continue up and L (V+) to a stance on the edge

13 40m A short slab (V) and a move L leads to an abseil in a shallow corner, landing on a small ledge

A direct finish is possible up the cracks above (V+,VI-)

14 30m Traverse slabs L (V+) to reach a chimney (IV) and a stance

15 40m Turn the OH above on the L (IV) and continue (V) to easier ground

16 40m Scree covered rock to the ridge (III) a few m L of the summit.

SOUTH PILLAR

Micheluzzi, Perathoner, Christomannos, 1929.

This old classic route is best climbed in late season. Some loose rock, stonefall and ice plus three pitches up a waterfall make it a serious undertaking, to be avoided in uncertain weather. Starts just to the R of the New S Pillar (7.04) to the R side of the cave.

Base hut – Contrin or Biv Marco del Bianco 1½ or 5min to the start 550m 9hr

7.05

VI/A0

44

1 25m Climb the OH and an oblique chimney crack (IV-)

2 25m Continue up a smooth narrow chimney (IV) to a pulpit

3 30m Climb a smooth slabby dièdre (V) by a hidden crack on the L to the terrace

4 30m A pillar above is formed by two cracks. Climb the R-hand crack, partly OHing (V) to the top of the pillar

5 25m Climb indefinite cracks (IV), traverse R along a short ledge past a shallow chimney to the top of the second pillar

6 35m A few m R a line of faint cracks up the yellow wall gives magnificent and exposed climbing (VI-) to a big niche

7 35m Climb an OH on the L and continue to a tiny pulpit (V+)

8 30m Difficult climbing up small indefinite yellow cracks (VI-) leads to a small niche. Next traverse R (VI-) to a small ledge at the foot of a series of grey cracks (not obvious) which are deeper and less difficult

9 100m Three pitches (IV+,IV,IV-) lead to the second terrace

10 40m Above is a wet gully between yellow ribs. (The chimney 20m L is taken by the New S Pillar 7.04). Climb the wet gully turning the first OH on the R wall, just R of the water, by a smooth crack (V+)

11 30m Continue by a vertical crack (V). (Beware of stonefall in this section)

12 30m Take the L-hand crack via an OH (V+)

13 40m Continue up the deeper sandy gully above (IV-) to a big cave blocked by an enormous block OHing 6m

14 20m The OH is turned on the R (A0/V) by a variety of rope moves etc. (In icy conditions a crack further R may be climbed (VI))

15 40m Move easily up the icy gully bed

16 30m Continue up the gully forking R (IV)

17 30m Climb the R-hand crack in the gully bed (VI)

18 40m Easily to the summit (II).

SOUTH FACE
Bettega, Zagonel, Tomasson, 1901.

This is a popular and classic route. The difficulties are mainly in the lower half but there is stonefall danger at mid-height, and bad weather can make the upper section hard. The alternative Leuchs finish is rarely climbed.

Base hut – Contrin or Biv Marco del Bianco 1½ or 5min to the start 650m 5hr

7.06
IV+
44

For the start descend E from the col past a first deep corner (alternative start) and a smooth nose to an easier line of chimneys just R of a memorial plaque.

Enter the chimneys by a gangway from the L and climb for several rope lengths, passing a few OHs on the L (IV-). The chimney closes at a big black OH which is climbed by a thin crack (IV+). Follow a 45m chimney with small walls and then a 45m chimney closed by an OH (IV+). A small chimney leads to the beginning of the first terrace.

A less popular alternative start avoids the first chimneys which are notorious for stonefall. From the Ombretta Pass follow the path down to the foot of the wall. Start 45m R of the huge gully up the R-hand side of a leaning pillar. From its top traverse 4m R. Climb 6m to ·each a stance. Leave this from the L end and climb to reach a chimney/crack . Climb this to reach a convenient stance and continue in this crack line to the first terrace where it joins the original route.

Traverse L on scree-covered ledges to near the gully overlooking the pillar (not too near, because of stonefall down the gully). Reach a prominent smooth, grey slab and climb it (IV+) direct. Under a high yellow tower traverse downwards to the R for a rope length to a steep gully and climb this to a corner. Go up the corner and the slab on its R in a line of cracks to the second terrace (IV). Traverse R (beware of stonefall) along this for several easy rope lengths and pass below a huge pinnacle. On the other side of the pinnacle climb the R-hand of two chimneys (IV) and then easier rock. Continue through a cleft in a block and via a small corner to a short steep wall, and after this on less difficult rock. More cracks and little chimneys are climbed to continue in the direction of the col between the Punta di Rocca and the Punta di Penia. Climb up the easy ridge on the L to the summit.

SOUTH FACE (VIA OMBRELLO)
Reiser, Mariacher, 1982.

*A modern free route with very few pegs . 50m double rope recommended.
First ascended in winter when the wall was dry. In summer and autumn
some pitches may be wet hence the route name! Some poor rock.*

*Base hut – Contrin or Bivouac Marco del Bianco 1½ or 5min to the start
680m 6hr*

7.07
VI
44
Start midway between the original S Face (7.06) and Sudtiroler Weg (7.08) Routes, below a line of cracks leading up the R-hand side of an obvious pinnacle at 250m.

1 40m Get onto a rib and climb it (IV-) and easier rock (II) to a ledge below the corner proper

2 50m Over an OH, then a smooth crack (V+) to a dièdre with three bulges (V)

3 40m A chimney (III,IV-) to a yellow niche

4 40m Another chimney on the L (IV-), traverse R (IV) and a chimney (III) to a stance at the foot of a ramp

5 40m Climb the ramp R and a curving chimney (IV-)

6 45m The corner crack (IV) then on the R (III) to a final dièdre (IV+) to a stance level with the top of the pinnacle

7 40m Move R up a loose wall (IV+) and then a loose crack up yellow rock (V+) to a higher ledge

8 25m Traverse R across the wall below OHs (II)

9 50m Climb a shallow, smooth, dark grey corner (VI-) then a loose OH (VI) to reach and climb a chimney with jammed blocks (IV-)

10 40m Continue up the chimney (III) for 20m and then break out R across the wall (V-) to a small stance

11 40m Move up L to reach a higher chimney (IV,IV+) and climb this (IV)

12 40m Ignore the gully above and climb a crack on the R wall (III) to a ledge, move R on this (II) and take a steep crack on the L of the arête (III)

13 50m Climb a loose crack (V), an arête (III) and finally a corner crack (IV-) to reach the middle of the second terrace

Finish up the original S Face Route (7.06) 200m.

SOUTH FACE (SUDTIROLER WEG)
Messner, Renzler, 1969.

This interesting route climbs the wall below the terrace of the original S Face Route (7.06), taking a line up the slabs below and R of the great bulging wall and a steep dièdre to join the second terrace at its R end. The dièdre can be very hard after wet weather.

Base hut – Contrin or Biv Marco del Bianco 1½ or 5min to the start 700m 7hr

7.08 Start directly below the R end of the second terrace, 50m L of the
VI/A0 water stripe which marks the start of the Gogna route (7.11)
VI/A2

1 20m Scramble up easily and traverse ledges past two caves to the foot of a dièdre (I)

2 40m Climb the dièdre (V+) move R below a little roof and continue to a pulpit (IV+)

3 40m Ignore the chimney on the L and climb a dièdre (IV+,V) to a ledge on the R

4 30m Move up R to a dièdre (IV) to ledges

5 40m Climb the cracked dièdre above (V+), continue to a roof then move L (IV+) to pass the top of a pillar and reach a stance in a dièdre

6 25m Easily up L (III) to a stance at the start of the slabs leading up R below the main OHing face

7 25m Climb a slab on the R (IV) to a stance back L

8 45m Continue past a yellow bulge (V) and a chimney (IV)

9 45m Slabs lead diagonally R (IV+)

10 50m Continue up R on steep slabs (IV+,V) to a stance on the R

11 90m Two long pitches (IV) lead Rwards to the end of the first terrace

The route now strenuously follows the great dièdre slanting back L

12 40m First climb slabs on the R (V) then continue up a smooth chimney with jammed blocks (IV+)

13 50m A difficult green chimney (V) and then a dièdre/chimney (VI or A0/V+)

14 30m A short slab (V) then various ways up or inside past three jammed blocks (V+ or A1) to a cave stance

15 30m Leave the cave with pegs (VI-/A0 or A2) and continue (VI- or V+/A1) to a stance below a chimney

16 25m Chimney/dièdre (IV+,V-) to a stance below the final roofs

17 40m Traverse diagonally L (III,IV,V-) to reach the second terrace

Finish up the original S Face Route (7.06) 200m.

DESCENTS

7.09 a To the F d Marmolada via the W ridge via ferrata. Follow the ridge W and reverse 7.02.(I,½hr)

To Lago di Fedaia via glacier and chairlift. Descend due N until a descent R into Pian dei Fiacconi is possible (7.01 in reverse). Usually well tracked but not easy in bad weather. (2hr)

Marmolada di Rocca 3309m

NORMAL ROUTE – GLACIER
Grohmann, Pellegrini, 1862.

With modern uphill transport the old route via Pian dei Fiacchi is now less popular, and the glacier is climbed either from the Pian dei Fiacconi chairlift or the cablecar middle station or the top station between Marmolada di Rocca and Marmolada d'Ombretta. (2hr or 1½hr or 30min)

7.10 From Pian dei Fiacconi head SE (L) across the glacier towards the
PD middle station of the cablecar below Piz Serauta then turn W (R) and follow easy snow slopes up the line of the cablecar to the ridge. Continue W along the ridge with a short rock section near the summit.

SOUTH FACE (GOGNA or VIA DEL CINQUANTENARIO FISI)
Gogna, Dorigatti, Giambisi, Allemand, 1970.

A fine route, climbed free in 1982, which does not suffer from water and ice in the upper section. It climbs the walls and slabs to the R of the wet

chimney to the first terrace and then finishes up a beautiful arête to the summit of Punta Rocca.

Base Hut – Contrin or Biv Marco del Bianco 1½ or 10min to the start 800m 12hr

7.11
VII–
VI/A1
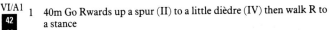

Start below the wet chimney 50m R of the Sudtiroler Weg (7.08) and 100m L of the Vinatzer Route (7.13)

1   40m Go Rwards up a spur (II) to a little dièdre (IV) then walk R to a stance

2   40m Climb a steep, damp dièdre/crack over a bulge (VI- or A0) then either continue up the crack to a pillar top (V) and then traverse R below roofs (VI or A0), or take a thin slab R (V)

3   35m Traverse R (V+) on slabs, move up (V) and then up a ramp L (IV) to a stance near a niche

4   25m Climb a dièdre on the L (IV+) then a crack (V-) to a stance at a pillar top

5   45m Climb a crack L, (V) then another short crack (V-) to reach a slab. Traverse this L (V) and move up (IV) to a stance

6   45m Climb a slabby gully/ramp L (III) until a traverse back R (IV) leads to a corner stance by a pillar

7   20m Go over the pillar, down R (V) and up a steep crack (VI- or V/A1)

8   30m Go R over a bulge (V) to a good ledge then back L (III) to a stance in an easier section

Two possibilities are available to the first terrace. The original R-hand route is more direct but can involve a wet chimney in early summer, the L-hand slab is easier and highly recommended.

DIRECT ROUTE

9   40m Climb to the top of a small pillar on the R, traverse R (V) and continue direct up a steep slab (V-) to a niche below roofs

10   20m Traverse R to reach and climb a crack (V+)

11   50m Step R (IV+) and climb the steep wet chimney (V+,VI- or V/A1) to a stance on the R

12   60m Easily up slabs (III) to the terrace. Walk 20m R to near a good bivouac site.

SLAB VARIANT

9 50m Continue up the easy ramp (II) then a steepening crack (IV+,V) to the pillar top

10 45m Climb the unprotected slab with a short traverse L at 30m and very small holds (V+)

11 35m Continue up the slab to a roof (V). Traverse R 20m to a poor stance

12 40m Over the roof (IV+) and up a slab, then R to the terrace (the final dièdre of the Messner Route (7.14) is 20m L). Walk R 70m to a good bivouac site.

This is a popular site. Modern Zeiten (7.12) reaches it direct whilst the Vinatzer Route (7.13) is just round the corner on the R, as is the Messner S face finish (7.14). (The best escape from here may be to abseil down the Vinatzer Route (7.13)).

13 35m Climb the corner crack (VI- or V/A1) until it is possible to break through the roofs R via an OHing crack (VII- or VI/A1) and continue to a stance at the base of a slabby ramp

14 100m Climb the ramp (III) and move L to the foot of a dièdre

15 20m Climb the dièdre (IV) to a good belay on the edge of the arête

16 40m Climb steeply past a bulge (V+) and then by a crack (IV)

17 35m Traverse R below a bulge (V+ or V/A0) to a crack (IV) which leads to another stance L of the edge

18 30m Take a short steep crack (V+) then move gently R on poorer rock (V,V+) to reach a very small stance

19 20m Continue up a crack to a stance on the shoulder (IV)

20 50m Climb up to a yellow bulge (V-), over this (V+), then a loose crack (VI- or A1/V) to a stance below a bulging wall

21 30m Climb a steep wall (V) then traverse R (VI+ or A2) to reach a chimney (V) leading to a stance on the R of the edge

22 30m Traverse R (VI) and then up (V) to a ledge. Continue up a crack (VI-)

23 40m Climb a steep wall (VI- or A0) then a slab (V+) and step L to a stance L of the edge

24 40m Up steeply (VI) then more easily (III) to the top.

SOUTH FACE (MODERN ZEITEN)
Mariacher, Iovane, 1982.

One of the hardest and most beautiful free climbs on Marmolada S face. Possible early in the season as there are no exit chimneys. As the name implies this is a modern free climb. Some pegs for protection may need to be placed. The first pitch is possibly the hardest. 50m double rope recommended.

Base Hut – Contrin or Biv Marco del Bianco 1½ or 10min to the start 800m 12hr

7.12
VII+
 42

Start 50m R of the Gogna Route (7.11)

1 50m Climb a shallow grey corner (II) then scramble R over scree to the foot of a groove and up this (III) to a pinnacle. Next climb the wall above to reach an obvious horizontal fault. Walk R past two caves to the foot of a very steep wall in a shallow corner

2 30m Climb the steep wall and a thin finger crack (6 peg runners, VII+)

3 30m Continue up a steep wall (VI) and then a smooth crack (IV-) to the top of a pinnacle

4 35m Step down R to reach another smooth crack, up this (IV-) and easily R to a stance on a narrow ledge

5 35m Climb the crack behind a flake (V+), then go L past a roof (VI-) and up a wall (V+) past a good thread (VI) to a good stance

6 35m Make a descending traverse back R (IV,V,VI-) to a stance below a pinnacle

7 40m Step R across a wet groove and climb a pillar (V-), then traverse a slab R (V+) and continue up a chimney (III) to a stance halfway

8 40m Break out onto smooth slabs on the R and climb these (III) to a stance on the L of a little niche

9 40m Move R towards the niche and climb a smooth crack (IV) and a ramp (II) until near the top of a pinnacle. Climb R across a steep wall (VI-) to a stance on a spur

10 40m Step up L to a ledge and climb a steep dark grey slab near a water stripe (4 peg runners) moving into the stripe (thread) for the final 10m (VI+)

11 35m Straight up to a roof, move L (V) and layback a steep crack (VI)

12 30m Continue up a smooth wide crack (V) to below a bulge and thread belay

13 40m Move L and up (III,II) to the great terrace near the bivouac site (junction with Vinatzer (7.13) and Gogna (7.11) Routes)

14 35m The Gogna Route takes the R-hand crack in the shallow corner, but this route takes a line a few metres L, over a bulge and up a cracked rib (4 peg runners) to the loose OH (VII-). Cross this and easier climbing (III) leads to a stance on the Gogna Route ramp

15 30m Do not follow the ramp L but climb direct up the wall (IV-)

16 30m Climb the water worn slabs (IV) moving L

17 30m Continue in the same line (V) to a stance on the L of a smooth crack beside a slight pillar

18 35m Climb the crack (V+) and the wall above (V) to a cave and large thread belay

19 30m Move down L and across (VI) to reach a second cave. Cross this and traverse round an OHing nose, climb up to a roof, turn this on the L and climb a crack to a poor stance (VII)

20 30m Climb a crack (V+), step L and then direct to a better stance

21 35m Step R, go up and then R (IV)

22 35m Climb a sloping slab with two threads (V)

23 35m Continue direct (V)

24 30m Zig-zag L up the wall (V+) round a loose flake with thread runners to a niche in the smooth wall (bong belay)

25 30m Move easily L, climb a small OH past a thread and up a steep pocketed wall (V+)

26 40m Move R to a peg, climb a steep wall on crystal holds (VI-), and then a very thin section (VII-) to a small slanting roof. Go over this, up a short crack (V+,IV-) to a thread. Finally traverse R for 5m on pockets (V+) and climb direct (V) to a stance

27 45m Climb a short crack (V+); move R to climb a pocketed wall (V-) leading to a little bulge with poor protection. Climb over this

(VI-) and continue up a thin crack (IV,VI), then make a delicate traverse L (VI) to reach a tiny resting place just below and L of a large niche. Continue direct (V-) until it is possible to move R on pockets, past a thread (VI-) and finally up to a higher niche

28 25m Exit L and climb more easily (III) to the ridge and by this to the summit.

SOUTH FACE (VINATZER ROUTE)
Vinatzer, Castiglioni, 1936.

A classic route up the lower wall, in its day the hardest route here. Now possible free as a 'genuine' grade VI route. All pegs needed should be present. The upper wall can be icy in early summer, whilst a storm can make the normal finish impossible and put a weak party in real trouble. The only possible escape from the middle terrace is by abseiling back down the route (45m double rope useful).

Base Hut – Contrin or Biv Marco del Bianco 1½ or 10min to the start 800m 8-10hr

7.13 Start below the only real weakness in the lower wall, a hidden
VI+ chimney up red rock about 80m R of the Gogna Route (7.11)
V+/A1
42 1 30m From the cave at the foot, bridge up the chimney (V+) and then the shallow dièdre above (V)

2 30m Climb a steep smooth slab L (V+ or A0) by a crack and step R to a stance

3 30m Start up the deep chimney (IV) and then take its L edge to a pulpit

4 35m Climb a steep little wall (V) then either take a crack on the L or move R round a roof (VI or A0) and go up a steep slab (V+)

5 35m Above is a series of corners. Climb the first direct (V+ or V/A0)

6 30m Climb the L wall (VI- or V/A0) by a vertical crack

7 30m Continue up the next smooth corner (VI+ or V+/A0) to a niche

8 20m Finally out of the niche (VI- or A0/V+) and up the short corner to finish over a loose OH (VI or V+/A0)

9 40m An easy ledge leads L and then up (III) to a stance just below a roof

10 35m Turn the roof on the R to reach a smooth dièdre. Up this (VI- or V+/A0)

11 40m Easier chimney (IV) and a bulge (V) to a ledge and pinnacles

12 25m Traverse a slab L then regain the corner (V)

13 40m Take the L-hand chimney (IV) not the one on the R

14 25m Continue up a short chimney and waterworn rock (V) then R to a good stance

15 35m Another smooth chimney (VI- or V+/A0)

16 40m A final strenuous chimney (V+ or V/A0)

17 30m Continue in the chimney for 10m (IV-) then break out L (III) to the great terrace (bivouac/water).

Three finishes are possible. The original which is usually wet and sometimes icy, the Livanos variant and the Messner (7.14) which is the most appropriate for a quick party.
    For the original and Livanos, traverse well to R until an easy gully leads up R to a ridge. From the ridge traverse across the great gully (water) and continue up it to a junction. The Livanos finish branches R here and reaches a ridge with a hard pitch (V+,IV) and then continues up fairly easy ground, and is recommended as the easiest way out. Otherwise continue up the L fork for 4 or 5 pitches of IV,V and A0 or VI-. These final pitches are sure to be wet and sometimes blocked with ice. Then the wall falls back and 3 or 4 easier pitches lead to the summit.

SOUTH FACE (MESSNER VARIATION)
Messner solo, 1969.

This fine route provides the ideal continuation to the lower half of the Vinatzer (7.13). It is possible early in the year as it has no exit chimney. 50m double rope and some belay pegs advised.

7.14
VI+
VI/A1
42

Start from the great terrace about 40m R from the top of the Vinatzer chimney.

1 30m Climb through the OHs at a break (V+) and then easily up slanting L

2 25m Continue Lwards up a smooth slab (IV-)

3 30m Up and then Rwards via a smooth crack (III)

4   30m Climb up to a niche and continue L (IV+)

5   35m Up and past a bulge on the R then back L (V-) to a good stance on water-grooved rock above some small roofs

6   40m Traverse L across a slab to a crack (IV+), up this to a pocketed slab (VI-) and so to a very poor stance on the R

7   25m Continue steeply (IV)

8   25m A slab sloping slightly L (IV)

9   30m Continue in the same line (IV) to a stance at the foot of a ramp

10   30m Climb the ramp R (IV-)

11   40m The crux pitch. Climb the steep yellow wall above by a narrow crack (VI+ or VI/A1)

12   35m Two steep cracks (V) lead to a col on the ridge

13   60m Up the ridge (IV) and so to the summit.

DESCENT

7.15
I   From the summit go NE down easy rock to the glacier (metal hut). Follow the flat ridge E to the cablecar station (30min) then descend the ski runs towards the halfway station (NE) (1hr) and then turn NW to reach Pian dei Fiacconi (1½hr)

Marmolada d'Ombretta

SOUTH FACE (VIA DELL'IDEALE)
Aste, Solina, 1964.

A hard serious route up the wall direct to the cablecar station. It was originally climbed with many pegs and 14 bolts. Now, owing to missing bolts, it has to be climbed free, particularly the pitch to the bivouac cave at half height. Some protection pegs may need to be placed. The upper wall involves a waterfall chimney which gets very icy in bad weather, so it is only recommended in very settled periods. Extra problems are created by the habit of the cablecar staff of tipping refuse down the wall, so it would pay to warn them of an attempt. Not usually in condition until August; often the route is dry in autumn. However it is still very serious due to its length and difficult route finding near the top. 50m double rope useful as an abseil descent is possible from the bivouac cave.

NOTE: 'Abrakadabra', a route just to the L, gives an excellent lower climb at V/V+ but its upper section, by an obvious dièdre, is extremely loose with poor belays at VII-!

Base Hut – Falier 1½hr to the start 850m 1-2 days

7.16
VII–
VII–/
A1

43

Start L of an obvious brown water stripe directly in the fall line of the cablecar station. Scramble up scree-covered rock to below, and 15m L of, an obvious corner on the L of a yellow/grey pillar.

1 40m Climb up below a roof (V) and then move R to the top of a pinnacle (IV). Continue up an OHing corner (VI-)

2 35m Climb a short gully (III) to a col. The original route now goes straight up the corner (VI-/A1). Instead move L out onto a steep slab and climb it (VI-) to a stance on the L

3 25m Continue up the crack L (IV) to a stance near a roof

4 35m Climb a wall and OH (V) then easily to a horizontal break (III)

5 140m Move R to rejoin the original route and follow a shallow line of corners and grooves direct for 4 pitches (IV,IV,IV/V-,IV) to a damp niche

6 25m Another similar pitch leads to a stance below the line of some small roofs

7 30m Continue up a thin wall R of the OHs (V+) to a corner stance. (Variations are possible in this section to the L)

8 40m Climb the corner (III), move L below the roof across a steep slab (V)

9 20m L and up (IV-) to a stance on a ledge which leads L to a cave marking the end of the lower half of Abrakadabra

10 30m Move L on the ledge for 3m then up to an OH which is turned on the L (V,VI, 1 bolt)

11 25m Move R and climb a crack up a flake in a corner (V), then R again to a stance on easier ground

12 40m Easily R on ledges (II) to a red/yellow pillar just L of the water stripe

13 35m Climb up direct (V-,V) to reach a smooth slab with some bolts. Climb this (VII-) and continue (V) to the bivouac cave. (Up to here the route keeps R of the brown stripe)

14 40m Leave the cave on the L, go up 10m (VI) then traverse 20m R (IV) across the water stripe

15 35m Easily up R (II) to a yellow rib

16 25m Start up the dièdre then break out L

17 20m Continue L to the foot of the waterfall chimney

18 35m Get into the chimney (VI+) and climb it (VI-)

19 35m Continue up the chimney (IV+)

20 30m Ignore the wet L fork and continue to reach a gully (IV+)

21 40m Early ascents continued up the gullies above and R, to reach finally a chimney very near the cablecar station. However it is quicker and much more pleasant to take a variant up the rib on the L, so take the gully for a few m then traverse L to reach a dièdre on the rib. Up this (III)

22 40m Continue up the dièdre (III)

23 40m Continue in the dièdre for 15m then break R to climb slabs (IV)

24 40m Follow the slabs until level with the end of the dièdre then traverse L (V) to reach a dièdre starting from a shoulder

25 40m Climb the dièdre (III) and the chimney above (IV) to a stance below a jammed block

26 40m Pass this and continue to a final gully (IV+)

27 30m Easily to the top of the spur.

SOUTH FACE (FISCH)
Koller, Sustr, 1981.

This route takes the middle of the imposing slab face between the Ideale (7.16) and the Conforto Crack (7.18). It is one of the most difficult and beautiful routes in the Dolomites. Only 7 points of aid were used on the first ascent, and the free standard is very high. Most belay points need placing and 50m double rope is recommended. The route is on excellent rock, and the ledge at 500m marks the end of the major difficulties.

Base Hut – Falier 1½hr to the start 850m 2 days

7.17 Start 50m R of an obvious brown water stripe directly in the fall line
VII/A1 of the cablecar station. Scramble in above the lower rocks

1   30m Climb direct over a bulge (V+)then R over another (V) and easily (III) to a ledge below a shallow dièdre

2   25m Go 10m L and climb a L slanting groove

3   45m Climb a crack (V), then L and back R (IV+), and finally direct (V) to another ledge

4   25m Go easily L (II)

5   45m Climb a crack (V-,IV+,IV) to a good stance between roofs L and R

6   45m Zig-zag up to a bulge (IV+), over this (V) to a groove leading L (IV+) and finally back R (IV) to a stance below a big bulge

7   30m Go round the bulge by a groove on the L (IV) then back R 8m on a marked ledge. Continue a few m (V) to a stance

8   45m Climb a shallow dièdre, at first on the R (IV+,V)

9   35m Continue up another shallow groove Rwards (V,V+) to a stance below a Rwards slanting bulge

10 25m Over the bulge (VI-), L a little (V+), then direct (VI) and L again to a stance level with a line of small niches on the R

11 35m Continue direct (IV) then tending R (V,V+) to reach a crack passing a bulge (VI-,VI+)

12 40m Climb a crack (V+) and wall (VI-) to reach a shallow groove. Up this (IV) to below a bulge. Traverse R 7m and go up round the bulge (VI-) and back L, then direct (V+,V) to a stance beside a pinnacle below bulges on the R

13 20m Move up to level with the bulge and then traverse L across white stripes (VII) to reach a crack. Up this (A1,V+)

14 30m Traverse L (V+) and then up (peg move then VII-) and L towards two shallow niches. Step L (V) to enter the L-hand niche and then go direct (VI-) to a stance

15 40m Above is a faint dièdre. Climb up on its R (V+,VI-) and then R (V+) to a stance below a bulge

16 15m Traverse R (VI-) and move up with aid to a small hole, and then R (VI-) to a prominent fish-shaped niche (bivouac)

17 20m Exit the L end of the niche (A1) and continue direct (V+,VI,VI- with two points of aid)

18 30m Use aid to start, then continue (V+) to a faint scoop. Above move L (VI-,V+) and pass a hole on its R (A1). Finally direct to a stance below a steep slab (VI-)

19 35m Climb up the slab for 10m (V+,VI-) then make a rope move down L to reach a crack. Up this to a stance (VI)

20 15m Step R into a dièdre, up this to a bulge (VI-). Move R again across the bulge (VI+) and back L (V) to a stance

21 40m Step R (V) and climb a crack (A0,V+) past another bulge (VI) to a shallow corner which leads to the main horizontal break (V,IV). This break has a good bivouac site and marks the end of the major difficulties. It continues L to the Ideale (7.16) bivouac cave and abseil escape

22 15m To the R is a break in the roof. Climb a steep slab (VI-)

23 40m A shallow groove leads L (IV,V)

24 80m Two easier pitches lead up into a corner (III,II)

25 35m Get into the corner (V) and climb it (IV)

26 160m Four pitches lead up easier rock on the R of the corner (II,III,III,III) to a chimney

27 60m Two pitches up the chimney (III,IV-)

28 30m Climb the chimney which opens out (V+) and then move out R (IV)

29 35m Continue up a corner parallel to the chimney (IV+)

30 35m Move back into the chimney, up it (IV) and out on the R to a stance under a roof

31 40m Step into the chimney (IV) and up it (IV)

32 40m Easily up the final section (II)

33 50m A traverse L and an escape via a hole (Madonnengrotte) leads to the cablecar station.

SOUTH FACE (CONFORTO CRACK)
Conforto, Bertoldi, 1939.

A classic pre-war route up cracks on the R of the great central wall which was soloed free in 1979. Most pegs are in place.

Base Hut – Falier 1½hr to the start 850m 8hr

7.18
VI

Start below the L end of the great terrace just before the path rises above the lower foot rocks.

43

1 30m Climb easily (II) to reach a ledge below a chimney closed by roof

2 30m Take the chimney for 20m then a slab on the R (IV)

3 30m Climb a steep wall (VI-) until it is possible to traverse R to a stance above the cave at the top of the chimney

4 30m Continue up the chimney line (II) past an OH (V-)

5 30m Leave a niche (IV+) and follow an easy chimney (II) slanting L

6 25m Quit another niche (IV) for a gully which leads (II) to the end of a terrace and spike belays

7 40m Take a steep crack then slab R (V+) and reach a stance on pinnacles

8 120m Four chimney pitches (III,IV-,IV-,IV-). The final one is taken on the R and leads to a stance on a shoulder

9 30m Climb a slab first L then R (IV-)

10 40m Above is a dièdre. Climb its R side up a pleasant slab (IV-)

11 40m Another slab on the R (IV+) to a stance below OHs level with the great terrace to the R

12 40m Go over a brittle OH (V+) to a chimney (IV+) and a slab R below OHs to a stance at the top of a pillar

13 40m Move R below OHs to reach a chimney. Climb this (IV)

14 40m Above is a smooth Rward leaning corner. Climb the slabs on the R (IV-)

15 40m Continue until it is possible to reach the corner and follow this (IV)

16 30m An easy gully leads to a hollow near the main gully line on the R (this is the line of the not recommended Philipp Route)

17 90m Climb the chimney directly above for three pitches (IV+,IV+,IV) to below a cave

18 10m Exit R (V+)

19 35m Move L (VI) to rejoin the chimney and follow it (IV-)

20 30m A wider chimney leads to below a roof (IV-)

21 30m Go round a first roof on the L and a higher one on the R (V-)

22 40m An easy gully (II) leads to a jammed block finish (IV-).

SOUTH FACE (DON CHISCIOTTE)
Mariacher, Schiestl, 1979.

An interesting free climb on generally good rock up the walls and slabs between the Conforto and Castiglioni Routes (7.18 and 7.21). Few pegs were used on the early ascents, and belays will usually need to be arranged. A very large hexentric and a few pegs need to be added to normal kit. 50m double rope recommended. The route dries fast and goes throughout the year.

Base Hut – Falier 45min to the start 750m 7hr

7.19
VI
43

Start by scrambling R above the subsidiary rocks which run below the buttress until 50m below their highest point. A gully runs up L between pinnacles and the main face

1 80m Scramble up a ramp and a shallow groove to a shoulder on the pinnacles (III,II)

2 40m Climb on the L of a chimney (III,IV)

3 40m Take a slab on the R (IV-) and then back L (III) to a stance

4 40m Continue up a chimney/corner (IV+) to a stance on the R

5 40m Slabs to the top of a pillar below roofs (IV)

6 30m Climb steep slabs (V)

7 35m A difficult crack (V) for 20m, then move R and climb a cracked dièdre (V)

8 50m Move R across the arête (V) and up steep cracks (V,V+), until a step R leads to a poor stance on the arête

9 30m More easily up a shallow chimney (III)

10 40m Reach the great terrace either by slabs on the L (IV) or up to the R (III)

Above the terrace is a large yellow, loose buttress. Move R to the

163

start of a shallow corner below the R-hand of some obvious niches about 80m up.

11 40m Climb the dièdre (III) and then trend a little L

12 40m Continue up a smooth slab (IV+) to a stance at a little col below the niche

13 35m Move up into the niche, out of it (V+) and up the vertical wall above trending L (V) to a stance beside the loose yellow buttress

14 45m Continue up to the top of the buttress via a slab (IV) and short dièdre (IV)

15 40m Climb a corner (III+) and then go diagonally R to a ledge on the R of the arête

16 35m Continue via a slab (IV+)

17 35m Move R (IV+) and climb a cracked corner (IV+)

18 30m Continue up a difficult slab (V) and a crack (IV+)

19 40m Above is a Rward slanting crack. Start up this for some m (V+) and then move out L and climb a vertical wall (VI) and a flake (VI-) which leads to a stance on the R

20 40m Do not head for the gully on the L but continue up steep rock (V+) to a stance on the edge

21 40m Climb up (V-) then L and up again by a loose crack (V-) to a stance below a shallow chimney

22 40m Climb the chimney (IV) and slab on the R (III+) to the top.

SOUTH FACE (SCHWALBENSCHWANZ – SWALLOW TAIL)
Schiestl, Rieser, 1978.

This is an excellent free climb up perfect rock. Pegs are few and difficult to place as the rock is very compact. Belay pegs are not always in place. Threading slings and a large hexentric are useful. Most of the difficulties are situated on the six pitches above the terrace where some variations are possible, none much easier!

Base Hut – Falier 1½hr to the start 750m 8hr

7.20 Start as for Don Chisciotte (7.19)

VI

43 1 160m Follow 7.20 until it is possible to head R over slabs and scree to the foot of a large dièdre (III)

2   50m Climb the chimney/crack (IV+) past a bulge (V)

3   50m Continue (V,V-) to a stance on a shoulder

4   50m Continue up the corner either direct (VI,V-) or partly on the R wall (V,V+)

5   40m Go up to the roof which closes the dièdre and climb it via a hole (V-)

6   70m Move easily via a funnel and scree (III) to the halfway terrace.

The route continues up the wall above the terrace, starting about 20m L of the water stripe which marks the middle of the upper wall and about 10m R of 7.20

7   20m Easily R up slabs (III+) to below a corner

8   40m Climb the corner (IV+) and continue R then L (V+) past a good thread to a stance

9   35m Go direct to a roof (IV-), L below it (V) and then up water-grooved slabs (V+) to a niche with thread belay

10 30m Climb the corner above to a peg, tension R then climb diagonally R (VI) to a dièdre. Up this (V+) to a niche

11 35m Move R and up to a white slab (V). Climb this and various bulges (V+) to a stance on the R

12 40m Turn the bulge above on the L (V+) and take a water-fluted slab (V+) to a stance below a roof

13 40m Traverse R (III,V) and up a brittle corner and slab (V) in the line of the water stripe

14 180m Climb the Rward slanting chimney (IV) past various constrictions for 5 pitches to the ridge.

SOUTH FACE (CASTIGLIONI)
Pisoni, Castiglioni, 1942.

This was the original route of the wall and offers the easiest way up this area of the Marmolada S face. Its upper pitches could provide an escape from the halfway terrace for other routes in this area but the last two pitches are often icy.

Base Hut – Falier 1½hr to the start 750m 5hr

7.21 Start at the highest part of the grassy shoulder below the middle of the
V   great terrace, 50m R of 7.20

  1 40m Easy climbing leads to the foot of a steep OHing chimney
      (III)

  2 40m Climb the chimney past an OH (V) and escape L near the top

  3 40m Move L and climb a slab (IV)

  4 40m Continue in the same line to a shoulder (III). Move R and
      climb a bulge (V-) and then reach a stance below a gully (IV-)

  5 40m Easily up the gully (II). Exit L through a hole

  6 30m Climb back R (III,V-) to a stance below a chimney

  7 30m Avoid the main chimney by a chimney/ramp R (IV-) to a
      stance at the top of a pillar

  8 30m Climb a slab (III) and move L to the main chimney

  9 30m Climb the chimney (III)

 10 30m Take a ledge R and a gully to the terrace

      Walk 100m R past a spur to below easy scree-covered rocks

 11 30m Easily up R (II)

 12 30m Continue (II) then move L (IV-) to below a gully

 13 120m Ignore the gully and continue L above the spur (II,III,II)
      then up (II) via a smooth groove to a stance below a chimney in a
      great gully

 14 20m Climb the chimney and step out R (IV)

 15 40m Move up then return to the chimney (IV-) and follow it

 16 35m Climb the steep, loose and often icy chimney (V)

 17 40m The chimney continues past a jammed block (V) to a snow
      gully and the top.

SOUTH FACE (HATSCHI BRATSCHI)
Rieser, Schiestl, Mariacher, 1978.

Free climbing with few pegs left. First ascent in late November! One of many good modern routes in this area. This route climbs the lower wall R of 7.21 and then continues up the buttress just R of the obvious corner and L of 7.21.

Base Hut – Falier 1½hr to the start 750m 6hr

7.22
VI–

Start as for 7.21

1   40m Climb up to a stance in a col (III)

2   30m A slab leads up R (IV–)

3   30m Another slab back L (IV)

4   40m Climb delicately across a nice slab L (V–) until the bulge above relents and a direct ascent (III) to a stance in a niche is possible

5   40m Move R with difficulty (V) then up and L (IV)

6   30m Continue L and climb a slab L of a loose wall (IV)

7   120m Four pitches slightly R (III,II,I) lead to the terrace

8   20m Cross the terrace and take a R slanting dièdre on a spur below the obvious corner (III)

9   30m Avoid the cracked dièdre by a slab on the R (V–) returning to the dièdre for a stance

10   30m Traverse horizontally R (V–) to a crack. Up this (V–) to a stance by a pinnacle

11   40m Move R out of the crack (II) and climb a steep wall (V)

12   35m Continue in the same line (V)

13   30m Easier climbing (III) to scree ledges

14   30m A smooth slab (IV)

15   30m Continue (III) to a stance level with a col on the R which would lead to the bottom of the final chimneys of 7.21

16   35m Climb a crack (V) and move L to a niche

17   40m Move R out of the niche, up a crack (V), turn a loose bulge on the L (VI–) and then climb a steep wall to a spike. Move back R to a stance

18 30m Climb an unprotected wall for 8m (VI-), pass L of a bulge (VI-) and climb a steep crack (V) to a niche stance

19 30m Go out R past a bulge (V+) and climb a loose wall (VI-) to a good stance

20 40m Easily (III,II) to the top.

DESCENTS

7.23 It is fairly easy to reach the glacier from most routes, and then either climb up to the top cablecar station or descend to the middle station (7.15). However both 7.19 and 7.20 finish on pinnacles and require two abseils to reach the snow whilst the other routes may give problems with bergschrunds. Traversing the ridge is difficult with loose rock and is not recommended. (15min – 1hr)

Geografica 1:25000 Sheet 3

This group has a high concentration of difficult climbing with its NW face rivalling Marmolada S face and the faces of the Lavaredo group. Virtually all the routes described can be free climbed and the rock is generally good. Good paths encircle the group whilst via ferrata go to its highest point.

The group is shaped like an inverted letter Y with the Torre Coldai at the NE end and the Torre Venezia and Torre Trieste forming the SW and S ends. The ridge is over 5km long, with Monte Civetta being the highest point and the NW faces having a major concentration of big hard routes.

HUTS

Coldai Hut 2132m. At the N end of the group. Approaches– i)from Alleghe via Pian de Pezze and then either the Forcella d'Alleghe on paths 564,556, or the Col Negro and past Lago Coldai on paths 565,560 (both routes 3hr) ii)an easier approach is from Pecol, drive up the track to near Casere di Pioda (1892m) then on path 556 (45min from the car park)

Tissi Hut 2250m. Magnificent views of the NW faces. Baggage lift for rucksacks etc at Masarè. Some space for camping. Approaches– i)from Masarè, S of Alleghe, take the steep path which starts near the baggage lift and follow it through the woods on path 563 (2½hr), ii)from Alleghe follow path 565 up the Ru Antersas (2½hr)

Vazzoler Hut 1714m. Idyllically situated at the S end of the group. The easiest approach is via the track from Listolade going as far as possible by car up the Val Corpassa. Cars are often left near the Capanne Triesta at about 1100m. Walk up path 555 (1½hr)

Torrani Hut 2984m. A high hut 250m below the summit of M Civetta with a few beds, drinks and simple meals. This hut lies at the junction of the Normal route and the Via Ferrata Tissi. Approaches– see HUT LINKS below

Bivouac Tomè 2870m. Situated on the E flanks of the Punta de Gasperi, this hut is useful if caught out on the descent from Cima Su Alto or Cima della Terranova.

HUT LINKS

Coldai to: Torrani (558) 4hr←2½hr

Vazzoler to: Torrani (558) 4hr←2½hr

The Val Civetta which runs below the NW face offers a delightful walk from the Vazzoler hut, past the Tissi hut to the Coldai hut (560,3hr). A more strenuous return can be made on the Tivan path (557) then via F d Moiazzetta (558) along the E face of the group (6hr).

Torre Coldai 2600m

NORTH-NORTH-WEST FACE (DIRECT ROUTE)
Gervasutti, Boiti, 1932 (upper wall), Pollozzon, De Toni, Gavaz, 1935 (lower wall).

Base Hut – Coldai 30min to the start 400m 3½hr

8.01 From the hut cross Col Coldai to a point directly below the summit.
IV+ Start slightly L of the lowest point of the spur at a chimney which splits into two. Climb the chimney until it divides (III,IV). Go L (IV,IV+) to reach a ledge on the crest of a spur. Traverse R to continue by a chimney (III+) which leads to the top of the spur. Continue for 100m obliquely R and then L to finish at a ledge. Climb a wall (IV,IV+) obliquely L and gain a higher ledge. Continue by an obvious crack to reach another ledge (25m,IV,IV+). Climb a crack (IV) and at its end go diagonally R (III) towards the central summit and finally L to reach the easy rocks of the descent route.

DESCENT TO THE NORTH-EAST
8.02 From the summit scramble easily towards the col between this peak
II and the Torre Alleghe. Before the col take a series of ledges and walls leading to a gully on the L. Scramble down the gully to the track leading back to the hut. (45min)

Torre d'Alleghe 2649m

EAST FACE
Pedrazzo, Calemelli, Kelemina, 1968.

Base Hut – Coldai 45min to the start 400m 2hr

8.03
IV
Follow the Tivan path until 200m after a col, then go up scree to reach a ledge leading R to the middle of the E face. Follow it to its end.

1   50m Follow a steep cracked ramp R (III) then go L of a niche (III) and finally vertically to a ledge.

2   40m Move diagonally R for 20m and climb a small chimney (IV) to reach a stance and spike belay

3   40m Go 6m R and climb a chimney (6m,III) to reach a sloping ledge. Follow this R and then go horizontally L to a grass ledge

4   30m Take a chimney to a niche (III)

5   35m Go obliquely L to a peg (III+), traverse L (IV) and then direct to a terrace

6   40m Climb the easy gully R to its end, then the wall to the L and continue by a scree gully to a stance

7   35m Continue L up a gully

8   35m Finish up easy slabs to the SE ridge

9   100m Follow the ridge to the summit.

NORTH-WEST FACE OF THE SOUTH PILLAR
Franceschi, Bellodis, 1955.

The pillars to the L and R sides of the NW face provide excellent free routes, whilst the central fault provides another hard route (Philipp, 1957). The route takes the R-hand pillar whilst 8.05 follows the L-hand one. Friends could be useful for protection on this route.

Base Hut – Coldai 1hr to the start 400m (200m of difficulty) 5hr

8.04
VII/A0
VI/A2
Follow the path over Col Negro and continue over grass and scree to the foot of the face. Start in a hollow below the central depression and climb the lower half of the face up easy slabs and gullies bearing R until below the R-hand pillar. Finally move up L traversing ledges until the true base of the pillar is reached. Pitches of II,III and IV.

1 25m Go a little to the L (VI-) then take a crack over the OHs to a stance

2 20m Continue up the crack (VI+/VII/A0)

3 30m Follow the OHing crack to an area of grey rock and a niche (VI+/A0)

4 40m Take a steep chimney (IV/IV+), exit through a hole and continue up OHing friable rock (VI) to a stance

5 40m Go over a black, wet OH (VII) to a difficult crack (VI-) which leads to a niche

6 35m Continue up a chimney on the R (V), then after a hole go over two bulges (V)

7 30m More easily to the summit of the pillar (III,IV).

NORTH-WEST FACE OF THE NORTH PILLAR
Bellenzier, 1964.

Base Hut – Coldai 1hr to the start 400m (140m of difficulty) 6hr

8.05 Start at the central depression as for the S pillar (8.04) but
VII– immediately trend L up easy, loose rock towards the foot of the pillar.
VI/A2 Mainly II and III, a little IV.

1 20m Climb a chimney formed by a spur (IV)

2 25m Traverse 2m R and climb a yellow dièdre to a small stance on the L edge (VI-)

3 25m Ascend for some metres (V+ or A0), traverse 3m R then go direct to grey rock (V). Traverse R, past a big roof, to a bad stance (IV-). Large friends or bong belays

4 35m Climb up to a peg (VI). Traverse obliquely L to a better peg (VII- or A2) then move L to the arête. Go 3m direct then zig-zag R then L to a good stance (V,VI-)

5 25m Climb the ridge to a big ledge (V+,V,IV+)

6 25m Traverse 10m R to a crack. Climb this (V-) and an OH (V+)

7 40m Continue diagonally R to the top of the pillar (IV,III) and scramble R to join the normal descent route.

DESCENT BY EAST FACE AND NORTH-EAST RIDGE

8.06 Follow the NE ridge, keeping R a little to avoid the top of the N pillar,
II to reach a col. Now zig-zag down easy rock E to reach a traversing
path and follow this L until a descent to the screes is possible. Many
cairns. (1½hr)

Torre di Valgrande 2715m

NORTH-EAST PILLAR
Pollazzon, Rudatis, 1941.

One of the best medium grade routes in the group.

Base Hut – Coldai 1¼hr to the start 255m 3hr

8.07 Follow the Tivan path until below the gully between Torre di
V+ Valgrande and Torre di Alleghe. Climb L up scree until a traverse can
be made R below the E face. Follow this along a terrace until it is
possible to reach a col at the foot of the NE ridge. From here traverse
R for 15m to a faint crack which is 5m L of the pillar. The descent
route is a further 15m R whilst the Faccioli, Bellaz route (VI-) climbs
the arête to the L.

1   35m Climb the wall on good holds to a small stance (III)

2   40m Go obliquely R to an obvious crack which leads diagonally up
the wall. Continue to a stance (III)

3   30m Continue up the crack (IV,III)

4   25m Follow the crack to a steep wall (III). Traverse 8m L to a good
stance (III+). (The wall can be climbed (V+) by the OHing
crack)

5   25m Climb a dièdre for 12m then 4m L and vertically to a jammed
block (III+)

6   20m Go R to a col on the crest of the ridge (III,IV)

7   30m Climb a vertical crack (IV+), then obliquely R (IV) and
finally by a shallow chimney (III)

8   60m Traverse L and continue to the summit (II).

NORTH-WEST FACE
Carlesso, Menti, 1936.

This excellent route takes a direct line up the obvious crack in the middle of the cylindrical NW face. Usually a little aid is used but the route does go free.

Base Hut – Coldai or Tissi 1hr or 50min to the start 500m 6hr

8.08 Follow the Val Civetta path until below the gully between the Torres
VII+ di Alleghe and Valgrande. Reach the foot of the obvious grey/yellow
VI–/A2 dièdre up easy rock either direct or via the gully (some III and IV,
51 180m).

1   25m Bridge the dièdre to the niche (V)

2   25m Climb the OH either direct (A2) or on the L (N) side (VII+) and continue steeply for 15m (VI,V+ or VI–/A1)

3   25m Continue up the dièdre (V+ or V/A0)

4   50m Follow the dièdre past two OHs (V+ or V–/A0) to a good stance

5   40m Continue to a stance below an OHing crack (IV+)

6   25m Climb the OH and continue direct (V–,IV–)

7   30m Continue up a grey slab which leads to the final chimney (V or V–/A0,IV)

8   40m Take the chimney to near the summit (III+).

SOUTH FACE (VIA DELLE GUIDE)
De Toni, Pollazzon, 1941.

This is a difficult free crack climb. The rock on the crux is very compact.

Base Hut – Coldai 1¼hr to the start 200m 4hr

8.09 Follow the Tivan path and then follow scree to the base of the NE
VII ridge. Scramble L below the E face on ledges until below the S face.
VI/A0 Start on the L of a prominent pillar below a grey wall.

1   35m Climb a ramp leading R (III,IV)

2   15m Continue up a short yellow crack (IV+,V) to the top of the pillar

3   40m Climb the OH (VI+ or V+/A0) then a water-smoothed,

strenuous crack (VI-) and another OH (VII or VI/A0). Some pegs but friends useful

4   40m Continue up the wider crack above (V) past a bulge (V+) and a higher crack (IV+/V-) to a stance below a dièdre

5   45m Climb the dièdre (V+), then a crack past a flake on the L (V)

6   20m An easy ramp leads to the summit plateau (II).

DESCENT BY NORTH-EAST FACE

8.10   Go down NE to follow the couloir on the E flank (one abseil) and reach the screes below. (1hr)

Pan di Zucchero 2780m

EAST FACE
Schober, Liebl, 1938.

An excellent free climb on steep rock. Strenuous.

Base Hut – Coldai 1hr20min to the start 370m 5hr

8.11
V+
From the Tivan path follow scree and sometimes snow to the L end of the E face at the highest point of the screes.

50

1   50m Climb easily L until a ledge leads from L to R to a stance at its end (II,III)

2   40m Go vertically until below a roof, move R for 3m and then return L climbing an oblique ramp past a large block (V)

3   30m Move L on vertical grey rock for 3m, then direct for 2m (V) and then L to a chimney. Climb this (V) and step L to a stance below a yellow OHing crack

4   40m Climb the crack or the wall on its R to an OH (V+). Over this (V+) to reach the base of a chimney

5   35m Follow the chimney (IV+) to easier rock

6   50m Climb a R slanting crack to the prominent big slab (IV), then direct over an OH (V) and continue up the crack (IV+) passing a bulge on the R

7   30m Either continue direct by a crack (IV+) to reach the SE ridge or go up a ramp (IV) to reach a yellow bulge. Over this (V-) and then continue up easier rock to reach a good ledge (III)   175

8   40m Traverse L to reach the SE ridge (III)

9   70m Follow the ridge to the summit (III,II).

NORTH-WEST FACE

Tissi, Andrich, Rudatis, 1932.

A classic route in two parts. A lower buttress of 300m of IV/III and an upper wall of V+/IV.

Base Hut – Coldai or Tissi 1¹/₄hr or 45min to the start 600m 6hr

8.12   Approach from the Val Civetta path (560). Start just L of the lowest
V+   point of the buttress.

52

1   40m Climb a 10m corner, traverse R and up 15m to a stance (IV-)

2   40m Move L and up, then R to a higher stance

3   20m Climb a short loose dièdre L to easier ground (IV-)

4   200m Easily up L via chimneys and gullies to the foot of a grey chimney (II). The NW Face Direct route (VII or V+ with a rope move), goes up the centre of the face to the R of the chimney, whilst this route leads to the arête on the L

5   35m Climb the chimney L(IV/V-)

6   40m Continue in the chimney (IV/V-)

7   25m Climb a wall to an OH (V), turn the OH Rwards (V+) and finish direct by a steep crack (IV-)

8   25m Climb an OH on the R (V+) and then move R and down (V) to a small stance

9   25m Step R to a dièdre (IV+) and climb this (V-)

10   30m Continue up the crack (IV+,V)

11   40m Go diagonally L to the arête (IV)

12   40m Continue near the arête to the foot of a chimney (IV) on the L of the edge

13   35m Climb the chimney (IV+,V)

14   50m Continue up the chimney (V) to a possible stance. Go over the final jammed block (V+) to a col

This col is passed by the descent route (8.13). The summit lies up to the R.

DESCENT BY NORTH-EAST RIDGE

.13
I
From the summit descend 30m to the NE and then make two abseils to a col between this peak and the next (Torre da Lago). Climb down 35m on the E side of the col by a chimney (III) and slab (III) and then abseil to a sloping ledge. More climbing and 4 or 5 abseils lead to the screes. Care is needed with rope retrieval on the abseils. (1¾hr)

Punta Civetta 2920m

NORTH-WEST FACE (ANDRICH ROUTE)
Andrich, Faè, 1934.

This face is split by two tremendous crack lines which make this and the following route. Both routes are hard but the Andrich suffers more from poor conditions in its upper chimneys. Both routes are serious, sustained and strenuous. Protection is usually in place and both routes go free, although if needed the Andrich Slab can be avoided at A1 on the L.

Base Hut – Coldai or Tissi 1½hr or 40min to the start 800m 8hr

.14
I+
V/A1
52
Start immediately below the summit at a characteristic gully. Climb just R of this using an easy angled ramp L for 45m to join the main gully. Continue for 150m, walk L along scree to a shoulder and follow this to below and L of the start of the cracks proper (II,III).

1   25m First R up a short awkward wall (IV-) then L to a stance below an OHing crack. (Aste Route 8.15 goes R from here but this route takes a variant L)

2   35m Go L round a bulge (IV-) then R and L to use two cracks (III) above. Finally over a bulge (IV) to a stance below a slabby corner which is not the route

3   35m Make a hand-traverse R (V-) and continue round a corner (IV) to an obvious thin crack

4   20m Climb the L wall of the corner above (V,VI- or A0)

5   35m Continue up a smooth slab (V+) back to the crack (VI- or A0) and over a bulge (V)

6   35m Follow the crack over two OHs (VI,V) to a cave stance

7   35m Go L over an OH by an impressive chimney (VI-) and then climb a crack (V)

177

8 35m Continue up a looser crack to a stance by a pinnacle (V-,IV)

9 30m Follow the steep crack with moves on the L wall (IV+,V)

10 30m Take the crack (V-) to a stance below a yellow crack

11 35m Climb the yellow crack to a stance in a niche (VI or V+/A1)

12 35m Turn the next OH on the L (VI or V/A0), and continue on the L on finger jams (VI), until a traverse R across a steep yellow wall (VI- or A0) leads to an exposed, narrow ledge (IV) (the aid variant goes direct from halfway up this pitch)

13 30m Move a few m L past a bulge (V+ or A0) to reach a smooth grey slab. Climb this, the delicate Andrich Slab (VI), on the L and continue (V+) to a good stance

14 35m Continue up a crack on the R of the main chimney line (IV,V+)

15 35m Move up (III) and L into the chimney (IV). Possible bivouac on a large block below a black roof

16 30m Continue up the chimney turning an OH on the L (IV)

17 20m Climb a crack (IV+), then move R and up (VI or A1) to a bad stance under a roof on the rib overlooking the chimney

18 30m Climb the rib for a few m (VI- or A1) then traverse L into the chimney and continue below a bulge (V,IV) where a rotten flake blocks the chimney

19 30m Go round the bulge on the R (VI- or A0) or on the L (usually wet) and continue more easily (II)

20 35m Go over the jammed block (IV-) and continue up the chimney (II)

21 35m Climb a short chimney (III) to an awkward move (IV) and reach the ridge near the via ferrata.

NORTH-WEST FACE (ASTE ROUTE)
Aste, Susatti, 1954.

This excellent route up the R-hand crack line has the advantage of drying quickly after wet weather. A free climb of comparable difficulty to the Andrich (8.14) but with one harder section. After lower cracks and walls it follows three dièdres to final chimneys.

Base Hut – Coldai or Tissi 1½hr or 40min to the start 800m 8hr

15 Start as for 8.14 at the top of pitch 1

V+
V/A1

2

1 35m Follow a cracked corner R over a bulge (V) towards a grey/yellow slab (IV-)

2 35m Up L over two black OHs (V-,V) to a niche

3 40m Step L from the niche (IV-) then direct to a higher niche (V)

4 35m Climb the L wall to a third niche (IV) then go back to the groove (9m) to a fourth niche; go 4m R on a smooth slab (V). Traverse L round the edge and go up a parallel dièdre (V+) to a small stance

5 30m Climb the R side of the dièdre to yet another niche (V)

6 35m Go some m up to a yellow slab. Traverse L (V) to a crack. Up this for 4m (V+) to a spike then descend L to the first dièdre

7 50m Up the cracked dièdre (IV+), which becomes a chimney, to a small tower. Then L to the second dièdre (V-)

8 30m Up the dièdre to a niche (V+,V-)

9 35m Continue in the dièdre for 20m (V+), traverse 10m L to an adjacent dièdre (IV) and up 5m (III) to a good stance

10 35m Return R to the main corner and follow this (IV+,V-)

11 50m Up the dièdre to a pinnacle (V-,V) then traverse L (V+ or A0) to the third of the dièdres

12 30m Follow the dièdre until its concluding roof (V+,VI)

13 25m Move R (VI+ or A0) across the wall, up and L to a niche (VI+ or V+/A0) above the roof and finally up an OHing crack (VI or A1) to a good stance at the foot of the final chimney

14 130m Three or four pitches up the chimney (V+,V,IV) to the ridge near the summit.

DESCENT

16 Join the well marked Via Ferrata des Alleghesi and follow this down to the Tivan path and so to the Coldai hut. Some unprotected sections and possibly some snow. (2½hr)

Punta Tissi 2992m

NORTH-WEST FACE (PHILIPP-FLAMM ROUTE)
Phillip, Flamm, 1957.

*This justifiably famous route takes a diagonal line to the L of the main
Civetta face. Ascents vary in style from those by fast lightweight teams to
conventional bivouac-prepared parties using the odd aid peg. Ice, snow or
water may give problems in the final chimneys although an escape L along
ledges may be possible. The route is in three distinct parts. First 300m up a
grey/black wall just R of the main groove, then 300m up the dièdre between
OHing yellow walls on the R and grey slabs on the L, and finally 300m of
icy chimneys and grooves.*

Base Hut – Tissi 50min to the start 950m 7-16hr

8.17 Start just R of the line of the dièdre.

VII
VI-/A1
46

1   80m Climb the shallow gully (III,IV) to a stance. (The Friends
Route 8.20 goes R from here)

2   40m Move L, climb the OH (V) and the crack above (IV+) to a
stance R

3   40m Enter a dièdre 5m L and climb it (V-) and a chimney (IV)

4   35m Continue up the chimney (V-), then move easily up a ramp L
towards a chimney between a tower and the face (II)

5   40m Climb the chimney to the top of the tower (IV)

6   30m Traverse 5m horizontally L to reach a grey dièdre (V), climb
this (V+) on the L for 10m and move back R 10m to climb a crack
(V-)

7   40m Move up L to a chimney (IV); climb it (V)

8   30m Continue to a small terrace (IV)

9   130m Climb a crack (IV+), dièdre and higher crack (V+)

10 25m Up a chimney (IV) for 15m, R to the arête, then R to another
ledge

11 40m Climb up (IV), then by a crack (V-) to a big niche at the foot
of the yellow/red dièdre

12 45m Climb the dièdre, first on the L (V), then direct (V+)

13 30m Continue up a steep slab (V+), then R and up a red chimney
(V+)

14 30m Another chimney (V), dièdre and slab (V+)

15 35m Continue up the dièdre over two roofs (V+,VI-) to a stance below a roof

16 20m Go up to the roof (V+) and pass it on the L (V)

17 35m Move L (IV) and climb a steep black crack (VI) to a niche

18 30m Do not continue upwards but traverse L (V+) and get round the yellow ridge (VI- or A1)

19 35m Up a groove (V+) and an OH (VI+ or V/A1) to reach easier ground

20 40m Start up the gully (II) but do not continue. Instead move R (III,IV) to a stance L of a big cave (direct variant is V,VI+)

21 35m Move L to a corner, climb it (V+ or A1) then a roof on the R (VI)

22 45m Move R and up (III+) then back L (IV+) to reach the main chimney line. (The Comici Route 8.19 joins here from the L)

23 45m Easily up slabs in the gully (III)

24 50m Over the OH (V+) then direct to a forking (III,IV). (Comici Route now goes R)

25 40m Climb a narrow chimney to reach a big niche under a great vertical chimney (IV+)

26 35m Get out L via a hole (V+) and reach the upper chimney

27 30m Slab (V,IV) and a dièdre (V+)

28 20m Move R to the R-hand chimney (V) and climb this (IV+) past a block

29 25m Climb a steep corner (IV+)

30 30m Continue up the corner (IV-,V-)

31 40m Climb the black OH on the R (VII or A1) then back L to a stance in a small niche

32 40m Follow slabs up the final gully (V,IV)

33 40m A final OH (V+) and slabs (IV) to the top.

DESCENT

18 Move L (NE) a little below the ridge to reach the via ferrata.

Then either follow this down as for 8.16 or follow it up over the main summit and so down to the Torrani hut on the Normal Route. (3hr t Coldai hut or 1hr to Torrani hut)

Monte Civetta 3220m

This, the highest point of the group, is easily climbed by the Via Ferrata degli Alleghesi from the N (5hr from Coldai hut), or by the Via Ferrata Tissi to the S (5½hr from Vazzoler hut), or from the E from the Tivan pa by the obvious Normal Route. The small Torrani hut lies 250m below the summit and is useful if late off a major NW face route. See 8.22.

The NW face has three important routes on it, each typical of its time. The Comici Route (8.19) starts well to the L below Punta Civetta, crosses diagonally over the face cutting the Phillip-Flamm Route (8.17) and finishing direct to the summit via the Solleder Route (8.21) which takes a line past the ice field (Cristallo) from a spur directly below the summit. Th Friends Route (8.20) starts as for 8.17 but then climbs the steep walls dir to join the other routes for their final pitches and is more typical of the modern style of climbing.

NORTH-WEST FACE (COMICI ROUTE)
Comici, Benedetti, 1931.

A very long, sustained route involving 1500m of climbing. Not very frequented it offers a major undertaking for those seeking a Western Alps type route.

Base Hut – Tissi 45min to the start 1500m At least 12hr

8.19 The start lies directly below the Punta Civetta above a shoulder whic
VI   hides a gully. The first difficulties lie on a whitish/grey wall on the L
VI–/A1 of a long red wall.

1   50m Climb the wall for 25m then a crack on the L over an OH (V,IV,V)

2   45m Direct delicately over poor rock, then slant R and finally climb a crack (IV,IV+)

3   50m Obliquely L then direct up a vertical crack (IV,V-). Slant R 10m, then ascend direct for 5m to a yellow/black roof (V). Climb this on the L by a yellow OHing crack (VI-)

4   50m Follow a groove for 20m and an OH to a ledge (III,IV).
    Continue in the same line past another OH to a stance (V)

5   100m Two easier pitches over cracked grey slabs to a scree ledge
    below a roof (III,IV)

6   50m Climb the OH (V) and continue direct (IV). Climb down L
    and then via a crack to a stance (V,IV)

7   50m Go 20m direct until below a roof, then slant R and climb it
    (IV,V). Move 5m L (IV) then direct to a small terrace (V) under a
    rock tower

8   55m Reach the tower and climb a 15m crack (III,IV,V). Go 7m
    diagonally R, then take a hard wall (15m,V) and finally R to a
    good stance (III)

9   80m Two pitches. The first on poor rock obliquely R for 25m
    (IV), then a loose red wall and a crack (V). Then diagonally R over
    difficult wet rock and continue R to a good ledge (IV)

10 35m Go up L via ledges to a chimney and continue past a roof to a
    stance below a yellow wall (IV+,V)

11 50m Up a chimney to a stance on the R by a block (III,IV).
    Continue L and leave the chimney (IV)

12 45m Go R by an indistinct ledge to reach a cave (V-,III). Go R
    over an OH on the R (V+ or A1). Continue up a corner (V) and
    then move R to a ledge below a bulging yellow wall (VI)

13 30m Move R under the roof and then reach an OHing corner and
    follow this steeply to the ridge on the R (A1/VI- or VI)

14 30m Slant R over a slab then up R by an obvious crack (IV+)

15 60m Two hard pitches up the crack passing frequent bulges
    (V,V+) to a good stance on the R

16 60m Make an awkward traverse R over an OH (A1 or VI),
    continue direct for 8m and then R to a large chimney and stance
    (VI-,V+). Climb strenuously up the chimney to a sloping ledge
    (V). Bivouac site common with 8.17

17 40m Climb the R wall of the chimney past OHs, then R across a
    rib to a ledge leading to a stance (A0 or VI,V)

18 60m Two pitches up the crack in the gully finishing in the gully
    (V,V+)

19 30m Climb an earthy chimney, go through a hole to break out R (IV+)

20 120m Three pitches up less difficult rock on the L of the pillar (III/IV)

21 30m Obliquely R to reach a chimney (II,III)

22 50m Climb the chimney (III,IV) and then go obliquely R again to the foot of a chimney/crack below and L of a great pillar

23 90m Two pitches on the L of the pillar using chimneys and corner (IV)

24 30m Continue with two rope moves to reach the edge of the pillar (V) and follow this to the top (IV)

25 80m Traverse R by scree ledges to reach the final gully of the Solleder Route (8.21)

26 70m Up the chimney/gully for two pitches (IV,V) to the summit.

NORTH-WEST FACE (FRIENDS ROUTE)
Messner, Holzer, Mayer, Reali, 1967.

This 1100m climb follows the prominent dièdre between the Solleder Route (8.21) and the Phillip Route (8.17). Not often repeated, it gives mainly free climbing at V or V+ and a section of A2 at the end. The free climbing may be found to be hard for the grade.

Base Hut – Tissi 45min to the start 1100m First ascent 21hr

8.20 Start as for 8.17. From the recess in the wall, generally filled with
V+/A2 snow, bear up a gully to the L (in parts IV) and later bear R into the
46 conspicuous dièdre system. At the point where the dièdre is blocked
by an OH, climb up R and after 8m go L into a crack in the dièdre
system. From here climb a further rope length to a ledge. Turn first R
then bear L (small ledge) to a large niche. After climbing the OH via a
dièdre continue on to the ledge below the enclosed grey/yellow wall.

Continue climbing up the pillar and up the dièdre between the
pillar and the main wall. First climb the L-hand wall of the dièdre
then continue a few m in the dièdre and finally cross the broken
R-hand wall of the dièdre, which is generally wet, to a small ledge (V).

From here climb L up a concealed crack (V) to a stance in the
dièdre. Now continue a few m up the dièdre and then move R to a
small ledge on the crest of the pillar. Go across the ridge and the
smooth bulging sections of rock (V), and continue up to the top of the

pillar. A bivouac site, used on the first ascent, can be found to the L beneath the crack/dièdre.

Climb on from the top of the pillar to the beginning of the yellow, OHing pillar, which here flanks the main wall to the R. First cross the sharp ridge (V+), then continue climbing more easily to a stance. Now bear R for one rope length upwards (V) over rock which is brittle in parts, and continue to a large platform to the L of the Solleder Route (8.21). Go straight up from the ledge and continue bearing L across smooth slabs (V+) to the beginning of a narrow crack. Follow the crack (V+) to a slab and bear R (V) to a further tier.

Climb up a small dièdre ,then over a bulge (A1), then straight up with less difficulty to a small ledge. Continue to the L below the crest of the pillar, crossing the crest, partly by free climbing (V) partly by means of pegs (A2) and go on with less difficulty to the Solleder Route (8.21) which should be followed on to the ridge and summit.

NORTH-WEST FACE (SOLLEDER ROUTE)
Solleder, Lettenbauer, 1935.

This is one of Solleder's three great classic climbs of the Dolomites. It is a long, serious free route and continuing or retreating in bad weather can be very serious. There is some stonefall danger on the middle section late in the day, and the scale makes route finding difficult. It is popular and usually many pegs are in place.

Base Hut – Tissi 40min to the start 1300m 10-14hr

8.21
VI
VI–/
A1
46

Start on the R-hand side of the well-defined little buttress which stands out from the face directly below the summit. Usually a snow gully to here.

Traverse L on to the buttress at half height (II) and scramble up it, trending R to a gap behind a yellow tower. Continue on the R (III) to reach a second gap between a black tower and the main face by an earthy cave. The much photographed first pitch leads L from here. Move up and follow the crack L first by a hand-traverse (V) then bending vertically (VI-) and finally past a roof (VI- or A1). Follow the continuation of the crack until it opens out to a wide chimney closed by a roof (V). Climb the back of the chimney (III), then get out onto the L wall and regain the chimney above the roof (V+,VI-).

Continue up the chimney (IV) to a large ledge. If the chimney is wet a variation is possible 40m L up a dièdre (VI-). The chimney continues as a smooth, black waterfall and is avoided on the R by a shallow grey groove and then a wet crack in a slightly OHing wall

(V+,VI-) to reach a narrow ledge. Follow the ledge (slightly down) for 50m to reach easy angled rock in the middle of the face. Climb up slabs and loose chimneys (some stonefall danger, III,IV) trending R to reach a prominent sloping ledge which leads to the L edge of the ice field (Cristallo).

At the R-hand side of the ledge are two diagonal red cracks, parallel and quite close together, and to the R of these is a large grey dièdre with a black dripping cave on its R. Start at the cave and traverse L across a vertical wall to reach the grey dièdre (VI-). Climb the corner for several pitches (V+) until it becomes a chimney (IV) and continue to a little shoulder below the upper walls. (From here a long couloir R (the Penzo Variation) offers a possible escape to the col between Civetta and Piccola Civetta (V, loose)).

Go across the scree ledges heading for a shallow dièdre slanting L. Climb this for two pitches finishing over a small OH (IV,V) to reach the final chimneys.

Follow the back of the chimneys (III) then over two wet OHs (V+), or up dièdres further L (VI-), to a third OH. It is also possibe to miss this wet chimney on the R by a hidden chimney, a slab and an OH (IV,V). Now go L along a ledge and climb a 20m crack (V) which leads to a ledge on the L arête of the chimneys. Follow easy rocks up the arête to another gully on the L of the main one. Where this secondary gully is closed by OHs traverse back into the main gully. Several variations are now possible – a wall (IV) on the R is the easiest. Next continue obliquely to return to the main chimney line. Use a crack (V) to reach a chimney blocked by OHs. Climb it (IV,V-) and exit L (V) to a ledge about 100m below the summit. Climb the wall on the L (25m,IV) then follow a loose gully (III+) to a bulge (V). Continue direct to reach the ridge 30m N of the summit.

DESCENT

8.22 From the summit descend directly down easy scree slopes SE, by a marked and protected path, to the Torrani hut which is hidden from above. The winch used by the guardian can be used as a landmark. From here either go down S to the high cwm known as the Van delle Sasse by the Via Ferrata Tissi or continue E down the well marked Normal Route to reach the Tivan path. (20min to Torrani hut then 2½hr to the Coldai or Vazzoler huts)

Cima Su Alto 2951m

NORTH-WEST FACE (LIVANOS DIEDRE)
Livanos, Gabriel, 1951.

This hard route takes the obvious yellow dièdre direct to the summit of this peak, which is the middle of the three S of the Tissi hut. The lower buttress is fairly easy for 350m but the upper 450m may be hard, with missing pegs and some poor rock in the final chimneys.

Base Hut – Tissi 30min to the start 800m 12hr

8.23 From the path from the Tissi hut go up scree to a start a little to the L
VI+/A2 of the lowest point of the lower buttress, at a little chimney with a

47 jammed block. Climb this (IV), then obliquely R for 2 pitches and then 60m up a chimney. Continue R then straight to reach a couloir on the R blocked by a big roof. Traverse R for 30m (V,IV) and continue by cracks for 70m (IV,V) to reach a cave still L of the line of the dièdre.

Continue R (V), then direct (V) for 25m, then obliquely across a slab (V-) to reach a good ledge at the foot of the dièdre.

Climb the yellow dièdre above for 5 pitches to a high roof which blocks it (150m,V/V+/A1/A2). Climb the roof on the L and follow OHing cracks to a small sentry box below a yellow OH (VI/A1). Traverse round the bulge on the R (V) to good ledges which lead to the top of a pile of blocks (V). (Bivouac a short abseil R). From the top of the blocks reach a grey crack and climb it, moving L to the foot of an open couloir (A2/V+).

Now the character of the climb changes and the couloir forms a tall chimney with loose walls. Continue direct for 30m past an OH. Avoid the next two OHs on poor rock on the L. Continue for 35m, moving R at the fourth OH to a niche. Climb out of this on the R wall to another niche 15m higher (IV,V,A1). Here the chimney divides. Do not go direct (A1,V) but reach the L-hand chimney by going up 7m and then by traversing L for 2m, and continue to a sloping scree ledge. Start up L for 2 pitches towards the ridge (V) to reach a rotten chimney round the corner. Climb this for 20m (IV) and then, half way up the corner above (V), break out L to easy rock leading to the summit.

NORTH-WEST FACE
Ratti, Vitale, 1938.

A classic and very popular free climb up the walls between Cima Su Alto and Cima Terranova. Difficulties are all in the upper part and whilst the climb is possible free, artificial means are often used although the number of pegs found in the route varies considerably.

Base Hut – Tissi 40min to the start 800m 10hr

8.24
VI
V+/A1
47
Start at the foot of the central spur, and climb up the crest of the ridge or sometimes on the R-hand side (pitches of IV). Avoid the last step in the ridge on the L, then go up a black and red section by an obvious slanting crack (V) a little to the R of the crest of the ridge and 35m L of the large red bulge. This leads to grey easy-angled slabs which mark the upper part of the face. In the upper part is a large yellow dièdre capped by a large roof (not the route), the R-hand wall of which is marked by parallel cracks. Go up the grey slabs, first L then R (IV). Climb a wall with OHs at its lower point, about 30m R of the yellow dièdre and continue a few m (VI- or A1).

Traverse 20m to the R (V,VI-) to a good ledge on the L-hand crack line. Go up this for four pitches, the first up a well marked dièdre (IV+), the second with a small roof then 20m up a very exposed wall (V,VI), the third with an OH (V) and the fourth a cracked wall (V) to a good ledge at the foot of a dièdre 10m below a big roof. Go up the dièdre (loose blocks) and traverse R on a steep cracked wall (VI+ or A1, V+) to reach a small ledge below a roof situated above and the R of the other. Then traverse R into the second crack line. Go up these cracks, over a large OH (V+) and follow the crack for another 20m (V) finishing on the R over a final OH (IV+). Then go up ledges separated by smooth walls on the R of the cracks, starting up a slight depression (V-) which leads to a peg stance. Then traverse L to a small ledge (VI) and climb up for 20m (IV,V+) to a peg at a stance which marks another traverse. This leads L for 30m to the final dièdre (V+), which is climbed in five pitches, with some OHs of V, to the top.

DESCENT BY EAST FACE

8.25 Descend on the E face for 100m to reach a large scree ledge which leads N towards the little Giazzèr Glacier. There is a bivouac hut (Tomè, 2800m) on this ledge. Descend the glacier and continue easily to the Vazzoler hut. The glacier can be tricky and it is also possible to descend mainly by abseils down from the col between Cima Su Alto and Cima Terranova. (3hr to Vazzoler hut but only 20min to the bivouac hut).

Cima della Terranova 2900m

NORTH-WEST FACE
Livanos, Gabriel, Da Roit, 1954.

Another modern route with good stances, not as sustained as 8.23. Much of the route is in chimneys, so it could be awkward in bad weather and nasty to retreat from. Possible with only one aid pitch.

Base Hut – Tissi 1hr to the start 700m 10hr

8.26 The best route up the lower section starts up the gully which leads to
VI/A2 the col on the R of the Cima della Terranove. Climb it for 3 pitches
47 (II,III) and then climb a crack (IV) which leads to a L traverse.
  Zig-zag up the spur to reach ledges below the steep, yellow upper
walls. This wall has two obvious chimneys in its lower part. Start
below the L-hand of these.

1 35m Climb the yellow OHing wall by a shallow dièdre past two
    roofs (A2). Under a third roof traverse R to a niche beside a small
    pillar (VI-)

2 15m Continue by a crack (V+) to a stance below the L-hand
    chimney

3 30m Climb up the chimney for a few m then avoid a roof on the L
    (VI-). A short crack (IV) leads to easier climbing as the chimney
    widens

4 45m Do not continue up the chimney but get onto a ledge on the R
    (V+). Traverse 15m R (IV) and then go direct by a slab and little
    chimney (V+),exiting R to a good ledge

5 45m Traverse R to a crack, climb this (V-) to a wide scree-covered
    ledge which leads R to the R-hand chimney

6 30m Climb the chimney (IV)

7 40m Continue up the chimney past an OH (V)

8 35m Climb the OHing chimney, then go R round the big roof (VI
    or VI-/A2) and then back L to reach a stance below a chimney
    with an OH with a hole through it

9 35m Go round the wet OH on the R (V) and then follow a crack
    diagonally R (VI or V+/A1)

10 35m Move up R (V) and then go obliquely L (VI or VI-/A2) to
    reach a wide crack which leads to the final chimney

11 35m Climb the chimney (VI- or A1,V)

12 45m Continue in the chimney (V,II) to the ridge.

DESCENT BY NORTH RIDGE AND EAST FACE

8.27 Follow the summit ridge N to the col between Cima della Terranova and Cima Su Alto. Descend on the E side a little, until a large scree ledge leads N to the Bivouac Tomè. Now descend as for 8.25. (30mins to bivouac hut)

Campanile Brabante 2252m

NORTH-WEST RIDGE

Tissi, King Leopold of the Belgians, Andrich, Franchetti, Rudatis, 1933.

This is the most sensational of three pinnacles which lie just off the main ridge, in a S-facing hollow W of Cima di Mede. The base is entirely surrounded by OHs giving a hard free first pitch. The descent is amusing! It can be combined with routes on the adjacent pinnacles to give excellent training or bad weather climbing. Note that abseil descents on all these pinnacles need double 40m ropes.

Base Hut – Vazzoler 45min to the start 180m 2hr

8.28 From the hut follow the path (560) to near a col, then go E up the
VI–   screes to the col on the N of the tower.
          Start at a jammed block and then climb the wall on the L of the N ridge until it is possible to traverse round the ridge to a stance (VI-). Now climb either up slabs near the arête, or the middle of the slab on the R, (both IV+) to reach a stance in a niche under the roof. Move R up to the OHs and hand-traverse R to the W ridge. Follow this easily to the summit.

DESCENT

8.29 Descend the SW face to the lip of the OHs and abseil 30m to the summit of the middle pinnacle (Boccia Rudatis). Another 30m abseil leads to the ground. (30min)

Guglia Rudatis (Guglia della Legione Alpina Piave) 2702m

NORTH-EAST AND NORTH-WEST FACE
Andrich, Vianini, Ghelli, 1935.

Two short interesting free climbs can be made on the third pinnacle.

Base Hut – Vazzoler 45min to the start 80m 1¹/₂hr

8.30 Start from the col between the Boccia and the Guglia.
V+   Climb 6m up the NE face then traverse R for 2m until near the N ridge (IV+). Continue straight up the wall for 8m (IV+) then traverse horizontally round the ridge R to a ledge (V+). Climb the NW face above trending R (IV+,V-) to below a line of OHs. Traverse R and climb these at the R-hand end (V) and then by easy slabs on the SW ridge to the top.

SOUTH-EAST RIDGE
Faè, Rudatis, 1931.

Base Hut – Vazzoler 45min to the start 75m 1hr

8.31 Start at the col between the Boccia and the Guglia at a block to the R
V- of the SE ridge.
    Climb obliquely up the wall (III) past a little bulge (IV) and up a L-ward leaning crack (IV) to a niche. Now take a steep crack to a higher ledge and finally move up L and direct over two OHs (V-) to a good ledge (40m in all).
    Go to the L end of the ledge, then climb direct for 7m, and traverse 3m L below an OH (IV+). Climb round this (V-) to a higher ledge, then go 2m L (III) and then direct, still steep (IV) to the summit.

DESCENT BY EAST FACE
8.32 Abseil down to the halfway ledge on the SE face from a rib a little below the summit (40m), then to the ground (40m); or a similar descent down route 8.30. (30min)

Pulpito di Pelsa 2210m

This peak and the next lie behind the Torre Venezia and present a small, well cracked face to the W. Good climbing on short routes for doubtful weather. The W face is marked by numerous cracks.

WEST FACE DIRECT
Goedele, Rieu, 1960.

This route takes a direct line up the centre. Another good climb, the Holtzer Crack (IV+) takes the R-hand line.

Base Hut – Vazzoler 1hr to the start 200m 2hr

8.33 Start 10m R of the obvious L-hand dièdre, at the foot of a crack.

IV+

1 30m Climb the crack (IV) to an OH which can be passed on either side (IV+) to a stance below a chimney

2 25m Exposed climbing up the chimney (IV+) to a stance beside a pinnacle on a scree ledge

3 30m Climb the wall (IV+) and crack above (III)

4 30m Follow sloping slabs R below the OHs (IV-) to a stance below a chimney

5 30m Climb the smooth, narrow chimney. Strenuous (IV+)

6 60m Easier rock for two pitches to the summit (II)

DESCENT BY EAST FACE
8.34 Climb easily down the E face to a col. Now go L (N) to reach a gully which leads down to the foot of the E face. (40min)

Punta Agordo 2290m

WEST FACE (AGORDO DIEDRE)
Da Roit and others, 1941.

This popular route climbs the big dièdre directly below the summit.

Base Hut – Vazzoler 1hr to the start 360m of climbing 2½hr

8.35 Start on the L of slabs below the corner.

IV+

1 60m Scramble up the slabs to the foot of the corner (II)

2 45m Climb a ramp on the R of the corner (III), pass a bulge on the R (IV) and move L back to a stance in the corner

3 25m Continue up the corner (IV,III)

4 40m Move up a crack on the R wall (IV) and then back in to the corner (III)

5   30m Climb a crack (IV) bridging past a bulge (IV+) to a peg. Move R to a stance on easy ground

6   90m Easily L and R to reach a short chimney. Up this (II) and move R to below steeper rock

7   40m Start up the R-hand crack, move L at the bulge, round this and back R to finish up a higher crack (IV)

8   30m A chimney and gully lead to the summit plateau (II).

DESCENT BY EAST FACE

8.36   From the summit descend N 10m to a ledge. Abseil 20m into a gully and climb up to a little col. Traverse 15m through a natural arch and then descend obliquely R to reach a gully. Move R to another gully and so join the descent from the Torre Venezia (8.41). (1½hr to the hut)

Torre Venezia 2337m

WEST FACE
Castiglioni, Kahn, 1929.

A classic, popular route on good rock.

Base Hut – Vazzoler 1hr to the start 300m 3hr

8.37
V
48
Follow the path (560) round below the W face of the tower. Then climb screes to the gully on the N of the tower, between it and Punta Agordo. Climb the gully to reach the start of a slanting corner, closed by OHs, on the R. Start at the foot of the corner.

1   30m Climb the corner and sloping slabs to finish below OHs (II,III)

2   25m Traverse R below the OHs (II), climb a ridge (III+) and then a crack (III+)

3   30m Traverse horizontally R across an exposed wall (IV-) to reach and climb a vertical crack for 15m (III). Care needed to protect the second

4   35m Follow cracks which widen to a chimney (III)

5   35m Go directly up the slabby wall to a little terrace at the top of the pillar (II)

6　25m Climb obliquely R (II) to the start of a long chimney, slanting slightly L, which cuts the upper wall

7　30m Climb the chimney to a place where it narrows (III)

8　40m Continue up a tight, smooth, often wet section (crux, IV) which eases to a stance below yellow OHs (III)

9　40m The OH direct is V so avoid it by ledges on the R wall (II) to a scree ledge. Continue R round an edge to a big ledge which runs right round the peak.

Follow the ledge R for 50m, then easily up to the summit or continue to join the descent.

SOUTH-WEST BUTTRESS
Andrich, Faè, 1934.

A classic free climb, on good rock, climbing the S side of the SW ridge up to a grey dièdre in its upper half.

Base Hut – Vazzoler 1¼hr to the start 300m 5hr

8.38
V+

Approach as for 8.37. From the foot of that route a ledge with small trees leads R for 80m to a peg stance near the ridge (III).

1　45m Climb a vertical crack for 15m (V+). Move R round a roof (V+) and up R to a little niche (V). Next move obliquely R (IV) to reach easier ground and a vegetated ledge below a steep yellow wall

2　30m Climb the steep crack using the wall on its L (V), then the wall above (V+) for 6m to a small ledge. Finally obliquely L to a good stance (IV)

3　35m Climb direct up on an OHing crack (V+) passing a roof on the L (V+). Continue up the crack passing another OH on the L (V)

4　45m Continue direct for 15m (IV) then slant R for 30m (III) to a large ledge (escape to 8.37 possible L)

5　40m Traverse the ledge R (I) to below the big dièdre

6　25m Do not climb the main dièdre but climb up R to a parallel dièdre which leads up the edge of the buttress to below yellow OHs (III, IV+)

7   40m Follow the crack for 3m to below the OH (V+). Traverse 3m L and climb 5m vertically to a ledge (V+). Now go direct then slant back L towards the main dièdre (V+) and a stance on a pillar

8   30m Climb the dièdre (IV+,V-)

9   40m Continue up the corner starting by a pinnacle below the final roof (V-). Traverse L and move up (IV+) to the circular terrace.

SOUTH-SOUTH-WEST FACE
Ratti, Panzeri, 1936.

A very exposed and interesting free climb.

Base Hut – Vazzoler 1¼hr to the start 420m 5hr

.39

I–

48

Approach and start as for 8.38.

1   45m As for 8.38 (V+)

2   20m Continue easily R along the ledge to a spur (II)

3   25m Go direct to a peg via a short yellow dièdre (V) then traverse R on reasonable holds (V-) to a crack leading to a stance

4   30m Climb direct for 10m (V+) then slant R (V)

5   35m Traverse L to reach an obvious dièdre (V-) and climb this to the top of a pillar (IV)

6   40m Traverse ledges R (II,III)

7   30m Continue R (II), descend a crack (IV+), move R on a narrow ledge (III) and up to a pinnacle below a dièdre

8   30m Climb the wall above for 7m (VI-), step 1m L and then go direct to the dièdre (V). Up this for 10m to a niche (V-)

9   40m Continue direct (IV), pass a bulge (V), and then go first R then L (IV+) to reach the end of a ledge below a yellow wall

10 40m Traverse the ledge R and climb a crack up a black wall (V) until it is possible to move L to a crack which leads (IV+) to a stance

11 35m Continue up the crack to a gully (IV)

12 30m Follow the gully (IV) to the terrace below the summit.

SOUTH FACE (TISSI ROUTE)
Tissi, Andrich, Bortoli, 1933.

An excellent free climb with an exposed and justly famous crux traverse. It climbs the grey rocks to the R of the huge, central, yellow dièdre (the Schubert Direct, VI-/A2 and A3 at the big roof). In good weather an early start is recommended for the wall can get very hot.

Base Hut – Vazzoler   30min to the start   600m   6hr

8.40
VI–
V+/A0

48

Start in a direct line with the final chimneys, to the L of a large block stuck against the wall near its lowest point. Alternatives are possible further L. These are harder but, if the grassy lower slabs are wet, a start can be made up the huge central dièdre for 40m then diagonally R (V+) to join the described route a pitch below the tree stance on pitch 7.

1   40m Climb onto the block (III) and follow slabs L to a stance below a short dièdre (IV)

2   50m Climb the dièdre (III) and move up L to a tree (IV). Continue L by a crack

3   30m Obliquely L up a crack (III) and traverse L (IV)

4   40m Again L (II) and then back R up a ramp (III+)

5   30m Climb a crack until below a yellow OH (IV). Traverse L to a stance (III)

6   35m R then L up vegetated slabs to a vertical chimney (III). Up this (III)

7   35m Up the wet grey wall by a vertical crack on the L of a small slanting dièdre (V+), ending at a tree stance

8   40m Move up and R above a small roof (V), slant R for 12m to a peg (VI-). Go up again slanting R for 9m (VI-) then finish on the R at a small ledge (V+/A0 if the pegs are used for aid)

9   35m Continue direct for 20m (V-) then go a little L (IV+)

10   35m Avoid a direct variant (V-) by going diagonally L (III) and then back R (IV-) on a ramp.

11   40m Climb a short crack, traverse 10m R (IV) then diagonally L to a stance below another crack

12   40m Climb the narrow crack for 15m (IV+), traverse 7m R, then take a groove (III) to a stance near the upper chimney/corner

13 35m First climb the yellow wall on the R (IV+) to below an OH, then L across a steep grey wall (V-)

14 30m Continue direct for 15m (IV+) then climb over a small OH on good holds (V-) to a stance in a niche

15 30m Continue up the chimney using the wall on its R (IV+) to the ledges below the summit.

DESCENT BY EAST FACE

.41 This descent involves quite tricky route-finding especially in mist.

From the summit descend N to the large ledge which encircles the peak. A well marked path leads down for 30m to a 15m abseil. Continue to climb down a gully (II) to the R (S) to reach the top of a chimney. Descend this for 10m and continue R (S) to a shoulder. Climb 60m down a wall and gully (II). Well before the end of the gully a ledge leads L (N) behind several pinnacles to the col behind the Torre (Forcella di Pelsa). Continue down the gully to the NE (II+) to easy ground and a path down to the hut. (2½hr)

Cima del Balcon 2346m

EAST FACE
Da Roit, Gabriel, 1953.

This route lies on the upper face of this subsidiary peak on the L of the Val Contrin. It is broken into three parts, a lower wall (mostly III), a very steep middle section above the first terrace (originally mainly aid climbing but now mostly free), and above a second terrace a final chimney section. Two similar hard routes lie up the walls to its L and the area provides good climbing early or late in the season, when the big N face routes are out of condition.

Base Hut – Vazzoler 45min to the start 450m 8hr

8.42
VII–
VI/A1
The E face is in the form of a wall on the L, a groove leading to two OHing dièdres in the middle, and a steep, grey wall buttressed by easier angled grey slabs on the R. The first terrace slants up from the R across the wall with the L-hand routes finishing on it.

Start on the R of the grey slabs at the lowest point of the wall. Climb Lwards taking the easiest line for 300m to the first terrace. Mostly II,IV but a final pitch of V-. Move L up the terrace to a wide crack below yellow roofs.

1　25m Climb the chimney for 10m (IV) then over a slab and a short crack (V) to a ledge

2　20m Climb up to the yellow/white roofs and then move R over them, via a thin crack (VI), and reach a niche by a short crack (V+)

3　20m Go R out of the niche and up a vertical wall by a crack (V+)

4　25m Traverse L 5m and go obliquely R up a smooth slab (VII- or V+/A1) to reach a ledge. Move R 8m to a stance

5　30m Go obliquely R past two small OHs (V), then more easily (IV) to the second terrace. Walk R 25m (good bivouac 30m further R)

6　40m Climb a friable OHing crack (VI-) and move up on poor rock into the start of a poorly defined chimney slanting L. Climb this past two OHs (V+) to a stance

7　35m Climb the chimney until it widens (V)

8　40m Climb up on the R, then go 5m L, and finally slightly L to the terrace below the summit.

Climb easily up the ridge to the highest point (III).

DESCENT TO WEST
8.43　Scramble down the main ridge, on its W flank, until it is possible to scramble down the great gully on the R to where it peters out in terraces and ledges. Continue down and to the R until it is possible to traverse across to the descent from the Torre Venezia (8.41). (1½hr to the hut)

Torre di Babele 2310m

SOUTH RIDGE
Solda, Solda, 1937.

This route lies on a subsidiary peak just off the main ridge on the L side of the Val dei Cantoni. It is due N of the hut and the climb is visible from it. Classic climbing on sound rock, free, sustained and exposed. The lower half of the route is on the L of the edge, the upper part on the R.

Base hut – Vazzoler 1hr to the start 300m 4hr

8.44 Start below the S ridge at the top of the screes below a gully leading
VI– up L. Go up the gully, passing under a chockstone, until a ledge leads
out R onto the ridge.

1   25m Traverse the ledge R, move up then continue R to a stance
   (III+)

2   35m Traverse horizontally R to near the edge, go up 5m and then
   traverse back R

3   40m Climb a steep slab for 10m (V+) and continue direct to a
   ledge (V)

4   40m Move L and climb a loose corner (V-) to an OH. Move L and
   then go direct over another roof (V+) to a ledge

5   35m Climb obliquely R (IV+,V-) to reach a stance in trees on a
   big terrace

6   50m Walk R to a stance below a crack line a few m R of the edge.
   (Escape possible R along the ledge)

7   40m Climb the crack obliquely R up the wall (V+,V) to a stance
   on the R

8   40m Move 2m L to a smooth corner. Climb it for 10m (VI-) then
   go L up the wall (V+) to finish at a very poor stance on the edge

9   15m Climb a short corner to a niche (V)

10 35m Move up R (IV) to a marked corner crack (V) leading to a
   shoulder

11 35m Traverse 10m R (III). Climb direct for 5m, traverse L to
   reach a crack which ends at a stance (IV+)

12 15m Easily R (III) to the big shoulder (Pulpit di Babele). Continue
   up the brittle S ridge (III) to the summit.

DESCENT TO SOUTH-WEST
8.45 Descend the S ridge to the Pulpit di Babele, then descend the SW face
to reach and descend a gully further S, which leads down to screes
100m L of the start of 8.44. At least three abseils of 40m needed, or
grade III climbing. Some parties abseil back down the route instead,
to avoid stonefall danger. (2hr to the hut)

Cima della Busazza 2894m

WEST FACE
Gilberti, Castiglioni, 1931.

An excellent free climb on good rock up this face on the R of Val dei Cantoni. It climbs the easier lower slabs to reach a gully and chimney leading direct to the summit. Some danger of ice in the chimneys early in summer.

Base hut – Vazzoler 45min to the start 1000m 8hr

8.46 Walk up the Val dei Cantoni and then go direct to the foot of the W
VI– face.
      Start 100m L of the bottom of the W ridge at a snow patch under a high steep wall.
      Climb easy ledges to below a vertical wall cut by a crack with a black OH near its start. Climb up 20m, then go round the OH on the L to rejoin the crack and continue up this (V) to the foot of a yellowish wall. Climb this by a thin crack (IV+) and continue to reach big grey walls which get progressively less steep. Climb direct towards a gully which marks the centre of the wall (IV,III/II).
      Next climb a crack from the R and follow the groove above until it splits. Take the L branch and follow a series of cracks, which get steeper and harder (V), to a marked tower below the final chimney.
      Climb the chimney above for about five pitches (IV,V+, one section VI-) until it ends at a little pulpit. Finally take the ridge on the L (a bit loose) to the summit.

DESCENT BY SOUTH-EAST FACE
8.47 This is easy, and goes SE from the summit to a hollow. Descend a chimney (II) and go obliquely R by ledges to reach screes leading to the Van delle Sasse path (558). (1½hr to the hut)

Castello della Busazza 2592m

SOUTH FACE
Holzer, Messner, 1966.

This peak lies directly behind the Torre Trieste, and the route lies above the end of the descent (8.53) from Torre Trieste.

Base hut – Vazzoler 1hr to the start 800m 7hr

8.48 Approach by going round below the Torre Trieste and climbing the
V+ gully under its E face to reach the base of this S wall. Climb up easily
by ledges then Rwards heading for an obvious corner in the steeper
wall ahead (II, a pitch of IV-). Move 30m L to a crack. Start of the
hard climbing at the level of the second ledge on the Torre Trieste.

Climb a chimney closed by a roof (V) and continue for another
pitch (IV+) until a traverse L leads to a dièdre. Climb this (V+,III)
up a thin crack to an OH. Now go R and up the corner above (V+).
Continue L up an OHing corner on poor rock (V+) to scree on a band
of slanting rock. Go easily up this for 100m slanting L (II,III) to reach
a ledge below steep walls. On the R of a pillar climb a crack (V,IV) for
35m. Continue for 5m and then traverse R to a dièdre. Up this (IV) to
a stance. Two more pitches up the dièdre (IV+,IV) lead to a ledge
below a yellow pillar. Traverse 30m R to another corner. Climb this
for two long pitches (IV,V) to the foot of a final chimney. Climb this
(V-) to the top.

DESCENT TO THE EAST
8.49 Descend to a col to the SE and go down two little chimneys. Next
down big blocks and slabs to reach scree after a final chimney.
Descend L down the scree to a col. Finally go L to the Van delle
Sasse. (1hr to here)

Torre Trieste 2458m

WEST RIDGE
Tissi, Andrich, Rudatis, 1931.

*A long classic route, unfortunately broken in the middle, but recommended.
No extreme difficulty, but its length plus the difficulty and length of the
descent make it a serious affair.*

Base hut – Vazzoler 45min to the start 650m 6hr

8.50 Start 45m R of the base of the big gully between the Torre Trieste and
VI the Castello della Busazza.
V+/A0 The W ridge ends in a steep spur and it is first necessary to reach
a groove on the R of this. Climb across vegetated rock to a terrace with
bushes. Traverse R 30m onto the true W face and to a spacious stance
under an OH.

1 50m Go up the wall to a tree (III+) then slant R to a stance under
a yellow OH (II)

2   40m Climb the yellow wall and OH, and move 3m R to a ledge
    (V+). Continue up a very steep corner until below a roof. Move R
    along a slabby rake to a poor stance (VI or V+/A1). Beware rope
    drag on this pitch!

3   40m Slant L to a stance below a long steep corner crack (IV)

4   50m Climb the corner past a bulge (V), then 6m R to a loose
    groove and up this (IV+), and finally slant L (III) to a stance

5   50m Obliquely L for 10m then vertically (III,IV) to easier ground

6   70m Continue walking and scrambling over two shoulders to
    reach a stance below steeper rock (I with a move III)

7   50m Climb a bulge direct (IV+) and continue up the wall above
    (II)

8   40m Slant L (III) and then direct up the ridge. Traverse 10m R to
    a good stance below a white slabby corner (III+)

9   50m Climb the dièdre (V) and then the shallow crack above (V)

10 40m Slant L (IV) then climb a vertical holdless wall for 5m to a
    pinnacle. Move L to a flake stuck to the wall. Up this by a crack
    and continue to a stance below a little roof (VI or V+/A1)

    Two finishes are possible. The original goes easily by the gully
    round to the L or the Couzy Direct up the wall above.

    ORIGINAL FINISH

11 20m Traverse L (II) and climb awkwardly down a crack (IV-) to
    reach a stance in the gully

12 100m Continue up the gully and chimneys above to the summit (I)

    DIRECT FINISH (Couzy, Schatz, 1948.)

11 40m Climb the roof above the R-hand end of the ledge, then a
    wide crack for 25m to a ledge on the L. Strenuous (A1,VI)

12 80m Climb a short wall on the L to a sloping ledge. Traverse R
    under a small OH (V+) to easy ground. Up dièdres and a blocking
    chimney to the summit.

SOUTH FACE
Carlesso, Sandri, 1934.

One of the classic hard routes of the Dolomites. Usually some artificial climbing, although it has been de-pegged at least twice and has been done with only one short aid section. Because of the de-pegging some holds have been lost and some pegs are not replaceable, so protection bolts are appearing. Enquiries at the Vazzoler hut are recommended concerning the latest state of the route (and the art!)

The seriousness of the route is reduced by the various possibilities of escape and the choice of finishes but it is still a major undertaking.

Base hut – Vazzoler 1hr to the start 700m 9hr

8.51
VIII–
VI+/A2 the R. Traverse out (II) on the highest terrace above the easy lower
53 rocks until grey rock and belay pegs mark the start of the route.

Take the Van delle Sasse path (558) until it is possible to go up to below the R-hand side of the face. It may be best to follow a stream on

1 45m Climb up R to a stance (IV+)

2 35m Obliquely R and then a ledge R to finish below a yellow OHing wall (IV)

3 20m Climb over the roof above and move R 6m to a stance (VII- or VI-/A2,V)

4 50m Various routes are possible up this hard pitch. The most free linetraverses 5m R and climbs the wall for 10m (VI+). Now traverse 5m L (VI) and move up under a black roof (VI+). Traverse 3m L and go over the roof (VII-,VI-). Finally traverse 4m L and finish direct over a roof (V+) to a small ledge. Other possibilities go more direct and use aid (VI/A1)

5 25m Traverse 8m L and go up for 6m (IV+). Traverse R then continue direct. (The Cassin Route (8.52) goes R from here)

6 40m Traverse L to the end of the ledge (III), climb a little roof (V) and continue L to a ledge (IV)

7 40m Continue L up a wall with a narrow ledge (IV,V) to a yellow niche below a roof

8 35m Climb the roof and continue direct for some m, then traverse L (V+). Regain a black crack on the L and follow this (V+) to a stance below a roof

9 30m Climb the OH (VI or A1) and continue by a crack (V) and then by an easy wall (III) to the first terrace

Note: Escape is now possible R (N), but when the ledge disappears do not try a direct descent (stonefall danger) but climb the gully for three pitches to reach the second ledge and follow this R to the normal descent (8.53).

10 40m Traverse the ledge L to finish at the base of a great grey dièdre

11 30m Climb up cracks on the R side of the dièdre (V)

12 40m Go a little L and continue by wall climbing (VI+ or VI-/A1) until easier rock (III) leads to the second ledge

Note: Escape again possible R (N) to the normal descent route (8.53). Good bivouac site 10m R.

13 30m Traverse L and climb up 3m to a grassy ledge (III) below a big, grey/yellow dièdre

14 35m Climb the R wall of the dièdre and continue direct (VI- or V+/A0)

15 30m Go obliquely R to the bottom of a very smooth slab (III)

16 35m Climb direct 10m (V+,VI+) to a little ledge, then towards the R 5m to reach a peg (VI,VIII- or VI/A2) and continue vertically by a crack for 15m to another peg (V+). Move 5m R (VI) to a little stance at the base of an OHing dièdre

17 35m Climb the yellow dièdre and continue by a chimney/crack to a niche (V+). Traverse 5m R to reach the continuation of the crack and up this to below an OHing wall (V) on a detached flake

18 15m Reach a horizontal crack and hand-traverse L to the foot of a grey dièdre (V,V+ or A1)

19 40m Climb the back of the dièdre (V)

20 80m Continue on easier slabby rock still slanting L (III) and finally horizontally L (IV-) to a pulpit made of big loose blocks at the base of the final head wall

Two finishes are now possible. A grey chimney on the L is normal whilst the Hasse Direct Finish goes up the yellow chimney above and is difficult and delicate.

NORMAL FINISH

21 25m Climb down a chimney behind the pulpit (IV-) to a ledge and traverse L to the final chimney (IV-)

22 90m Three pitches up the chimney (IV,V,V) lead to the summit

HASSE DIRECT FINISH

21 30m Climb the OHing dièdre to the top of a pillar (V)

22 30m Continue up the corner (V+) over two roofs (VI or A2), the first on the R, the second on the L, to continue to a stance below a chimney

23 30m Over the initial OH (VI-) and up the chimney (V)

24 25m Over a little OH and up a steep slab to a roof (V). Traverse L and up another slab (IV+) to a gully and the top.

SOUTH-EAST RIDGE
Cassin, Ratti, 1935.

A tremendous free climb of similar difficulty to the S Face (8.51) with which it shares the first five pitches and escape possibilities. See comments for that route.

Base hut – Vazzoler 1hr to the start 700m 8hr

8.52
VII+
VI/A2
53

Approach and start as for 8.51 as far as the end of pitch 5.

6 40m Move R below OH (V-) and continue obliquely R up little walls and ledges to reach a ledge under an OH. Climb R to a stance and thread belay on the ridge (IV+)

7 45m To the R of the ridge climb an OH (VI- or V/A1) and continue by a crack (IV+) which finishes obliquely L by a higher crack to the bottom of an obvious chimney/dièdre on the L of the ridge

8 50m Climb the chimney/dièdre past some OHs (V) and continue (IV) to the first terrace (escape R as for 8.51)

9 15m Traverse L 10m round the ridge to a stance below a big roof

10 45m Climb direct by a yellow crack to finish under a roof (VI+ or A1,V). Move L and up (III+) to a stance and thread

11 50m Avoid a direct route above by continuing some m obliquely L (IV) and then direct to a hollow under a roof (IV+). Climb the

OH on the L to a block ledge, which leads to a crack leading to the second terrace (escape R as for 8.51)

12 25m Climb up easily at first on the R of the ridge (III). Then climb a steep grey corner (VI-,V+) to a niche on the R

13 40m Move L and continue up the corner to a good ledge (VI,VI-,IV+). A harder variation takes the R wall (VI+ or V+/A2)

14 50m The slab above is grey and compact with occasional pegs, and there is a big yellow corner round the ridge to the L. Either is possible:-

a Follow the ledge 10m L and climb the dièdre (V+,V,IV-) to an uncomfortable stance at 30m. Then continue until under a yellow roof (VI or A1) and climb this (VII+ or A2) to continue R to below a big roof (VI or A1). Traverse under this for 5m to a good stance

b Stay R of the ridge. Climb to a ledge some m to the R, go up a short dièdre closed by a little roof (V+), move R onto a slab (VI+ or VI-/A0) and continue obliquely R by cracks to a niche (V+). This is below and R of the stance on (a). Continue to a higher niche on the L

15 50m From either stance reach and climb a crack on the slab above. Then go obliquely R (V+) and climb a crack (IV+) which leads to a good stance on a terrace on the edge of the ridge

16 25m From the ledge traverse R on a compact slab (V) to a cracked chimney. Up this (IV+) to reach a higher terrace on the ridge

17 30m Continue gently R by an attractive slab (V+) and then by a wall and crack (IV)

18 40m Climb a crack (V+) leading to a cracked dièdre formed by an obvious detached tower. Go up this (V-) moving R at the top

19 50m Ignore a chimney on the L and reach the final chimney R by difficult and delicate climbing (V). Continue up it (IV-) to a boulder on the R

20 100m Take the ridge and easy gully to the top (II).

DESCENT BY EAST FACE

8.53   This is a serious and complicated descent. Care on the abseils is vital. Good pegs have made it less dangerous, although some trees may have to be used but great care is still needed especially in poor visibility. There is some stonefall danger from other parties and in bad weather.

From the summit descend for about 50m over easy ground on the W face. Traverse horizontally NE and go round a ridge to reach a `platform at the top of a chimney (Cozzi Chimney). Descend this in two abseils to a ledge at the foot of the chimney. Traverse across a narrow ledge along the ridge N towards Castello della Busazza. Climb round L of the first pinnacle (II,III). Ignore the first pegs and from the next col between the pinnacles descend a little on the E side to a peg. Abseil 20m to a col then a further 25m. An abseil of 40m and a descent of 5m leads to a short abseil of 10m followed by another of 40m. Now descend 10m to an abseil diagonally L from a peg in a big block. A final 30m abseil leads to the second ledge level with a rock spur. Cross to the gully on the N of the spur and descend 80m to a fork. Continue down the gully on the L for 30m to a peg on the R. Abseil 15m and then descend to a shoulder. Keep traversing and descending N down a gully of big blocks, leading to a gully which in 200m leads to the starts of 8.51 and 8.52. Continue down to the hut. (Allow at least 4hr)

Geografica 1:25000 sheet 3

This is a compact massif lying NE of Civetta and S of Cortina. It is in the form of a horseshoe facing SE.

HUTS

Venezia de Luca Hut 1946m. This popular hut is situated to the SE of the group. Approaches– i)easily by car from Borca di Cadore. It may be possible to drive up the rough track to within 15min of the hut or cars may have to be left near Tabià de Tiera (1271m) then by 470 (1¾hr), ii)from another road near Zoppe di Cadore (c.1600m) then by 493 (1½hr)

Citta di Fiume Hut 1917m. A small hut situated to the N of the group. The farm, Malga Fiorentina, below it has accommodation. Approach by a track from near the F d Staulanza.

Monte Pelmo 3168m

ORDINARY ROUTE FROM SOUTH-EAST
John Ball, 1857.

The traverse of the Ball Ledge at the start is quite exciting, the rest is a strenuous walk up scree slopes. Fine views from the summit.

Base hut – Venezia de Luca 15min to the start 1000m 5hr

9.01
II
55
Follow path 480 steeply NW over scree slopes to the start of the Ball Ledge which runs across the lower part of the E face. Reach it over broken ground and follow it to its end. There are two awkward places, the Passo dello Stemma and the Passo del Gatto towards the end of the ledge where it is necessary to crawl for about 6m along a low passage below an OH. The ledge ends on the great hollow of the mountain. Go along above the scree slopes of the lower section and continue over wide ledges in the middle section to reach the large amphitheatre from which the small Pelmo glacier comes down. Go R from here and up to the summit ridge. Now go easily along the summit ridge to the central and highest of the three peaks of Monte Pelmo.

SOUTH-EAST PILLAR (FRANCESCHI ROUTE)
Bellodis, Franceschi, 1955.

*A fine free climb up the prominent pillar which leads to the secondary
summit of Monte Pelmo at a height of 3017m. An easy ridge joins the
peaks. The climb is in three sections, a lower introductory buttress, the steep
middle section and an easier upper section. The rock is generally good
where it matters.*

Base hut – Venezia de Luca 15min to the start 800m 9hr

.02 Start as for 9.01 but after 50m on the Ball Ledge head R up
I–/A1 scree-covered rock towards a gully running from L to R. Climb this
55 for 50m and continue up a series of chimneys (III) for 70m on the R
side of the ridge. Continue for 100m up broken rock to a large scree
ledge below the steeper upper walls.

Near the centre of the wall climb diagonally L to R across a
smooth slab (V) to the start of a flared crack. Climb the OH at the
base (V+) and continue for 35m to a ledge below yellow OHs.
Traverse R below the OHs for 20m to a good peg belay, climb a
vertical crack on good holds for 25m (V) and continue by a crack **and**
a yellow flake for 30m (V+). Next climb a smooth chimney (V) **for .**
12m to a spike belay and continue 15m up an OHing dièdre to a b.
roof (VI-,A1). Traverse R (A1) and climb up to a niche (V+) in 20m.
Now go horizontally R to an OHing chimney which starts with an OH
(V+) and in 20m leads to a scree-covered ledge.

Continue in the same line for 70m (V+,IV+) on good vertical
rock and pass another OH to reach a ledge. Climb up and Lwards
close to the crest of the pillar for 80m and then finish by a chimney
onto the summit ledges. Go along the terrace under a roof then
straight up to reach a long chimney and in 80m reach the summit.

SOUTH-EAST PILLAR (ANGELLINI ROUTE)
Angelini, Vienna, 1931.

*This route takes the R flank of the E ridge pillar and is quite serious due to
its length and route-finding difficulties. The climbing is not sustained. Not
a popular route.*

Base hut – Venezia de Luca 30min to the start 850m 6hr

.03 Start as for 9.01 but continue up the path below the E face to near the
V foot of an obvious couloir. After a preliminary spur reach a gully
which runs parallel with the E ridge and climb this going L to a large
scree ledge. Climb the next step from L to R and continue up a little

gully. After another steeper pitch go obliquely L to reach a well
marked **ledge on the L** about one third of the way up the buttress.
(This **ledge can be** traversed L across 9.02 to reach the main Pelmo
amphitheatre and 9.01.)

Next go R in **zig-zags** then L to avoid OHs and finally R to reach
an arête at the edge of the NE face.

Good route-finding is now essential. Take the easiest line up
little **walls and over** ledges to below a big wall, traverse L and ascend
by gullies to **another** steep section which is climbed more to the R of
the arête.

Return L by ledges to near the arête and climb a steep little
black gully. Traverse L to the edge to a place where the S face is in
view and climb the exposed ridge above and finally easy steps to the
final terrace below the red summit tower. Move L onto the S face and
easily to the top of the pillar.

NORTH FACE
Rossi, Simon, 1924.

*This is a classic free climb and is a serious undertaking due to its length and
situation. It takes a fairly direct line up the pillar in the middle of the N
face, first climbing gullies, chimneys and slabby terraces on the R of the
pillar then taking chimneys and corners on the L. The rock is generally
good but ice and some stonefall maybe found in the upper sections whilst a
bergschrund is usual at the base.*

*Base hut – Citte di Fiume or the road at F d Staulanza (1776m) 2hr to the
start 850m 11hr*

19.04
V+
54

Follow paths (480 or 472) to the foot of the glacier below the face and
ascend it to a steep snow indentation just R of the lowest part. Climb
the snow to its top edge.

1   130m Get onto the rock and follow a ramp diagonally L to the top
    of the subsidiary spur (III,IV+)

2   100m From the highest point move up some m to reach a
    horizontal fault line. Follow this R across water streaked rocks
    (IV) finishing with a hand-traverse (IV+)

3   130m Climb direct up cracks and chimneys (V) until an exit L is
    possible to a big ledge. An alternative start comes up to here from
    the R up a slanting ledge

4   100m Move L for 25m until it is possible to climb up to scree

ledges below a black wet crack. Climb this for 6m, traverse R round the arête (V) and finish up a smooth slab (V-). Continue in a cracked dièdre to reach a gap in the edge of the big sloping ledge which is an obvious feature here and which descends from the central pillar

5   80m Climb easily up the ledge L to a stance below OHs (II)

6   80m Start on the R of the pillar, climb an OH and then go obliquely up slabs to the base of the main arête (IV,III)

7   50m Above are two dièdres, a yellow one on the L which cuts a little buttress and a grey one parallel to it on the R. Move up from a niche on the R to the yellow dièdre and climb it to a ledge (V+). Move round a little pillar to the L and climb a chimney to its summit (IV)

8   35m Traverse horizontally R for 10m to a shattered slab (V) and climb to the R via an awkward niche (V+,V) to another terrace

9   60m Climb more easily L to reach a stance on the edge below big OHs (bivouac site)

10 45m Traverse L round the edge and continue for 15m delicately towards a red chimney (V). First climb the wall on its R past an OH then move L until it is possible to reach a stance in the chimney (V+). Continue up the chimney (loose) climbing a gap in a roof (V+)

11 90m Climb OHing cracks then grey slabs (V+,V) to reach a line of OHs and traverse 12m R below these to a dièdre

12 60m Climb the dièdre (V+,V) and move L to climb another dièdre past OHs to a stance in a niche (V) (bivouac site)

13 80m Traverse R round the edge to reach and climb an icy crack in the back of a dièdre/gully (V+)

14 80m Go slightly R and follow a loose diagonal crack to the L (V) and continue to the ridge (III) 50m E of the summit.

DESCENTS
9.05 From the main summit descend SW towards a col and go L (SE) to the snow slopes of the great central amphitheatre. Continue following cairns and a path to the lowest part of the hollow to reach the Ball Ledge and follow this L (NE) with two awkward places to the screes. (2hr to the hut)
      From the SE pillar head NE to a col and then descend L (SE) to reach the amphitheatre. (2hr to the hut)   211

Pelmetto 2990m

NORTH-WEST RIDGE
Cascara, Visentin, 1936.

Less difficult and much less popular than the N face of Pelmo this route is nevertheless serious and quite bold for the standard. It follows the line of the ridge for most of its length and route-finding up the various alternatives needs alpine skill.

Base – road at F d Stanlanza 1½hr to the start 850m 9hr

9.06
V
54

Follow the higher path from the col SE until it is possible to scramble up L through a little valley with small pine trees and up a scree couloir below the W face. Keep traversing L until a ledge leads out onto the NW ridge. This point is at least 100m above the actual foot of the ridge

Start 60m R of the ridge level with a deep gully. Climb the gully and a chimney on its L exiting through a hole (III+) and continue L to below a loose red crack just R of the arête. Climb this and a grey wall L (IV-) to a col. Now go L of the ridge up a gully leading to jammed blocks by a white flake (IV). Continue on the L to reach a big scree terrace.

Continue above the terrace for 30m on the R of the edge then go R and finally L. Continue towards the vast hollow formed by a smooth wall flanked by detached pillars.

From the col behind the R-hand pillar descend 10m, traverse L and climb easy rocks to reach the edge of the ridge and a view of Pelmo N face. Traverse into the N side and climb the second chimney encountered past a jammed block (IV-) and continue easily up the ridge passing various cols and gullies to reach a higher col.

Now get into a big corner to the R of a red tower and climb it past various niches and holes to a big roof. Traverse L to a crack and climb it to a col. This is the key section of 100m (V). Move L 15m on the N side and continue near the ridge up red cracks and walls. A dièdre (IV), a 15m traverse L and a chimney with a hard exit (V) lead to easier ground and two more pitches (III) lead to the easy upper ridge and the N summit.

DESCENT
9.07 Go to the S peak and descend scree SW to reach a ledge leading to the R. A steep step separates this ledge from a lower one, Salto del Mago. Either climb down it or abseil 12m. Follow the lower ledge round the SW and SE faces to the start of the S gully and descend it to path 472. Go E for the Venezia hut (3hr) or W for F d Staulanza. (2½hr)

Geografica 1:25000 sheet 4

Although only 20km from Civetta this area has, until recently, received little attention from climbers and yet, for those seeking hard climbing on fine faces at low altitude, its peace and seclusion makes it a very attractive area. However, this isolation does mean that those attempting the hard routes should be fully competent. Most routes are accessible from the Boscanero cirque to the NW. The main peaks form a reversed L shape. To the W is Rocchetta Bassa di Bosconero (2047m) then F d Rocchetta Bassa (1950m). The main climbing peak is Rocchetta Alta di Bosconero, a wedge-shaped peak with a N pillar (2309m) separated by a small col (2371m) from the main summit (2412m) to the S. It has steep faces on three sides and an easier E slope to F Rocchetta Alta. Next to this col is Sasso di Toanella (2430m) with its excellent East Crack route (260m, V+) then another col, F d Toanella (2150m) between it and the continuation of the ridges N. Sasso de Bosconero (2436m) comes next although some maps call it Monte Rocchetta (2468m). It has easy ascents from E and S but a good NW ridge and after a final col, F Matt (2063m), comes the imposing mass of Sfornioi (2409m) which has excellent routes up its E face (V+) and SE dièdre (V).

HUTS

Bivouac Casera di Bosconero 1457m. This lies to the NW of the group in the Bosconero cirque. Approach from the Forno di Zolda road near Lago di Pontesei (800m) and follow paths E through the woods. (1¾hr)

Bivouac Casera di Camestrini 1649m. This lies to the NE of the group. Approaches– i) from Biv Boscanero by via ferrata over Sasso de Bosconero (2431m) or by F Matt (2063m), ii)from Ospitale di Cadore by a little road then 483 (2hr)

Rocchetta Alta di Bosconero 2412m

SOUTH FACE
Geihs, Goedeke, 1965.

An elegant and exposed climb following a line of least resistance Rwards up this narrow yellow/grey buttress which is well seen from the road between km 116 and km 115 S of the Lago di Pontesei.

Base hut – Casera di Bosconero 2hr to the start 400m 4hr

10.01
V– From the hut take the path towards the N face but leave it on the R to cross under the W wall over scree and grass. Ascend a snow and scree gully to the F Rocchetta Bassa (1950m) between the Alta on the L and the Bassa on the R. From the col descend 100m on the S side to a gully. Climb the R branch of the gully (II,III) to its upper limit and traverse across the wall on grass and vegetation for 200m to a prominent pillar covered with dwarf pines. Start at the col between the pillar and the S face.

1   35m Climb the wall to a ledge below a yellow OH and traverse 20m L to a chimney and cairn (II)

2   25m Climb the chimney (III) to a big ledge

3   30m Climb the black wall (IV+) finishing L under OHs to a stance

4   30m Climb obliquely R up a wall (IV) and cross a grass-covered ledge R to the foot of a black corner with a small roof, on the L of a loose crack (II)

5   20m Climb the black corner (IV) and go L (IV+) to a stance below a chimney

6   35m Ascend the chimney (IV) and the gully above (II) to a terrace

7   35m Move L (II), go up to a ledge and up a chimney to a yellow niche (IV)

8   20m Now climb a thin partly OHing crack to a black OH (V–,IV+) and traverse diagonally R to reach a chimney (IV)

9   40m Climb the chimney (IV+) and a cracked dièdre with a flake (III) to a big ledge below a yellow wall

10   50m Walk R until below a big dièdre/gully

11   180m Climb the gully and ledges L (II,III,II) then the ridge above (II) for 50m to the summit.

WEST PILLAR
Geihs, Goedeke, 1965.

A serious route for its standard which climbs a pillar and the W face to join the summit ridge near the descent col.

Base hut – Casera di Bosconero 30min to the start 750m 5hr

10.02
V
60

Start up the W gully as for 10.01, zig-zag up to the first dwarf pine-covered terrace and traverse R. Climb a gully with a jammed boulder (II,III) for 65m to reach a second vegetated ledge. It may be possible to solo to here.

Climb for 15m over small OHs on the R of the edge of the pillar (IV+) and continue up a corner crack (IV). Follow the edge for 130m (III) to a great pine-covered shoulder below the point where the ridge steepens and scramble up to a yellow niche which may contain a dwarf pine just R of the centre of the wall.

Traverse 6m R and climb a 10m wall (IV+). Trend back L to the beginning of a crack system and follow this for 50m (V-,IV) to a ledge which lies R of the base of a 30m high tower. Climb a crack for 15m to the R of the tower (V) and the 15m chimney above (IV+). Finally climb 15m up another crack (IV) to a ledge below OHs. Traverse 20m L on the ledge to a peg and either hand-jam up the crack above (V) or continue the traverse then ascend (IV) to the stance.

Scramble over scree-covered rocks for 35m (III) to a stance below a large pillar. Climb the OH in the dièdre/gully on the R of the pillar (IV+) and continue L below a yellow wall. Climb a yellow corner on the R (III+) to a stance. Continue by a further corner (IV-) followed by broken rock to a chimney/crack with jammed slabs and climb this for 35m (IV+) to a big ledge.

Go R along the ledge for 20m then move Rwards over scree-covered rock for 80m to a stance below a grey wall. Climb the wall first direct (IV) and then diagonally L below roofs for 35m. Continue L and then R for 60m past the OHs to reach a wide terrace (III) with bivouac sites under OHs.

From the R-hand end of the terrace an easy scree gully leads to the ridge which can be followed in 15min to the main S summit or a direct descent can be made (10.05).

NORTH-WEST RIDGE (SPIGOLO STROBEL)
Menardi, Da Pozza, Lorenzi, Lorenzi, Zardini, 1964.

A superb route with hard free climbing in exposed situation on good rock with good stances. The ridge lies on the edge of the N wall and   215 *is reached by a traverse from the R and climbed by cracks and corners a little R of the actual edge.*

Base hut – Casera di Bosconero 45min to the start 600m 9hr

10.03 Start as for 10.01 but scramble up below and R of the NW arête.
VII Climb 120m up a series of gullies first R then L (II,III) to a large ledge
VI/A2 marking the start of the difficult climbing. Start about 40m R of the
60 edge of the NW ridge.

1 50m Climb a small OH (VI- A0) and then go obliquely L for 8m
to a black dièdre which is usually wet. Climb the R wall (IV) then
the crack in the back (V) to a large ledge

2 30m Move L along the ledge for 15m and then ascend slightly for
15m to a stance near the arête

3 45m Climb a grey wall for 10m (III), avoid an OH by the wall to its
R and continue up the yellow wall (V+) to a stance

4 15m Go along the ledge L to a crack near the arête

5 35m Climb the crack and the fine wall to its R (V+,V) to another
ledge

6 35m Traverse L for 8m and climb diagonally R up a grey/yellow
wall (VII or A1) to a leaning corner (IV) leading to a good stance

7 20m Continue in the same direction by a dièdre and a wide crack
(V) to a ledge below OHs

8 35m Some m L climb an OH then slant R to a shallow crack (V+)
and continue (VI-) to a yellow crack and a platform stance

9 35m Climb an OHing crack for 8m, go round a rectangular roof
on the R (VI) and continue up an OHing corner (VII- or A1) to a
pinnacle and stance

10 15m Climb diagonally R to a terrace (VI-). Bivouac site. Escape R
possible (IV+) to join the W Face Route (10.02) or another nearer
line

11 25m Climb a dièdre (V,V+)

12 35m Continue up the dièdre (V) which gets harder and climb the
final roof on the R (VI or A1). Return to the corner and climb
direct to a stance

13 30m Climb the widening crack and chimney passing a roof on the

R (V+,IV,VII- or A1)

14   35m Move L 4m and climb grey rock to a roof. Traverse (tension?) L round the arête and follow another OHing crack to a ledge under a line of OHs (V+). Belay pegs high L

15   30m Climb direct up a corner (IV) and then traverse L (IV+) to a good ledge

16   25m Climb a short wall for 15m (III) and reach a larger ledge

17   150m Follow a gully for 100m taking the R branch to reach a col on the ridge (II). Follow the ridge to the top of the pillar.

NORTH FACE (VIA DELLA GROLE)
Navasa, Dalbosco, Baschera, 1965.

This is a fine route with mainly free climbing. The face is made up of horizontal beds which create ledges or roofs and vertical walls cut by dièdres. Take plenty of rope. There is a second route on this face, Via KCF, which starts L of this route but intermingles in the upper half of the wall. It may cause some route-finding confusion but is of a similar standard.

Base hut – Casera di Bosconero   30min to the start   700m   10hr

10.04   Approach direct from the hut to the centre of the face.

VI/A1

60

1   90m Climb a ramp towards the R leading to a ledge (III)

2   25m Traverse 25m L to a leaning pinnacle

3   25m Climb a crack on the R side of the pinnacle to its top (III,IV)

4   50m Descend some m and traverse R across a grey wall, then climb R in the direction of a yellow corner (V+)

5   20m Climb the corner to a good stance (IV)

6   45m Continue up the corner to a belay below a large roof (VI)

7   12m Traverse L below the roof to a ledge (A1)

8   50m Climb diagonally L for 10m (IV) to a thin crack and climb this (V+) to a ledge

9   20m Move L 8m and move up R via a rib (IV) to a grey crack. Climb this (IV) to a ledge

10   50m Move L into an OHing corner crack and climb it (VI/A1) to a roof. Turn this and go up a short grey crack to a terrace

11 40m Climb a rib to a scree ledge. Continue R of a detached block to the foot of a smooth slab (V,IV)

12 25m Climb the short smooth slab (VI) and a crack (IV) to a small stance

13 45m Above are two dièdres. Climb the R-hand one for 10m to a peg (V-), tension L to reach the L-hand corner and climb it (V+) to a roof and niche (bivouac)

14 20m Leave the niche and follow a ramp Lwards. Climb a corner/crack to reach a narrow ledge (IV)

15 25m Climb a grey crack for 2m, traverse R round an arête and overcome two steps to reach a prominent yellow corner visible from the start

16 45m Climb 20m to the first roof (V+). Traverse L under it and layback up the edge (VI). Climb a grey crack to a terrace (V)

17 40m Climb a crack (V) and the flake crack above (V+). The major difficulties are now over and if time is short an escape can be made L round the NE ridge

18 100m Move up and traverse R under a triangular roof. Continue by short cracks and gullies for two pitches to a col in the ridge and so reach the summit of the pillar. The main summit is about 15min SW.

DESCENTS

10.05 From the main summit go NE along the ridge to a col. Continue to another col overlooking the gully between Rocchetta Alta and Sasso di Taonella to the E. Descend and traverse R (S) over terraces to the col between the peaks and descend the snow gully or the rocks on its W, N to the valley. (1½hr)

   From the summit of the N pillar either go towards the main summit or from a notch in the ridge descend diagonally S across the great depression in the wall. By traversing and scrambling down a system of terraces join the normal descent above the col. This route can be difficult to follow in poor weather. (1½hr)

Sasso di Bosconero 2436m

NORTH-WEST RIDGE
Pellegrini, Pretto, 1964.

A sustained and exposed climb following an attractive arête.

Base hut – Casera di Bosconero 1³⁄₄hr to the start 600m 4hr

10.06 Follow the path towards F Matt on the L of Sasso di Bosconero and
IV+ break off R to a stance at a platform on a pine-covered spur on the
57 L-hand side of the W face.
First follow the sharp ridge for 300m. This is exposed and
interesting climbing (III+/IV+). When OHs block the line of the
edge follow a ledge R for 30m and climb a couloir which also gets
hard. Climb 20m of steep rock until a narrow ledge leads L under
loose yellow OHs. This leads to an arête which gives good exposed
climbing for 200m until 80m below the summit. Continue on the L
up easier rock to the top.

DESCENT BY SOUTH FACE
10.07 Follow scree and vegetated slabs S, possibly a marked path to the F d
57 Toanella (2150m), and descend snow in the NW gully to the path.
(1½hr to bivouac hut)

Kompass 1:50000 sheet 27

This is the most southerly of the groups included and lies just N of Belluno. The rock climbs are quite busy at weekends with local Italians and with German visitors. Schiara itself is well covered with via ferrata and surrounded by bivouac huts. The climbs on the Pala del Balcon peaks are quite short but further W the Burèl SW face gives a much harder modern free climb over 1000m long rivalling, at a lower altitude, the big Civetta and Marmolada climbs. This area is ideal early in the season as most of the good climbing is on the S side and certainly worth a visit.

HUTS

7th Alpini Hut 1495m. Situated below the S face and popular with walkers doing Dolomite Route 1. Approach by car from near Belluno to the Case Bortòt (750m) then 501 (2½hr)

Bivouac Sperti 2100m. No water near the hut! Approach from 7th Alpini hut by 504, Via Ferrata Sperti (1½hr)

Schiara 2565m

WEST TO EAST TRAVERSE
An excellent day out on via ferrata and good paths.

Base hut – 7th Alpini 45min to the start 700m 6hr

11.01 From the hut follow a path towards a prominent black cave-like gully,
II Il Portòn and join the Via Ferrata Zacchi on its R at a height of about 1800m. First start up R then head L past a deep chimney to a green platform. The descent route joins here. Continue L until a big scree ledge leads R to join Schiara's S face and continue L across the face to a shoulder and a bivouac box – the Bernardina hut (2320m) quite near a prominent rock needle, Guséla del Vescovà (see 11.08). This is about 3hr from the start. Now take Via Ferrata Berti which starts a few m R (S), and is clearly marked, to the summit (cross). To descend follow the rounded E ridge and branch R (S) down to the Màrmol bivouac box (2266m). (L leads to Bianchet hut on N side – Dolomite

Route 1). Descend another obvious path (Via Ferrata Màrmol) past a gully until it meets the ascent route and reverse that to the screes. Down these (30min) to the 7th Alpini hut.

SOUTH PILLAR
Gross, Hiebeler, 1962.

A fine climb leads direct to the summit with only a few moves needing aid.

Base hut – 7th Alpini 1¼hr to the start 500m 5hr

11.02 Start as for 11.01 until directly below the pillar on a grassy shoulder.
VI–/A2 Move up and R to reach a smaller shoulder (cairn), then climb a gully (III) and go R to another cairn, and finally return L to reach the base of an obvious dièdre. A direct approach to here up the wall may be better (IV+). Climb the corner (III) and easy rock above to reach an OHing crack. Pegs go R here but climb the crack (V,IV+) for 30m and continue up the chimney above (IV) for 30m. The steep wall above has good holds and leads (IV-) to a good stance.

Higher, after easy rock (III), a scree hollow is reached and ledges lead L (escape possible to Bernardina bivouac hut, 11.01).

Continue direct first on grassy rock and then in a gully with a natural crack for four or five pitches (III,IV) to reach a large ledge with blocks.

Now head for the L side of a little tower and climb up to two cracks above. Climb these for 35m (IV-,V+) then a smooth chimney (III) and easier rocks to reach another good ledge (Sperti Ledge) below the prominent final OHs (Testòn). Again escape L is possible.

Climb the OH by a crack (A2) and from a niche traverse 6m L (IV-). Climb for 4m (A0) then obliquely R (VI-) to a stance.

Continue up a dièdre for 30m (IV) then move gradually R for four pitches (IV,III) up the R side of a ramp to easy rock and the summit. Descend by 11.01.

Second Pala del Balcon 2371m

WEST PILLAR BY SOUTH RIDGE
Cusinato, Rossi, 1952.

The ridge which runs from Schiara SW to Burèl has a fairly steep S face and easy broken slopes to the N which provide in part the route for the Via Ferrata Sperti (path 504) which passes through the col (F Viel 2250m) between the Second Pala and Third Pala. The whole of this face and various towers and pinnacles around it have been developed as a climbing area. Easy access and descent make the face popular and the holds are a little polished. The Second Pala lies W of the bivouac hut and has two pillars leading from the path to separate summits.

Base hut – Sperti 40min to the start 250m 2hr

11.03 Follow the path around the W pillar and start up an easy couloir on
IV the L to reach a black niche (II). Climb three 30m pitches on the L side of the ridge (II,III). Next climb a crack to a stance below an OH (II). Now go L up a short chimney to below a higher roof (III). Traverse R below the OH (III) and climb an exposed pitch up the edge (IV). Continue direct up the edge just L of a dièdre (III) until two easier pitches lead to the summit.

EAST PILLAR BY SOUTH RIDGE
Sorgato, Caldart, 1956.

There is a route up the chimney between the pillars (Cusinato, Vazzoler, 1952, IV) but this route climbs the face of the E pillar moving onto the edge at half height.

Base hut – Sperti 40min to the start 250m 4hr

11.04 Start from the path up a short chimney well R of the edge of the pillar.
V+ Head L for a slanting crack 50m above the path. Climb on the R of the crack up a grey wall for 40m (IV) to a fork in the crack, take the wall between the cracks for 10m over an OH (V+) and continue to a stance below a big yellow OH. Traverse 15m L (V) and go L again up an exposed wall (V) to reach the arête below a roof. Climb up L of the roof, go over a black OH and continue on the arête of a red crack on steep grey rock. Pass OHs and a smooth slab which is climbed direct (V+) to less difficult rock. After another hard pitch climb easily for 40m to the summit.

Third Pala del Balcon 2328m

EAST FACE
Goedeke, Herbst, Lukasik, Schuster, Wohld, 1967.

The Third Pala lies to the L of the F Viel behind a smaller tower, Torrione Bianchet, 2200m, which has a good hard climb on its SE face (Sorgato, Pellegrini, 1955, VI).

Base hut – Sperti 1hr to the start 220m 2hr

11.05 Follow the path past 11.03 until a big block forms a bridge. Take the
IV – second col in the ridge joining Torrione Bianchet with the Third Pala
and descend 40m in a gully to a secondary gully on the R. Start below
a prominent yellow nose visible halfway up the face.

Climb L for 70m on a steep grey face with good holds and
thread runners (III,IV-) to reach a chimney to the L of the nose.
Climb this for 70m (III,III+) to an OH. Go diagonally R up pleasant
slabs (II,III) for 30m to a stance above the nose. Climb 35m on
exposed rock up the arête to the R of a little chimney on excellent rock
(II,III). Continue for 50m to a col on the ridge and go easily to the NE
summit.

DESCENT
11.06 Descend S down a ridge to a col between the NE summit and the
central one. Now go R (NW) down a narrow gully (III or 2 abseils of
20m) to reach the Sperti path. (1hr to the hut)

Burèl 2281m

SOUTH-WEST FACE (MIOTTO ROUTE)
Miotto, Bee, 1977.

*This attractive tower rise out of the steep Val di Piero and has at least five
hard climbs on its SW and SE faces. The face is cut by a horizontal ledge
at half height offering an escape route but nevertheless gives some of the
hardest climbing in the area. This route is all free climbing except for a few
m on the smooth slab. It is long and hard and local advice should be sought
before attempting it. A bivouac hut is proposed at its foot (bivouac Arbam,
1000m).*

Base hut – 7th Alpini 2½hr to the start 1100m 16hr

11.07 Follow path 502 SW towards the F d Oderz (1716m). About 100m
VI/A2 before the col go R and climb a steep gully to a col on the ridge
(Forzeléte). Go down the other side (W) which soon steepens into a
deep gully with difficult (IV) rock steps. This leads to a path going R
below the S face of Burèl and grassy gullies leading to scree and snow
below the W face. This route climbs the dièdre on the L of the face
going quite near the W ridge in places.

Start on the L over an OH (V) then direct on loose rock for 10m
and finally 3m L (IV) to an obvious vertical chimney. Climb

223

this for 40m (III,IV) and continue for 80m on good rock obliquely R (III) to where the wall steepens. On the L, level with an isolated dwarf pine, is a yellow OH while on the R is a grey roof.

Climb a cracked slab for 5m (V) to reach an arête on the R and continue direct to reach a 6m traverse R (V+). Now climb vertically for 4m (V) and up a groove leading to below the grey roof. Traverse 8m R (VI) and go round the roof to a stance in a niche. Climb obliquely L for 40m (IV,V) to reach a stance at the base of a tower. Climb a ramp R (III,IV), traverse 15m R below a yellow roof (V,VI) and climb direct to a roof (V) where a traverse leads R round the arête (VI) to the base of an impressive dièdre.

Climb vertically on the L of the dièdre (IV+) on loose rock to some OHs which are passed on the L by a crack (VI/A2) and continue direct for 20m to a higher roof (V) which is climbed direct (VI). Continue up the dièdre until an obvious traverse L of 5m (difficult to peg) leads to a smooth slab. Take the arête and climb it past an OH (VI) to a stance on the edge which marks the end of the major difficulties.

Go round a roof on the L (V) and climb the most obvious dièdre above. This widens to a chimney (IV) and after 40m leads to a terrace. Move R 10m (V), climb an OH and continue diagonally L (V) to a ledge. Go L again then direct to a stance.

Climb slabs on good rock for 150m towards an obvious dièdre beside a tower above and continue up ledges with rock steps (IV,V). Escape is now possible R (III,IV).

Climb for 40m up a steep ramp to near the bottom of the dièdre (IV,V,V+) and reach it via a chimney with a jammed block in 35m (IV,V). Climb the dièdre first on the R wall then by a crack in the corner, go over a roof (very exposed) and continue in the same line to a chimney and a little col (IV). Above this a gully (V) leads to a good stance. Climb 120m up good rock on the L of a gully (III) until the gully divides. Next climb the wall to the R for 130m (IV,V) to reach the edge of the W ridge at the level of the big roof which cuts the central part of the SW face.

Climb the ridge for 5m and continue direct up an OHing crack (V). Traverse 5m R (V) and climb 10m (V) back to the arête. Continue up a chimney (V,IV) for 40m and stay on the same line for 80m up an obvious line of cracks and chimneys (II,III) to reach a final chimney. Climb this and two steep sections above, the first on the R the second on the L (V), and continue for 150m to the summit.

To descend go easily NE then R (E) to reach the Via Ferrata Sperti (504) near F Viel. Continue to the 7th Alpini hut. 2½hr

Guséla del Vescovà 2316m

ORDINARY ROUTE
Jori, Andreoletti, Pasquali, 1913.

This is a famous pinnacle the ascent of which is easily added to a route on the Pale del Balcon. Not advisable in thundery weather!

Base hut – 7th Alpini or Biv Bernardina 3hr or 10min to the start 40m 30min

11.08
V+
56
Approach by 11.01 and start below the R edge of the N side under a small OH.

Climb a smooth slab under the OH and go 2m further round the OH to a small ledge on the R (IV+). Move back L 2m past another bulge to a thin crack and climb this (IV) to a niche (20m in all). Now move L to the E face and climb diagonally L up a steep wall (IV) to an exposed crack which leads to the summit.

DESCENT
11.09 Abseil 20m from a good peg to the niche on the N side and make a second abseil 20m to the base.

Geographica 1:25000 sheets 1 & 5

This very interesting area stretches N from the Falzarego Pass and contains some excellent and unusual free climbing. Many routes can be reached from the roads or via the cablecar at the Pass or the chair-lift to the N of the group in the Val Badia at Pedraces.

HUTS

Scotoni Hut 1985m. Small, private hut. Approach from San Cassiano It is possible to drive up to the Capanna Alpina then walk (45 min).

Lagazuoi Hut 2752m. Small, private hut 80 metres below the top station of the Falzarego cablecar.

Fanes Hut and La Varella Hut 2060 and 2042m respectively. Approach these neighbouring huts from Rif. Pederu at the head of the Valle di Tamores. Walk up a private road (2hr).

Bivouac della Chiesa 2652m. In a col between the Lagazuoi and Fani peaks (ladderway). Approach from the Falzarego cablecar (1hr).

Sante Croce Hut 2045m. Small, private hut. Approach from the chair-lift at Pedraces (20min) or walk from San Leonardo (2½hr).

Piccola Lagazuoi 2778m

Directly under the cable car at the Falzarego Pass three crags have been developed British style by the local climbers giving free routes graded from IV to VIII. These give good training, none go to the summit of the peak and they are mostly under 200m long. Protection is generally with chocks and friends and chalk is in evidence. The hardest routes lie on the R hand buttress on a steep, triangular wall just L of a giant pointed boulder. All descents use the Martini ledge which crosses the face above the crags, incidentally the scene of much activity in the 1914-18 war!

Torre di Falzarego 2400m

SOUTH RIDGE OF PICCOLA TORRE AND SOUTH FACE OF GRANDE TORRE

Two towers, the Grande and Piccola which face the Pass. Usually busy with guides but a good introduction to Dolomite climbing.

Base – Falzarego Pass 20min to start 280m, 300m 2hr

12.01 Start above the remains of old barracks. The original start, a steep IV/V+ crack, is avoided and the Guides route starting 20m to the R is taken.

1   30m Go R across a wall then back L (II)

2   25m Continue horizontally L (II)

3   15m Up L to a stance by a tree (III)

4   60m A chimney ramp to a stance by a jammed block (III)

5   25m Move up and traverse delicately L to the arête (IV) and climb it (III)

6   50m Continue up the arête

7   20m Continue a little on the R (IV−)

8   20m Easily to the summit of the Piccola Torre (II)

Abseil 30m to the col between the towers. Now either descend down the gully on the L or continue up the harder Grande Torre by its S Face.

9   30m Climb the crack on the R (V, V+)

10 30m Continue L and up the chimney above (IV, V)

11 30m Climb easier rock on the R to the summit (IV+).

From the bottom of the descent gully the Grande Torre can be climbed by its excellent W Face (180m, II and III) which starts 20m up the scree.

DESCENT

12.02 From the Grande Torre descend N down an easy gully for 40m. Traverse to a col then continue W by a faint path.

Lagazuoi North 2804m

WEST FACE (VIA DEL DRAGO)
Barbier, Giambisi, Platter, 1969.

The two Lagazuoi peaks are well seen from the cablecar station. This fine free route lies up the triangular W face of the N peak.

Base hut – Lagazuoi hut, Biv della Chiesa or the cable car station 45min or 20min to the start 300m 4½hr

12.03 Start at the bottom R hand side of the face below an obvious chimney
VI– with a jammed block.

1 Climb the short grey dièdre (IV+) on the L then continue by a gully R (III+)

2 Take a black slab (V) then easier chimneys (IV) and slabs towards a higher black slab and a pulpit stance

3 Go L across the slab to a marked spike (V)

4 Reach a shallow, yellow crack and climb it (V+) and turn a roof to reach a ledge(V+)

5 Traverse the exposed ledges (IV+,III) (These are the obvious horizontal faults in the middle of the face)

6 Climb a ramp on the L for 25m (III,IV)

7 Continue for 35m (III,IV) to the start of the dièdre

8 Climb the dièdre, first by the R wall then the L (IV+,V–) to a stance on the R

9 Continue in the back of the dièdre (V+,VI–,IV) to reach ledges

10 Continue to reach a terrace (II,III–) which leads round to the descent route.

WEST-NORTH-WEST FACE (VIA DEL CONSIGLIO)
Consiglio, Oglio, Micarelli, 1954.

An elegant, exposed route. It takes the big grey walls with a gully on the L and a yellow pillar on the R.

Base Hut – Biv della Chiesa or cablecar station 5min or 45min to the start 300m 4hr

12.04 Start on the screes well up the L hand half of the face below the
IV+ bivouac hut.

`62`   Traverse the obvious ledge R to a chimney. Climb this, then
another with an exit R(IV+).
        Continue for a pitch R to reach a yellow pillar then obliquely L to
a little chimney. Traverse L past a bulge (IV+) and climb a grey wall
(exposed). At the top of this move obliquely L to reach a small ledge.
Go some metres L to reach a long grey chimney going diagonally R.
Climb this and then move easily R and up a dièdre formed by a small
pillar. Now follow a gully blocked at the top by an enormous jammed
block. Take a friable chimney with a bulge at 20m then below the
block move out R. Finally a 30m chimney leads to near the summit.

DESCENT
12.05 Easily down the NE face past old military workings (30min).

Cima Scotoni 2874m

SOUTH-WEST FACE (LACADELLI ROUTE)
Lacadelli, Ghedina, Lorenzi, 1952.

*This great route climbs the middle of the SW face above the Scotoni hut.
Climbed free it is one of the harder Dolomite climbs, most ascents use some
pitons for aid!*

Base Hut – Scotoni 40min to the start 550m 9hr

12.06 Start on an easier angled spur L of a yellow-black overhanging wall
VIII– below the R hand end of the first ledge.
VI–/A1 1 80m Climb up the spur from R to L(III,IV)

`63`
     2 20m Continue up a slanting grey crack (IV+) to the start of main
        difficulties

     3 30m Climb a yellow crack (V) and turn an OH on the R(A1 or
        VIII–)

     4 40m Move R across a black wall (V+) then direct past a niche
        (VI–) and finally by a hand traverse L to a stance at the foot of a
        dièdre

     5 40m Climb the dièdre (V–)

     6 40m Continue direct on friable rock (V–) until a confined

       crawling traverse L under a roof leads to the first great ledge

7   70m Walk L to belay pegs

8   45m Climb vertically (V) then get into a white dièdre above an OH and climb this (V+)

9   15m Move R to a stance at the foot of grey wall (V−)

10 30m Climb by an obvious chimney (IV+) to a stance on the L below yellow rock

11 35m Traverse R along a friable edge to a stance beside red rock

12 45m Climb 12m to a small spur, traverse R to a peg and descend 2m R (rope move or VI−). Now continue direct for 20m (V) to a stance on the L

13 20m Climb up to a roof and turn it by a little dièdre on the R (V,A1 or VI−)

14 30m Climb the yellow, cracked dièdre past an OH (V+,A1 or VI) to a stance on the R

15 35m Continue by a crack (IV) and a wall (V,A1 or VI) to a stance in a niche

16 50m Move R and up past an OH (IV) to reach easier rock (III) and the second ledge

       Four choices are possible from here, (a) is most preferable.

a   Go 60m L and then slant up R for 100m at III until a final section of IV,V leads to a col 50m from the summit

b   Go 120m R to a giant block and then climb dièdres L (II,II+), a ledge R and a chimney/dièdre at IV,V,V+ almost direct to the summit (loose in places)

c   Go even further R to climb a ramp and a gully to a col R of the summit at IV (snow?)

d   Walk round L to reach the descent route.

SOUTH-WEST FACE (VIA FACHIRI)
Cozzolino, Ghio, 1972.

Another good route up this wall, first climbed in winter with few pegs!

Base Hut – Scotoni 40min to the start 400m to the second ledge 6hr

12.07 Start on the R of the face at a grey spur.

√VI

63

1   80m Climb the spur (IV,IV+)

2   40m Continue first L (V) then direct (IV+,V)

3   45m Move up L (IV−) and then climb a dièdre on the R of a pulpit (IV+) level with the first ledge

4   70m Continue for 2 pitches to a higher stance (IV+)

5   30m Traverse L (III,IV,V)

6   35m Continue to traverse past a detached flake (V+) and a slab (V−) to a stance at the bottom of a dièdre (this is directly above the crawl pitch on the Lacadelli route)

7   50m Move L out of the dièdre (V) and continue to a stance on the L (IV+,V)

8   30m Step R into an obvious R sloping yellow dièdre and climb it (V+,V,VI) to a stance on the R

9   25m Traverse R then over a roof (V) and R again (V+)

10 40m Slant R (IV+) to a dièdre. Climb it (V)

11 40m Continue up another dièdre (IV+) to reach the big ledge 20m L of the great block below finish (b) of 12.06.

Finish by any of those for Lacadelli route (12.06).

DESCENT

12.08 Go NW down scree and friable rock to the col between Cima Scotoni and the Torre del Lago. A path then leads to the foot of the face and the hut (1½hr).

Col Boccia 2406m

WEST FACE
Breitenberger, Glatz, 1969.

This route on the face immediately S of the Scotoni hut gives good climbing on firm rock. Ideal for training, it can be approached from the cablecar and kit left at the top.

Base Hut – Scotoni or Lagazuoi 30min or 1hr from the cablecar to the top of the crag then 30min down to the start 250m 2½hr

12.09 Start below the summit on the R hand side of the face below an
V   obvious chimney slanting L to R.

     1   30m Climb the chimney and slabs (IV−,IV+)

     2   25m Take the wall L (V) and continue up an easier crack

     3   40m A vertical crack (V) then continue direct on easier rock and
        finally obliquely L on grey rock to a stance

     4   15m Climb directly to a ledge (IV−)

     5   40m Climb a crack slanting R which would lead finally to a pulpit
        on the R hand edge of the face. Leave the crack after 10m and
        traverse L to a small ledge. Continue L to a better stance and belay
        (IV+,V)

     6   40m Go L then R (compact rock with threads) then a slab to reach
        the base of the final dièdre (IV+)

     7   40m Good climbing up the dièdre (IV+).

     8   Easily to the summit.

Cima and Torre del Lago 2654m/2632m

WEST DIEDRE
Consiglio, Micarelli, Dall'Oglio, 1954.

*This route climbs the upper part of the dièdre which leads to the col between
the summits of this peak. It reaches it up the wall on the L until a traverse
on a horizontal band is possible.*

*Base Hut – Scotoni or road at Capanna Alpina or cable car 30min or 1hr
or 50min to the start 370m 4hr*

12.10 Start 50m to the L of the line of the dièdre.
IV+
58

     1   150m First climb a little L then directly (II,III+) to reach the
        halfway ledge

     2   40m Traverse R to a cairn 15m from the dièdre

     3   30m Climb a bulge and a short overhanging chimney (IV) and
        then move R into the dièdre

     4   50m Follow this to a niche at a fork (III,IV)

     5   30m Take the R branch on good holds on yellow & black rock (IV)

6   70m Two good pitches to the top (IV,IV+).

DESCENT

12.11 From the top of the route descend 40m NW to the side of two large blocks, then go R. Take a little gully, then a chimney, always moving R to the col between Cima del Lago and Cima Scotoni and a good path (II, 1¼ hr).

Sasso della Croce (Crusc) 2825m

This peak and the next one lie to the N of this area. Sasso della Croce is the name given to the W face of the ridge leading to Punta Cavallo 2907m. Spelling of the peaks seems to vary but their special character makes them easily recognised.

The Sasso della Croce dominates the Val Badia and the routes can be reached by chairlift from Pedraces. However the approach will take 45min plus another 30min for the broken lower buttress.

WEST FACE (GRAN MURO)
Messner, Frisch, 1969.

This route climbs the wall well to the R. Possible free with all the difficulty in the last few pitches.

Base Hut – Sante Croce 1¼hr to the start 300m for the lower buttress then 250m 8hr for the final wall

12.12 Start up the lower buttress by a dièdre/couloir on the R. Poor rock.
VII   Finally move R to the first terrace below a dièdre which splits into two
VI–/A1 chimneys higher up.

1   30m Climb the first dièdre (IV,V)

2   30m Move diagonally R past two friable pillars (III+,V)

3   30m Climb the R chimney/ramp (IV)

4   30 or 50m Either continue up the chimney (V–,IV+) or take easier ledges diagonally R (II,III) and walk back L on the second terrace

5   40m Move a little L from the top of the chimney to a stance below a steep yellow wall. Climb the overhanging crack (VI–,A1 or VII) and continue (V) to a good stance on the R

233

6   40m Climb a R slanting dièdre (V), traverse R (V+) on smooth slabs to reach a great flake. Finally descend a little (rope move or VI−) to a poor stance

7   25m Climb a short dièdre (V) then 10m direct until an 8m traverse L under an OH leads to a stance below a steep crack

8   30m Climb the crack (A1,V+ or VII−) moving R a little (A1 or VI+) and finally direct to the plateau(V).

WEST DIEDRE
Mayerl, Rohracher, 1962.

Another good route possible free up the great dièdre to the L of the Gran Muro. Rock a little friable. Pegs usually all in place.

Base Hut – Santa Croce 1¼hr to start of dièdre 300m of lower buttress then 250m 9hr

12.13 Approach as for the Gran Muro moving L to the foot of the dièdre on
VII− the first terrace.
V+/A2
59

1   35m Climb the friable corner (IV), continue direct (V) and then move L into a crack. Up this (V+)

2   35m Step L to a dièdre (V+) continue past a flake (VI−) to a stance

3   15m Climb a crack slanting R (VI) to a ledge

4   30m A yellow dièdre leads to a niche (A2 or VI,V+)

5   25m A grey dièdre (IV+) then move L (V) to a stance

6   35m A grey slab (V+) leads past some blocks to a traverse L and a stance at a flake by a higher niche

7   30m Get over the flake R into a yellow dièdre. Climb this (A1,V or VII−) ignoring an exit R to reach a stance below a chimney

8   20m Enter the chimney (VI−) but then get out R onto a grey wall and climb this R (V+)

9   35m Go straight up to the roof and move L below it. (A0/V+ or VI) to an easy chimney in the main dièdre . Up this (III)

10   35m Move up R past unstable blocks (V+) then continue (IV)

11   30m A chimney to the plateau (III).

WEST FACE OF THE CENTRAL PILLAR
Messner, Messner, 1968.

A very hard free climb. The original crux seems to be avoided by leaders who use the variant R!

Base Hut – Sante Croce 45min to start 500m 8hr

12.14 Start at the highest point of the screes directly below the central pillar.

VIII
VII−
59

1 Climb 5 pitches first easily (II) then up the obvious chimney (V+,V,V+)

2 Break out R (III), slant back L and up a slab (IV) to a stance below a large pillar.

3 50m Climb direct (IV) then slightly R (V) to the top of the pillar. This stance is directly below the nose of the pillar

4 45m Climb up then rise slightly R (VI) until a move down or a pendulum leads to holds leading to a stance below a small dièdre in a grey wall above a large roof (V+)

5 45m Climb the dièdre and move up to a horizontal crack (VII). Either continue direct (VIII) or traverse well R until it is possible to move up to a higher horizontal crack (VII−) and traverse back L to a stance below a large flake

6 30m Climb the 7cm wide crack (VI−) and then move R to a good ledge (IV+). An escape at V possible

7 30m Climb an OH (V+), continue to a roof and move R round it to a stance (VI+) below the final dièdre

8 Climb the dièdre (VI−,V+) to the plateau.

DESCENT
12.15 Follow a path S to the col and then back to the hut (1½hr).

Sasso Nove (Neunerspitze) 2968m

This peak gives a unique slab face to the S and adds a new dimension to Dolomite climbing. The routes are generally friction climbing with minimal protection and fairly difficult route finding. In May it is possible to approach on skis, climb dry rock and then get a good run back to Pederu!

The usual approach is from the La Varella hut via a path leading towards the Passo S'Antone. Once on the plateau tend towards the base of the slab.

SOUTH EAST SLAB
Kastlunger, Bottaro, 1948.

Base Hut – La Varella 1³/₄hr to the start 250m 2¹/₂hr

12.16 The climb starts about 80m L of a vertical line from the summit at a
IV+ crack where two slabs overlap.
61   Climb the slab to reach the end of an obvious ramp, 80m (III).
Follow the ramp R for 60m (III,IV) to below a bulge. Continue for 60m to reach the foot of a steep slanting crack (peg, IV).
        Climb the crack (IV+ crux, 30m) and continue up the wall (IV+) for 10m to below an OH. Climb the OH on the R (IV) and continue 20m to a stance under another OH. Move R 20m and over another bulge and then more easily to a big stance. Move L on this and then climb directly to the ridge which is followed easily R to the summit.

SOUTH FACE (DIAGONAL ROUTE)
Riello, Fratelli, 1962.

It reaches the obvious diagonal break below the summit from the L and continues up this.

Base Hut – La Varella 1³/₄hr to the start 300m 3hr

12.17 Start on the R hand part of the face climbing for 100m on easy rock to
IV the start of the diagonal crack. Follow this for about 7 pitches (II).
61   Traverse 15m L on a friable ledge then climb a short dièdre and then a higher dièdre on the L. An exposed traverse L leads to a crack which leads to a good stance (IV). Next take a thin, disappearing crack (IV) and in 20m reach a cave stance. Continue L and up to the ridge a short distance W of the summit.

SOUTH FACE (VIA DELLE PLACCHE)
Messner, Messner, 1965

This friction route takes a more direct line to the summit. It crosses the diagonal route at half height and so combinations can be made.

Base Hut – La Varella 1¾hr to the start 250m 3hr

12.18 Climb the obvious R facing dièdre (60m, III) to reach a ledge which is
V   followed L to a cairn just before its highest point.

61   Continue direct up the slab on small holds starting near a
vegetated crack then slightly R on smooth rock for 3 pitches to a niche
on the diagonal crack (IV,V). Move a few metres L to a peg stance.
Continue direct (grassy crack) for two pitches to a good ledge
(V,IV+,V−) then climb direct (III) to a higher ledge. Take a dièdre
on the L (III+) until the rock deteriorates then climb L up the wall
(III) to the final slabs (III) and the summit.

DESCENT
12.19 Easily down the E ridge then bear S by easy rocks to reach a gully
leading back to the foot of the face (2hr).

Geografica 1:25000 sheet 1

This compact group lies W of Cortina on the N side of the road over the Falzarego Pass. Although the Pilastro area gives excellent rock climbing and Tofana di Mezzo fairly obscure hard routes, the area's main claim to fame is the excellent via ferrata which go over or near most of the principal peaks,and its World War 1 associations. On the Cortina side chairlifts and cablecars aid access whilst a narrow road on the S side leads to an ideal start point.

HUTS

Dibona Hut 2050m. Approach by narrow road from the SE or 442 (1hr)

Cantore and Giussani Huts 2588m and 2561m. Approach from Dibona Hut by 403 (1½hr)

Tofana di Rozes 3225m

SOUTH FACE
Dimai, Eötvös, Eötvös, Siorpaes, Verzi, 1901.

An interesting and varied route but not very sustained.

Base hut – Dibona 45min to the start 800m 5hr

13.01 Start at the top of the scree cone below the central amphitheatre near
IV+ a big red hole.

1 300m Climb the slabs R of the central couloir keeping well R whenever the couloir steepens and using a chimney/crack up a pillar near the edge after 180m (II,III) (Some reports indicate a harder pitch (IV) on this section)

2 150m Just below the amphitheatre move across L and climb up behind the pillar which forms the L side of the lower couloir. Where the rock steepens climb a 20m crack and follow a ledge L (III+) to reach a second hollow. Move up this towards two caves in the vertical yellow wall above

3 20m Traverse L on a ledge below the yellow wall (belay peg)

4   25m Climb the vertical wall first R then L by a crack (pegs,IV+)

5   40m Climb a chimney to a grassy terrace (IV-,III)

6   50m Continue up the gully or the rocks to its R (III) to a final slab leading L to a peg belay below an obvious chimney

7   35m Ignore the chimney and follow a short ledge L to the beginning of an exposed traverse. Move across and down 2m into a niche. Continue L for 3m to a little ledge and another niche and follow the same line on good holds for 20m to near a gully (IV-)

8   30m Move 10m L and climb the gully to a terrace (cairn) and traverse under OHs L to reach a stance in a niche (III)

9   30m Climb the R-hand of two chimneys above, first past a difficult chockstone (IV-) and then inside

10 40m Easier chimneys and gullies lead to the SW ridge

11 150m Easy climbing/walking to the summit.

DESCENT TO THE NORTH
13.02 The descent is easy down a well marked path N until an even better path leads E to the Giussani and Cantore huts. (1hr)

Pilastro di Rozes 2820m

SOUTH-WEST RIDGE
Constantini, Ghedina, 1946.

This is a fine route up the L-hand edge of the face and is a little easier than the S Face Route (13.04). There are possibilities for variations and this can lead to route-finding problems.

Base hut – Dibona 40min to the start 500m 7hr

13.03 Start at the foot of the gully.

VI–
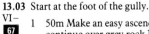
1   50m Make an easy ascending traverse R (II) to reach a ledge, then continue over grey rock L past a yellow patch to the base of a dièdre (IV)

2   50m Climb the dièdre (IV,V-) and exit R (IV) to a stance below steep walls

3   30m Traverse almost horizontally R (IV-)

4 25m Continue diagonally R up a slab to a big ledge (IV)

5 30m Go direct then slightly L (V) to reach easier climbing below yellow walls (IV)

6 30m Climb direct until below a series of roofs, traverse R and when possible climb direct to reach a ledge under a big roof (V+,VI-). (Traverse further R for easier variations)

7 40m Go 15m L (V) and climb an open crack for 10m (VI-). Move L round an arête to reach the start of a dièdre

8 30m Up the dièdre and then exit L (V)

9 70m Continue direct on poor rock (IV+) to reach a stance on the L edge near a gully which may be wet

10 35m Up the gully which cuts the arête to below a bulge (IV-)

11 50m Climb over the bulge on the L (V+) and continue up the L side of the gully (IV)

12 90m Traverse L and follow a crack, then easier rock with occasional bulges to reach a scree/snow gully. Up this to join 13.04 and so to a col below the summit.

SOUTH FACE
Constantini, Apollonio, 1944.

A popular, classic route usually climbed with aid on the roofs but possible free.

Base hut – Dibona 40min to the start 500m 7hr

13.04 The bottom of the face is marked by a pinnacle on the L. Start below
VII+ either side of this.
V+/A2
67

1 40m Climb a dièdre either on the L side (V+) or the R side (IV,V) of the pillar to a stance just below its top on the R

2 30m Move R up a grey slab for 12m to a peg (IV+). Now either traverse horizontally R to reach the obvious crack line (V) or descend 6m and traverse R (tension, V) and then up the crack to a stance

3 100m Follow the crack, past two small OHs, for three pitches. Beautiful climbing on excellent rock (V,V,IV+)

4 40m The bulge blocking the crack is passed on the L (VI or V/A1) to reach a stance on the first terrace. (Escape possible R along the

ledge with a 40m abseil into the gully and two more down it)

5 50m Go round the hole which descends into the face (III) and then climb 35m up the black wall and a yellow crack to a stance below the first roof (IV+,V-)

6 20m Climb the roof direct (VII+ or A2,V)

7 40m Continue up the steep yellow wall by cracks and mantleshelves (VI or V/A0)

8 25m Climb the second roof moving R (VII or A1,V) to the second terrace

9 40m The OHing nose above is known as the Mules Back. Go up into the cave (IV) and climb out up the OHing chimney either by strenuous bridging (VI+) or using aid on the R side (A2) until it eases past a chockstone (V)

10 40m Continue up the easier chimney above (IV)

11 35m Climb the vertical chimney (IV+,V-)

12 30m Move R and climb the light coloured wall moving R (V,V+)

13 40m A steep wall of grey rock leads to the final yellow walls (IV)

14 40m Traverse L easily (III) to a harder bulge (IV+)

15 40m Continue up a steep little wall on the R (IV+) and then reach the easy gully on the L of the buttress

16 60m Easily up the scree/snow gully to a col below and L of the summit of the pillar.

DESCENT

13.05 From the col do not descend R but traverse horizontally (N) heading for a gap behind a subsidiary peak (Punta Marietta) and then descend the scree/snow gully on the other side to the Cantore hut. (45min)

Primo Spigolo di Rozes 2650m

SOUTH-WEST RIDGE
Pompanin, Alverà, 1946.

A very popular fine, steep free climb with superb situations.

Base hut – Dibona 40min to the start 400m 4hr

13.06
V

67

Start a few m L of the dièdre which forms the first 80m of the arête

1 50m Climb the L side of the dièdre for 40m (IV), then traverse L past the arête to a stance

2 90m Climb the wall on the L of the arête by cracks past a little OH (IV+)

3 90m Continue obliquely R on easier rock to reach the edge which is climbed to below yellow bulges

4 40m Move up 4m then R onto the front face. Make an exposed traverse to reach and climb a crack up an exposed, vertical grey wall (IV+,V or A0)

5 30m Continue L to a large ledge (III)

6 40m Climb an OHing crack 2m L of a little tower on the arête (IV+)

7 40m Move onto the arête and climb it direct for 10m, then climbdiagonally L for 15m (IV+) and finally traverse 12m R to a stance on the R

8 30m Continue on the R of the arête (IV,III)

9 90m Follow the arête to the top (III/IV-)

Descend easily to the Cantore hut. (30min)

Tofana di Mezzo (Tofana II) 3244m

EAST FACE (CENTRAL SPUR)
Alverà, Ghedina, Pompanin, 1945.

This face looks towards Cortina and lies under the cablecar (Freccia del Cielo) from Cortina which leads to near the summit. The wall is divided into three parts by two enormous, wet, black amphitheatres. This route climbs the central spur and the next route takes the R-hand spur.

Base – Cablecar station at Ra Valles 1hr to the start 450m 7hr

13.07
VI
64
The steep yellow spur has a succession of OHs for the lower 200m. The only break is a dièdre which goes up this wall and is blocked by a massive yellow roof. Start at the bottom of the gully which lies on the L of the spur.

Climb the gully for 80m on difficult wet rock, then traverse R by a ledge to the dièdre. Climb broken rock for 30m to a ledge and continue up the dièdre for 20m to a niche. Traverse 2m R and climb a crack diagonally R through the large OH (VI). From the ledge above the OH continue vertically (VI) to reach a narrow ledge. Traverse 20m R on a narrow ramp and then climb vertically for 40m up an exposed wall. Traverse a ledge 6m R and then climb very exposed rock for 15m to a ledge at the end of the hard climbing.

Traverse R to reach a gully which divides the spur from the R-hand part of the wall and follow this over awkward wet rock for 100m to reach the final ridge. This leads quickly to the summit.

EAST FACE (RIGHT-HAND SPUR
Constantini, Pompanin, 1945.

A similar route to 13.07 but not as hard.

Base – Cablecar station at Ra Valles 1hr to the start 450m 1hr

13.08
VI
64
Start a little to the R of the spur.

Climb up for 15m to a ledge with a large niche. Leave this on the R and continue direct to a big ledge. Go obliquely R for 40m on broken rock to a second ledge. Move up 3m to reach a traverse line L for 30m ending at a rib. Climb this for a pitch to a platform. Continue obliquely to the start of a big dièdre well seen from below. Continue for 4m R of this dièdre to the start of a long black crack which is climbed until it ends on a narrow ledge. Traverse R for 50m to a wide chimney and follow this for several pitches until easy rocks lead up L to the summit.

DESCENTS
13.09 Either use the cablecar which ends a few minutes below the summit or descend the S ridge ladderway to reach the Bus de Tofana – a window in the ridge – and then either W steeply down boulders and scree to the Cantore hut, or NE down snowy corries back to Ra Valles. (Either way 1½hr)

Geografica 1:25000 Sheet 1

This famous group of towers, giving climbs of up to 220m, lies on the S slopes of the Falzarego Pass above Cortina, on a flat shoulder NE of Averau (2649m)

Despite the name there are many more than five towers. The Torre Grande is split into three blocks, Cima Sud, Cima Nord and Cima Ovest. The Torre Seconda is made up of Torre Lusy, Torre del Barancio and Torre Romana. Torre Latina is the third (Terza) tower. The fourth, Torre Quarta, has an Alta and a Bassa whilst the fifth, Torre Quinta, is also known as Torre Inglese. (See diagram 69)

As the climbs are short and the peaks low, they are ideal for short days, training, beginners or poor weather. Quite high free standards can be found and these routes need to be treated more as outcrop climbing.

Approaches are easy. Either drive up to the hut, Rifugio Cinque Torri 2137m, to the E of the towers then 10-15min walk to any route, or use the chairlift from the main road 3km E of the Falzarego Pass and walk for 5min. A pleasant alternative to these is to walk in from higher up the pass by path 440, which leads to the top of the chairlift and the towers in 1hr.

Torre Grande – Cima Sud

SOUTH FACE (VIA FRANCESCHI)
Franceschi, Constantini, 1936.

A very popular and spectacular route up the obvious crack which breaks through the OHs on the L of the face.

100m 3hr

14.01 Start on a large block below the crack.

VI+
V+/A1

73

1   30m Climb up to the first roof (V). Pass this and continue up to and over another roof of about 1m (VI or A1). Continue up the crack which eases and widens (IV+) then closes (V+) and leads past another OH (VI+ or V+/A1) and so to a stance. (Some abseil off here)

2   30m Continue vertically up the cracked corner (V+,VI- or A0). Higher it becomes a chimney/crack (V) which leads to a ledge

3   45m Continue by the crack, over a small OH (IV+) and then easier up a wall to join the descent route.

SOUTH FACE (VIA COL VENTO)
Dall'Omo and others, 1984.

A short, hard free route up the lower walls. Some bolt protection.

150m 2hr

14.02 Start a few m R of 14.01 below OHs.

VII+

1   30m Climb direct up the wall to reach a crack below the roof (V,V+). Traverse R for 7m (V) until above the start of 14.03. Climb the difficult OH (VII) and go obliquely R for 4m (V) to a stance

2   25m Move L a little and then climb direct for 4m (VII+). Next move back R and start direct up the wall above (VII-,VI) and then slightly L (VI-,VI) to a good belay. Now either abseil 50m to the path or traverse L to finish up 14.01, or traverse R to reach 14.04.

SOUTH FACE (DIRETTISSIMA SCOIATTOLI)
Alvera, Ghedina, 1942

An old aid route which now gives excellent free climbing.

150m 5hr

14.03 Start 10m R of 14.01 at the base of a yellow OHing corner.

VIII-

1   35m Climb over the bulge at the bottom of the corner (VII+) and climb it to reach the roof (VI+). Traverse R for 11m (V+) and then climb obliquely R to reach a pronounced roof (VI+). Climb the roof (VIII-) to reach a small peg stance

2   35m Go obliquely R for 10m (V+), traverse L for 2m and then climb direct up a thin crack for 10m (VI+). Where the crack vanishes climb a wall (VI-) to reach a ledge on easier rock

3   20m Go diagonally R up a slab (IV+) between the two alternatives of the Via Miriam (14.04), to reach a stance to the L of and slightly above the big OH which dominates the R-hand part of the S face

4   25m Climb obliquely R up a very exposed wall (VI) to reach a stance on the ridge above the roof

5   35m Climb a short OHing crack (VI-) and a corner (V) to reach easier rock leading to the top (II).

SOUTH FACE (VIA MIRIAM)
Dimai, Dimai, O'Brien, 1927.

One of the most popular routes on the group. The rock is good but worn and all peg belays and runners are in place.

210m 2¹/₂hr

14.04   Start a few m L of the edge between the S and E faces at an open
V   dièdre.

73

1   45m Climb easily up the dièdre for 6m to an OH. Bridge past this (V) and 2m higher move L and climb a second OH (V-). Now traverse a little R and climb a corner on grey rock with a step L halfway (IV). When it closes (5m) move R 3m to reach a slanting ledge. Stance at the end of this

2   35m Climb the little chimney above, at first inside then on the R for 5m (IV+), until an easy ramp leads L (III) for 25m to a stance below a reddish flake crack which leads up to the big roof

3   40m Go up the flake crack to below the roof (IV+) then traverse 4m horizontally L passing a corner (beware rope drag) until clear of the roof. Now go up a short chimney/crack for 3m to a ledge (stance 3 of 14.03) and step L to a stance at an obvious cracked block

4   45m Move up diagonally R for some m (IV) and then climb a big open corner past a lower OH, turned on the R (IV+), and a second (the Mules Back) climbed by layback or bridging (V). Continue to a red chimney/crack which is climbed for 3m (IV,III) then move L past two niches to a ledge near the descent route (14.07). 30m from here to the summit (II).

SOUTH FACE (DIMAI DIRECT)
Dimai, Degasper, Ghedina, Verzi, 1933.

This fine route takes a line up the arête which marks the junction of the S and E faces.

190m 3hr

14.05 Start as for Via Miriam (14.04).

VI+/A0

73

1   45m As for 14.04

2   20m Climb the little chimney (IV+) and continue direct to a stance on the prominent shoulder, also accessible by a traverse L from 14.06

3   35m Traverse L across the SE ridge by an exposed ledge for 8m (IV+),then go direct for 4m (V+), next a little L then R and finally L again on the ridge (VI) to a stance on the L. A variation to the R reaches this stance more directly (VII)

4   20m Climb obliquely L to reach a stance below a thin crack (IV+,IV)

5   35m Climb direct up the crack (V+,VI-) to a stance below a yellow roof

6   30m Traverse 7m L under the roof (VI), then climb the OH (VI+/A0) and continue diagonally L to the R end of a ledge (IV+)

7   20m Easily to the summit.

EAST FACE (DIMAI CRACK)
Dimai, Dimai, Degasper, 1932.

A very good free climb.

150m 3hr

14.06 Start at the foot of the gully between the Cima Sud and Cima Nord.

V+

1   30m Climb up the gully, over and under large blocks (II,III), until it is possible by a chimney to reach the big shoulder on the L below the E face

2   30m Start up a crack formed by a flake for 10m (V) and then step L to the base of a corner. Climb the corner (V) and then a crack (V+) for 20m to a stance in a niche

3   30m Climb for 7m in the base of the corner (V); go over an OH (V+) on the L. Return to the crack, which higher opens into a chimney (V+). Stance below an OHing crack

4   40m Climb the OH direct (V+), traverse R and then regain the crack (V+). Continue up this over bulges (V) to reach a good ledge

5   30m Go 15m L on the ledge, then climb a chimney (II) to the summit.

DESCENT

14.07 From the summit go down easy rocks on the S side, move across L and descend a short chimney. Move R to a large cemented abseil point. Abseil 10m to the start of a series of big ledges which lead to the big gully that separates the towers. Ignore the chimney on the R and move L a few m to the next gully which leads down to easy ground to the L. (40min)

Torre Grande – Cima Ovest

WEST-NORTH-WEST FACE (VIA ARMIDA)
Petrucci, Smith, Da Col, 1942.

This route climbs the face a few m R of the NW ridge. Just a few m below the start is a popular slab boulder with fixed belays at the top!

100m 2hr

14.08 Start at the base of two obvious broken cracks 6m R of the NW ridge.

VI
V/A1

1   30m Climb the L-hand crack finishing steeply to a stance (III,IV+)

2   25m Continue up the crack (IV+) then slant R (III+)

3   12m Climb diagonally L up a steep wall (V+,VI or A1)

4   30m Continue along the ridge to the summit (III,II).

NORTH-WEST FACE (VIA OLGA)
Lacedelli, Zardini, 1929.

A nice climb up the dièdre to the R of 14.08.

120m 2hr

14.09 Start at the foot of the dièdre.

V+
68

1   45m Start on the R wall for 4m, move into the corner and continue to a ledge after 12m. Continue a little on the L then direct to a stance in a cave below the roof (V/V+)

2   20m Move up a little then traverse R (V) for about 7m to the arête. Continue for 4m to a stance. A direct variant climbs the roof (V+)

3 45m Continue by the ridge and walls above moving R to the summit (III+).

SOUTH-WEST FACE (VIA DELLE GUIDE)
Dallamano, Ghirardini, 1930.

A popular route with good stances and belays.

140m 1½hr

14.10 Start at the highest point on the scree facing the chairlift station.

IV

68

1 35m Climb obliquely R for 12m (III,III+) to reach and follow a horizontal fault for 6m below bulges. Climb up through a weakness on the R (IV) for 3m, then traverse 1m L and continue direct (III) to a good ledge and block belay

2 25m Continue up a yellow groove climbing on the L of a big flake and then returning R to a stance below another bulge

3 35m Climb up L and over the OH (IV) then continue direct up the wall on easier rock (III). Block belay

4 35m Continue up short walls and corners to the top (III).

DESCENT
14.11 From the summit descend 5m to the E (towards the Second Torre). Then abseil 20m from a cemented peg to a ledge. Move 3m S to a second fixed peg and abseil another 20m to arrive in the gully. Follow this down to the base. (40min)

Torre Lusy

NORTH FACE
Pompanin, Lusy, 1913.

A delightful and popular little route with fixed belay pegs.

120m 1hr

14.12 Start at the centre of the N face.

IV

1 30m Climb up L to an obvious niche (III). Leave this on the R and go up the edge (IV) then back R to a stance on the R edge

2 30m Go diagonally L to the other edge and up this a few m (III)

3   20m Traverse L onto the E face (III) and then direct (III+) back to the ridge and up this for a few m

4   25m Traverse a little R then obliquely R to reach the NW ridge (III). Climb this for 6m (IV) then back L (III) to a stance on the edge

5   30m Climb up the ridge for 3m then go L and traverse to a crack (III) which leads to a ledge. Go L on the ledge then direct to the summit.

DESCENT

14.13 Either descend to the W by a little chimney for a few m to reach a ledge with cemented pegs and abseil 40m to the base or, if only one rope is carried, abseil back down the route (4 abseils of 20m) using the fixed pegs. (20min or 40min)

Torre del Barancio

NORTH FACE
Dibona, Apollonio, Stefani, 1934.

A similar climb to the previous one (14.12).   *120m 1hr*

14.14
IV+
Start at the centre of the N face.

1   30m Climb direct to a little niche on well marked holds (IV). Next go R of the niche and follow a slanting crack (IV+) to a stance

2   20m Go diagonally L for 5m to reach a slight niche at the start of two parallel cracks (IV). Climb the R-hand crack for 10m (IV+) to a horizontal ledge

3   45m Move R and climb up the middle of the wall past a fixed peg (IV). From here on good holds go obliquely L for about 30m to reach a ledge on the L of the face

4   15m Climb a little OH on the ridge to the summit (IV+), or move R on the ledge to reach the corner of 14.16 and climb 3m up this and so direct to the abseil peg.

SOUTH FACE (VIA GIOVANNA)
Constantini, Menardi, 1945

Not as popular as other routes in this area; it may be harder than the grade suggests or need aid.

80m 1hr

14.15 Start on the R side of the S face near the SE arête.

VI   Climb a chimney for 10m to a ledge on the L. Go 3m R to a

[66] yellow friable dièdre. Climb this for 12m until direct progress is
impossible. Move diagonally L round an arête and climb with
difficulty (little protection) up an OHing wall for about 15m to reach a
ledge (VI). Next climb a bulge for 8m to reach a higher ledge.
Traverse R to near the SE ridge and continue, keeping L of the edge,
for some m over an OH and up a difficult crack. Finally move R onto
the E face and climb a short wall to the top.

DESCENT

14.16 Descend easy rocks on the W face (II,III) to the gap between the
Barancio and Romana Towers and either easily reach the abseil peg on
the Romana SW ridge and abseil 40m, or reverse 14.18.

Torre Romana

NORTH DIEDRE

Scoiattoli, 1944.

*Another popular climb. Combined with 14.12 and 14.14 this makes a good
day out at IV.*

100m 1½hr

14.17 Start at the foot of the corner between the Romana and Barancio

IV   towers

1   35m Climb the corner, easy at first then awkward (IV-) to a stance
under a roof

2   20m Climb up under the roof (III), over it (IV) by a smooth
section to a stance above

3   20m Continue up the corner (IV) to a fixed peg

4   20m Continue to a stance on a ledge level with the ledge on the
Torre Barancio

5   15m Continue for a few m in the corner then easy rock R to the
summit.

Descend by 40m abseil as for 14.16 or reverse 14.18.

SOUTH CHIMNEY (NORMAL ROUTE)
Pompanin, 1912.

50m 30min

14.18
III
Start at the foot of the chimney between the Romana and Barancio towers.

1   30m Start over blocks from the L and climb the chimney to a large jammed block (III)

2   20m Continue up the chimney past a second chockstone to reach the gap between the towers (II). Easily up L to Torre Romana summit or R (III) to Torre Barancio.

Torre Latina

SOUTH FACE
Menardi, Zanettin, 1942.

Not yet a very popular route up this, the easiest of the towers.

70m 1½hr

14.19
VI/A1
Scramble up the gully below the S face starting from the foot of the SE ridge. Pass a cave to reach a large jammed block which closes the gully.

1   25m Climb the wall on grey rock following a wet crack leaning gently R (V-)

2   25m Continue up the OHing crack on poor holds for 3m (V) then the wider crack above to a cave. Climb over the roof on the R and up the holdless crack (VI/A1)

3   20m Continue on easier rock heading for a gap in the ridge and so reach the top.

Descend easily down the E face (I).

EAST FACE OF ALTA
Dallago, Menardi, 1966. Variation Dall'Omo, 1984.

A modern problem with bolt protection.

65m 40min

14.20 Start under the roof in the middle of the E face, either in the middle
VII+   or to the L.

72

1   25m EITHER: Climb up to the roof, first L and then direct
(IV+), and climb it direct (VII-). Then continue direct for a few
m to reach a higher fault (IV+). Traverse horizontally L 2m (III)
and then continue direct up a crack (III) to a stance

OR: Move up a few m L (IV) and climb the roof at a bolt (VII+).
Pass a higher bulge (IV+) to join the other start at the end of its
traverse

2   40m Either traverse R (IV+) then direct up the vertical wall (III)
moving R up darker rock to the summit ridge, or climb direct (V-)
then easier (III,II).

SOUTH FACE OF BASSA AND NORMAL OF ALTA
Girardi, Dibona, 1911.

Pleasant and popular little climbs combining both summits.

150m 1½hr

14.21 Start below the S face a few m R of 14.20.
IV-

1   20m Climb up the wall to a horizontal break. Various routes to
here (III+). Fixed peg

2   20m Climb a crack with good holds (III-) to a stance in the gap
between the towers

3   20m Climb direct R via a short crack to the summit of Torre
Quarta Bassa. Either go N down slabs and a little wall for 23m to a
peg and abseil 13m to the ground, or return to the 2nd stance

4   35m Climb 5m towards the E face of Torre Quarta Alta where it
leans against Torre Quarta Bassa. Then climb the wall on the L of
a ridge to a little stance and cemented peg below a little corner

5   15m Climb up to the corner and climb it with one little OH
(III+), to reach a fixed peg 2-3m L on the ridge.

DESCENT

14.22 From the Alta one or two abseils (20m or 40m) to the gap between the towers then another of 20m to the foot. (30min)

Torre Inglese

SOUTH-EAST FACE
Menardi, Majoni, Wyatt, 1901.

Another pleasant, short, beginners climb.

50m 2hr

14.23
IV-
Start either in the corner on the R of the S ridge, or in the gully further R.

74

1 25m Either climb the corner past bulges at 12m (II,III) or the wall on its R (III), or scramble up the gully and then climb the chimney/crack on its L (III+). Either way leads to a block belay on the shoulder

2 25m Climb diagonally L up the wall to join the S ridge (IV-). Up this to the top.

DESCENT

14.24 Go 4m down the SE face to a peg. Either make a long abseil (45m), or a short one to the shoulder on 14.23 and then a second from a block, down the R-hand start of 14.23 to the foot of the gully.

Geografica 1:25000 sheets 1 and 2

These peaks lie N of Cortina and the Tre Croci Pass. The routes described on Pomagagnon are low level rock climbs of a medium standard with easy descents which are useful at the start or end of the season or in doubtful weather, whereas the route on Cristallo although of low grade is a strenuous expedition needing a certain amount of experience and giving a step up from the via ferrata and cablecars which lead to its lower summits to the NW. Luckily there is no easy link from these to the main summit!

All routes in this area are climbed from the road so huts are not included.

Punta Fiames 2240m

SOUTH-EAST RIDGE
Jori, Broske, 1909. Castiglioni, Gilberti, 1930.

This attractive little peak offers a variety of routes covering a range of standards and so gives a pleasant day out for a mixed group of climbers. This route takes the R arête and by either of its starts gives interesting and fairly sustained climbing.

Base – road 2km N of Cortina 2hr to the start 350m 4hr

15.01
V
70
From the road it is possible to drive up a rough track E until below the main face of Pomagagnon. Head across below the face towards La Grava, a big scree gully descending from the ridge (descent route 15.04) and continue L towards a steep chimney/gully separating Punta Fiames from the peak to its R, Punta della Croce (2300m). Climb up to a col behind two rocky shoulders and continue L below the chimney/gully to reach vegetated rocks below the face.

ORDINARY ROUTE START
Continue L, over rock and vegetation, 100m to the centre of the S face beside a slanting gully. Climb 40m up grassy slabs to a ledge (II with a move of IV) which is followed R round an arête to reach a crack leading in 40m (III+) to a well used stance and a cemented peg. The Ordinary Route (15.03) continues direct from here but instead

traverse R on the ledge to reach the arête. This start is most popular.

CASTIGLIONI DIRECT START

From below the arête climb easily up vegetated slabs (I,II) for 150m to the first obvious ledge. Climb a chimney on the R of the arête, go L and continue for 10m in a yellow dièdre and go R of the arête again to a stance below a big chimney (40m,IV+). Climb an OH on the L via a smooth slab (IV+) then the chimney (IV) and finally take the slabs on the L (III) to reach the true start (35m).

1 30m Start up a little crack a little L of the arête for 12m (IV+) and then continue diagonally R to a good stance and spike belay

2 30m Climb a dièdre on the R (IV)

3 40m Continue up a crack on the R of the arête (IV+)

4 35m Climb a higher crack OHing at the start (V) and continue to a stance on a detached pillar

5 40m The slab above is split by a crack 5m from its R edge. Climb it with difficulty (V) and continue up the yellow slab above. Move R on a ledge and continue by a chimney (IV+)

6 40m Move R of the ridge and climb a crack (IV+) hard to start

7 25m Continue in the same line to a ledge (III) and move a few m R

8 35m Climb a vertical crack to a roof (IV+) which is avoided on the L (IV)

9 40m A final pitch up the wall to the summit.

SOUTH FACE – CENTRAL ROUTE
Dimai, Dibona, Degasser, 1933.

A hard variant up the final walls between the Ordinary (15.03) and Jori (15.01) Routes.

Base – road 2km N of Cortina 3hr to the start 200m 3hr

15.02
VI–
70
Follow 15.01 Ordinary Route Start to the cemented peg and traverse 40m R on the good ledge.

Climb a crack for 50m (IV) and then go R for 20m (IV) and finally some m diagonally R to reach a big grey wall cut vertically by a thin crack. Climb the crack for 50m (V) ending at an OH which is climbed on the L by a smooth flake with few holds (VI-) leading to a narrow ledge. The yellow wall above is cut by a deep crack which is climbed direct (V) and higher to the L to its end (IV).

Traverse some m L to a gully which leads to the W ridge and the summit.

SOUTH FACE (ORDINARY ROUTE)
Dimai, Verzi, Heath, 1901.

The original route up the wall and typical Dolomite climbing of its era.

Base – road 2km N of Cortina 2hr to the start 300m 3hr

15.03
IV
70

Approach as for 15.01 and climb the Ordinary Route Start to the cemented peg.

Climb a short chimney to a higher ledge. While it is possible to continue in a direct line it is usual to traverse L along the ledge to reach and climb chimneys for 70m (III) until a traverse back R on a higher fault line returns to the original line. Continue the traverse for 10m (IV-) to an exposed stance. Now climb up the chimney/gully above with some awkward sections to a narrower chimney ending at a jammed block and a ledge leading L. Climb chimneys 10m L until easier rock in a gully leads to the ridge near a little col. Continue easily up the ridge to the summit.

DESCENT BY VIA FERRATA STROBEL
15.04 Follow the Via Ferrata first N and then E passing the gap between Punta Fiames and Punta delle Croce and crossing slabs (wet sometimes with snow early or late in the season) until the big scree gully, La Grava, is reached. Descend this to paths and the road. (1½hr)

Testa del Bartoldo 2435m

SOUTH FACE (TERSCHAK CHIMNEY)
Terschak, Kees, 1913.

This face is cut diagonally from L to R by five ascending terraces whilst the walls between them provide various routes. The Third Ledge starts level with and to the R of the base of the great scree gully, La Grava, on the L of the face, whilst the Fifth Ledge, starts halfway up the gully and finishes on the R-hand summit. Both provide walking routes to the summits (about 3½hr from the road) whilst the walls between them give some of the best climbing. Directly below the summit of Testa del Bartoldo the Dibona

Direct Route (V) climbs a line of cracks and chimneys slanting L and the L arête of the final peak above the Fifth Ledge, whilst this route climbs chimneys above the start of the Third Ledge then follows the Fifth Ledge R to finish up the face of the final tower.

Base – road 2km N of Cortina 2hr to the start 500m 5hr

15.05
V–
71

Start as for 15.01 to near the base of the scree gully and move R to the top of a scree cone near the start of the Third Ledge. This route climbs the R-hand line of chimneys above.

1 30m Climb easily R up a ledge to spike belays

2 30m From the middle of the ledge climb on the L of a crack for 10m (III) and then move R (IV-) to a stance below a chimney

3 35m Climb the chimney passing a jammed block (III) and an OH on the R (IV)

4 40m Continue up the chimney moving onto the R wall after 20m (III)

5 40m Another chimney pitch past a jammed block (IV)

6 35m Climb on the R of the widening chimney to a roof and get past it via a hole on the L (IV+) to reach the Fourth Ledge

7 35m Climb a crack on the loose wall to the L of the chimney (III)

8 25m Continue up the chimney past two jammed blocks (II)

9 40m The chimney widens again, offering three cracks. Climb the central one (IV) and move L to climb an OHing crack (IV+)

10 35m Climb a crack (IV) until below a smooth OH. Move 5m R and climb the bulge (IV+) to a stance

11 35m Continue by scree and ledges (III) to a stance below a steep crack

12 25m Jam up the crack (V-,peg) to a big roof and traverse L below it past a jammed block (IV-) to a stance

13 70m Two easier pitches (II,III+) up chimneys with jammed blocks lead to the Fifth Ledge.

Now either descend the Fifth Ledge L (15.06) or go R for 150m and climb L of a big black chimney for 20m to a narrow red ledge. Continue direct for 5m to a little col and then by easy rock to the summit.

DESCENT BY THE FIFTH LEDGE

15.06 Go E to the col between Testa and Costa del Bartoldo and descend the
71 long ledge W, protected by wires in places, to the big scree gully.
(2½hr to the road)

Monte Cristallo 3221m

SOUTH-EAST FACE (NORMAL ROUTE)
Grohmann, Dimai, Siorpaes, 1865.

*An enjoyable mixed climb up a fine peak. Crampons and ice axes may be
needed.*

Base – road at Tre Croci Pass 3hr to the start 450m 2hr

15.07 Follow path 221 N to the F d Cristallo (2808m) with a steep final
PD section on snow. From the col climb a short snow gully to reach a big
ledge sloping up L across the SE face. Follow the ledge for about
20min until an easy ascent is possible on grey rock up the face
(cairns).

Move up and R for 60m to a chimney. Climb it (II) and traverse
30m L below yellow rocks. Now climb steep rock to the R (II) and
continue R to a col. Go 5m R, climb a 20m crack (II) and traverse 8m
R to reach a scree shoulder. Continue L on ledges to the S ridge (views
of Cortina) and follow this ridge for 15min. Finally climb a 10m wall,
La Lastas, (II) and continue along the ridge for 20min to the summit.
Descend the same way.

Geografica 1:25000 sheets 2 and 4

These two groups lie E of Cortina and S of the Tre Croci Pass. On Sorapiss the routes are generally wild and serious in a cwm of exceptional grandeur. The group is encircled by high level via ferrata served by two bivouac huts. These provide descent accommodation and safe routes back to the starts.

In contrast Antelao is a big mixed mountain. Here the routes require Western Alpine skills rather than the usual rock gymnastic ability.

HUTS

Vandelli Hut 1928m. Idyllically situated in the NE facing Sorapiss cirque just below the lake. Worth visiting just for an off day walk. Approach easily by traversing path 215 from the Tre Croci Pass (2hr)

Bivouac Slataper 2600m. Situated to the S of the Sorapiss group. Approaches– i)from the Vandelli hut by 247 to Tondi di Sorapiss then S by the exposed Via Ferrata Berti (242 sometimes marked 241), ii)laboriously for 1800m from the road at Albergo Dogana Vecchia directly NE on 241 (5hr), iii)from San Marco hut NW on 246 (3hr)

Bivouac Comici 2020m. Situated at the NW end of the Sorapiss group. Approaches– i)from Vandelli hut by 243, Via Ferrata Vandelli (3½hr), ii)from San Marco hut NE on 226 and 243 (4hr)

San Marco Hut 1823m. A popular hut situated at a low altitude S of the Sorapiss group. It is often crowded. Approach from San Vito di Cadore by road to Baita della Zoppa (1429m) then 228 (1hr)

Galassi Hut 2018m. Situated N of Antelao and a popular starting point for ascents of the peak. Approaches– i)from Baita della Zoppa (1429m) by 229 and 227 over the F Piccola (2120m) (1½hr, ii)from Capanna degli Alpini (1395m) to the E reached by road from Calazo di Cadore then 255 (2hr)

Bivouac Brunetta 2120m. Situated on a col at the foot of the SW face of Antelao. Approach from Borca and Corte di Cadore (1260m) by 232 (2½hr)

Bivouac Cosi 3111m. Situated just below and N of the summit of Antelao (see 16.13)

Punta di Sorapiss 3205m

NORTH-WEST FACE
Terschak, Degregorio, Ghelli, Armani, Betto, 1931.

A classic but fairly serious climb to the main summit. Usually some need for ice gear.

Base hut – Vandelli 3hr to the start 400m 7hr

16.01
IV
Follow path 247 until it is possible to traverse diagonally L to reach the small W glacier below the NW face which has a shallow central buttress with an obvious pinnacle, La Saetta, visible halfway up it. The L side of the buttress is cut by a steep ice couloir with a bergschrund across the bottom.

Cross the glacier to the foot of the ice gully. A direct start goes straight up the ice and friable rocks on the R zig-zagging up the main face. However it is safer to get out onto a ledge on the L-hand rocks and reach a steep chimney slanting from L to R which leads to a minute col in about 40m. Continue up a smooth wall then more easily up a slanting couloir which leads to the R and continue straight up to a large scree terrace under a smooth wall. This is the lower end of a big terrace which cuts this part of the face and is well seen from the glacier. From the terrace descend a little to the R and traverse across the large ice couloir to reach the main face.

Traverse to the R across narrow ledges then up the wall for 15m to a short terrace (cairn). From here go up 20m, first L then R, to a short horizontal ledge which ends on the L at a strange mushroom shaped rock. Climb a grey ridge on the L to a sloping terrace (cairn) then to the L up a smooth wall (shoulder needed). Continue up broken walls to the foot of the large pinnacle, La Saetta. Climb easily to a narrow gap between the main face and a smaller tower on the L of La Saetta. Continue up a loose crack on the L for 12m to a small terrace, then a delicate traverse under some yellow OHs leads to a very small ledge. Follow up a slanting groove and easy rocks to a terrace at the foot of the final wall (cairn). Traverse diagonally L (ice) to a gully which leads up to a col on the L of the summit.

SOUTH-EAST FACE (ORDINARY ROUTE)
Grohmann, Dimai, Lacadelli, 1864.

The Sorapiss group is encircled by via ferrata and this route to the highest point provides a fitting extension to the round tour with only one real climbing pitch.

Base hut – Bivouac Slataper 400m 2½hr to summit

16.02 From the hut descend a little and move N across the screes (Fond di
III– Rusecco) following paths to the highest point to the R. Get onto an
obvious sloping ledge and follow it L for 100m to reach a 15m
chimney with a smooth wall on its R and a jammed block at the top.
Climb it (II,III-) to an abseil peg. A little higher go L for 40m to reach
and follow the line of a gully on easy rock. Head R from a snow patch
and climb a gully which reaches the ridge just L of the summit. Move
R a little and climb up to the summit.

DESCENTS

16.03 The safest descent is to reverse 16.02 going first SW then S from the
summit until an abseil down a 15m chimney leads to a ledge leading E
100m to Fond di Rusecco and the bivouac Slataper. (2hr)
      Alternatively it is possible to follow the old hunters route along
the main ridge W over the Anticima (3191m) and descend into Fopa di
Mattia (snow possible) and descend this hollow to F Sora la Cengia del
Banco. From here follow path 242 and 247 back to the Vandelli hut.
(3hr)

Punta Zurlon 2720m

*This peak is marked on some maps as 3053m and much further S. The
peak with the routes on is quite near Dito di Dio.*

NORTH FACE
Mazzorama, Milani, Pagani, 1942.

*An excellent route in a beautiful setting. Less climbed than would be
expected, it should go entirely free.*

Base hut – Vandelli 40min to the start 500m 8hr

16.04 Follow path 274 round the lake and continue W until level with the
VI–/A1 base of the ridge. Cross scree and snow to the start.

▸75   Begin to climb some m R of the ridge up a short, loose, flared
crack (IV) and continue up smooth black slabs (V+) to a large open
dièdre. Follow this first on easy rock on the L then by little dièdres
and chimneys for 60m (IV) until a traverse is possible across black
slabs and round an arête to reach a vertical subsidiary dièdre. Climb
the dièdre (V) and a chimney (V) for two pitches to a scree ledge
below a light coloured wall with a thin crack up its R side. A direct
variation (Menegus, Bonafede, 1962) goes direct up the thin crack for
262 90m (V,VI/A1). However, traverse L with increasing

difficulty (V,A1) to return to the great dièdre/chimney which cuts across the NE face. Follow this to a large yellow cave which is passed on the L. Climb R to reach a vertical dièdre which narrows to a chimney and climb this (V,V+) to a scree ledge below steeper rock. Traverse back R round the arête and climb a dièdre formed by a big flake on the NW face which closes near the top.

The black compact wall above is cut by two cracks. Climb the L crack passing OHs on the R to a damp cave (V,V+). Move 3m L and continue up this crack to reach a big yellow window visible from the hut and near a terrace which crosses the upper walls. Move R 15m and climb a dièdre for 10m to a chimney. After 20m the chimney is closed by an OH (V). Move 2m R and climb a steep wall by a shallow crack for 25m (V+/A1) to a small niche. Move 8m R to another dièdre and climb it for 40m (V) to reach slabs (IV) and easy rock leading to the summit.

DESCENT BY SOUTH RIDGE

16.05 Follow the S ridge over short steps (III) abseiling 15m as required. Continue down the ridge and then E down a scree gully with a jammed block making a window to reach a hanging valley, Circo dello Zurlon, which runs NE. Descend this and at its end go along a ledge R (E) and abseil down an OHing chimney (III). Continue in the same line to the screes below the Central Glacier and follow paths to the hut. (2½hr)

Dito di Dio 2603m

NORMAL ROUTE
Von Glanner, Domenigg, Von Saar, 1899.

This route climbs into the hanging valley surrounded by fine looking towers to the E of the peak. On the R are Dito di Dio and Punta Zurlon, behind is Punta Emmy and on the L is Gusela del Rifugio. The cirque can be reached at its base by a Comici variation (16.05) with a chimney of III or by this route which goes through a col SW of Gusela del Rifugio and joins the cirque halfway up. From the cirque most of the peaks can be climbed at III although the Gusela ridge is IV from the col.

Base hut – Vandelli 1hr to the start 500m 5hr

16.06 Follow traces of paths up the glacier until below an obvious smooth
II yellow/red wall on the R. Follow scree ledges R to the col SW of

263

Gusela del Rifugio and go down the other side into the Circo dello Zurlon. From here climb Dito di Dio by terraces leading to a long crack which leads up to a col between Dito di Dio and the last slender tower on its SW ridge. The upper part of the crack looks unclimbable. Bypass the first step on the L and climb the second direct over a jammed block and traverse R to a buttress at the foot of a parallel crack. Climb this over an OH to the lower summit and cross a small col to the main summit.

NORTH FACE
Comici, Del Torso, Mazzorama, 1936.

A fine sustained climb.

Base hut – Vandelli 30min to the start 600m 7hr

16.07 Start at the top of a small snowfield below an OH which is itself below
VI/A1 big black OHs on the upper wall.

1 70m Climb two pitches up smooth slabs L then R (IV) to reach the obvious ledge

2 35m Follow the ledge L until below an obvious crack cutting the steep wall Rwards (cairn)

3 15m Climb the wall heading for the crack (V)

4 35m Continue up the wall on friable rock (V,VI or A0)

5 40m Climb in the same line past various small OHs (V,VI or A1)

6 20m Follow the corner to a good stance (IV)

7 35m Take the red crack in the dièdre (IV) to a stance on a shoulder

8 40m Climb a narrow chimney on the R past OHs (V,VI or A0)

9 40m Climb the OHing chimney above (V)

10 60m Continue up the crack passing OHs (V) to below a yellow roof

11 40m Climb obliquely R (IV)

12 40m Continue up a cracked wall to below an OH in the crack (V)

13 40m Take the double crack above (V+,VI or A0)

14 40m Follow the narrow chimney (V) to a scree col

15 25m Climb up and traverse R to reach a crack in a corner (III)

16 50m Climb the steep corner moving L to a stance below higher cracks (V+)

17 50m Continue direct (V) past a final OH (VI or A0) to the summit.

DESCENT

16.08 Descend the SW ridge and abseil over the lowest step. Continue towards a slender tower and finally descend SE down a slabby gully starting at a rocky gap which leads easily to the Circo dello Zurlon. Now either descend the cirque to its rim and take a ledge and an abseil R (SE) to reach paths leading to the hut as for 16.05 or reverse 16.06 over a col R of Gusela del Rifugio and then down R (S) to the Central Glacier. (2½hr)

Sorelle di Mezzo 3005m

NORTH-WEST FACE
Comici, Fabjan, 1929.

A serious route in a splendid ambience.

Base hut – Vandelli 1¼hr to the start 600m 8hr

16.09 Follow a path S and climb screes to reach the little E glacier. Continue V+/A0 up snow to the R of the lower rocks and the bottom of a R to L
| 78 | slanting ramp.

Climb slabs for 30m (III) on the R of the ramp below black OHs at a scree ledge and continue up a chimney with loose blocks to reach the top of the shoulder near red-stained rocks 100m from the start. Climb a short chimney to reach a higher ledge and follow it easily R for 40m until directly above the start and quite near the gully between Mezzo and Prima Sorelle.

Climb obliquely R by a chimney/crack for 25m (III) to reach a wet wall with poor holds. Move L across this (IV) and continue L by steep cracked slabs (III) to reach a col near the other edge of the buttress.

From the col climb direct for 30m up a difficult wall (IV+) to a higher red stain below yellow OHs. Next traverse 40m R on a series of detached flakes (IV-) to a chimney which is followed for 10m until an exit is possible R on a narrow exposed ledge. Climb the wall above for 25m (IV+) to a scree ramp and stance below a prominent triangular roof visible from below. The ramp leads to another shoulder but this is not the route. Instead climb up past the roof by a crack (IV), traverse R for 3m on a narrow ledge to a peg and abseil 15m down a white slab. Now climb a difficult OH (V) which is very exposed and continue up a chimney (III) for 25m. Finally take the wall on the R for 10m (IV) to reach the start of a 150m chimney which may be wet in the back.

Climb the chimney for five pitches past five OHs (III/V+/A0) to reach the top end of a snow-covered ledge. Continue in the line of the ledge easily L (II) for about 100m to below a yellow tower.

Climb a short chimney (III) and a vertical slab (V+/A0, crux) and continue for two pitches of 30m to reach a col between the yellow tower and the main face. Stance on a jammed block. Climb R from the col for 60m up walls and chimneys (V-) to reach a narrow ledge under a big yellow OHs. Traverse the exposed ledge, in places on all fours, (IV) for 30m and climb higher walls and a chimney with little OHs for 25m (IV) to finish at a higher ledge. Another 30m exposed chimney (IV) leads to below a final black OHing gully. Climb a very difficult crack on the R (IV+) and then a crack and wall lead easily to the summit.

DESCENT TO THE SOUTH

16.10 In theory it should be possible to traverse the Tre Sorelle NE, abseil and climb into, then descend, a fairly easy snow gully on the L of the main face, but this is rarely done. Instead head SE to reach an easy rock amphitheatre and join a scree terrace leading S below the yellow walls of Prima Sorella. Descend easy rocks and a couloir to reach a large grassy ledge across which goes Sentiero Minazio (243) and either follow this N to the bivouac Comici (2hr from summit) and continue from there to the Vandelli hut (3hr more) or descend S to join path 226 leading to the San Marco hut. (3hr from summit)

Antelao 3264m

NORTH-EAST FACE (MENINI ROUTE)
Menini, Zandagiacomo, Carrara, Pordon, Tuffoli, 1886.

This route offers an unusual Dolomite experience, a mixed route leading to a summit giving marvellous views. Best climbed early in the day to avoid stonefall in the couloir.

Base hut – Galassi 1½hr to the glacier 700m 3½hr

16.11 Follow path 250 to moraines leading to a 45 degree rock barrier below
AD the F d Ghiacciaio (2584m). Cables and steps lead up on the L to the col.

Start up the glacier (crevasses) and head for a large regular snow gully which is about 50 degree angle and 350m high and leads to the col L of the main summit, F Menini. Climb the couloir keeping R near the top to avoid stonefall from loose rock near the col.

Above the col traverse for 40m on poor rock, pass below some yellow rocks and continue L for another 20m to reach a large rock gully and climb it until it narrows (II). Pass an OH in a chimney on the L (II+). Continue over little walls on the L (II+) on exposed but firm rock to reach the blocks of the S summit (route book).

SOUTH-WEST FACE
Bettella, Scalco, 1941.

This is a major route on a big peak. Mainly free climbing but with snow in the upper reaches and on the descent. A short axe and crampons may be necessary. The rock on the hard section is good but there is some poor rock on the final easy section. The route follows dièdres on the L side of the large SW face and then an arête to the summit.

Base hut – Bivouac Brunetta 10min to the start 1000m 12hr

16.12 Descend from the hut and follow a ramp and ledges L towards the
VI–/A1 great couloir/chimney on the L of the face. Continue up ledges and
77 little walls for 200m (II, moves of IV) towards dièdres with obvious niches on the L of the wall about 120m in from the R edge. Finally climb a vertical 30m gully (III-) to a ledge below a grey/black dièdre. Although the dièdre has pegs go L up a steepening ramp for 50m (III+) and continue for 50m up a chimney on the R (IV-) to the base of a higher grey dièdre. Climb this (V-) past a roof (V+) for 55m and move a few m round the arête (III+) to reach another dièdre with

unstable blocks leading in 40m (V-,V) to a terrace with a big block in the centre. Climb a yellow wall by a crack (A1) and continue past a loose flake (V) and then a slab on the L to a poor stance after 25m. Continue by a higher dièdre and crack for 25m, sometimes wet (V-,VI-), until a final 45m flake crack (IV) leads to a big sloping snow field.

Traverse the snow R for 120m to a stance below a steep little wall. Climb this (IV) and continue up little chimneys (III+) towards a col between two pinnacles. Continue up the ridge by friable ramps until it is possible to go round a subsidiary summit to a col between it and the main peak (mainly III on poor rock).

Finally climb the obvious arête L past two snow patches and continue on the arête to the summit.

DESCENT TO THE NORTH

16.13 From the main summit descend NW over the summit rock down chimneys and walls with faint paths, cairns and a pitch of II. Now head for the bivouac Cosi (3111m) and continue direct down a gentle slab covered with scree and snow. At the base of the slab continue N along the ridge until a path R (E) leads down a steep wall to a scree hollow which is followed to F Piccola (2120m), and by path 227 go E to the Galassi hut (2½hr) or go W to the San Marco hut. (3hr)

Geografica 1:25000 sheet 2

This extremely popular area offers a variety of excellent climbs. From a rock climber's point of view there are five peaks, mainly with steep N faces and easier S faces, on which side the descents are found. Crowds tend to ruin the mountain atmosphere but nevertheless once on the routes the climbing may be worth the circus environment. Peaks are described from W to E.

HUTS

Auronzo Hut 2320m. A giant tourist hut. Approach: easy by toll road from Misurina. Large car park.

Lavaredo Hut 2344m. Private. Many climbers camp near here. Approach: a horizontal walk from the Auronzo Hut past the Alpine chapel (30min)

Locatelli Hut 2405m. Facing the great N faces, this hut is more popular with Continental hard men. Approach: 101 from Lavaredo Hut (45min)

Cima Piccolissima (Kleinste Zinne) 2700m

NORTH-EAST FACE (PREUSS CRACK)
Preuss, Relly, 1911.

A classic free climb on good rock. Polished rock at the crux.

Base hut – Lavaredo 15min to the start 200m 2¹⁄₂hr

17.01 The Piccolissima has a subsidiary peak on its E flank – Torre Minor.
V Start on the N side of this just L of the crack separating the peaks.

1   60m Climb up to a ledge. Follow it L round the E ridge and then up a short dièdre. Traverse back to the N side, pass behind a pinnacle and up to the shoulder where the peaks join. Cross the gap and follow a ledge R to a stance at the foot of a steep crack (III)

2 40m Get up to the crack and climb it (V) to a little hollow

3 35m Climb the corner chimney above (IV+)

4 35m Continue bridging up the chimney past two bulges to a stance in a cave (IV)

5 40m More OHs in the chimney lead to a jammed block (IV+)

6 35m Continue in the chimney/gully for 15m then break out R up easier rock (III)

7 20m Direct to the summit (II).

SOUTH-EAST FACE
Cassin, Vitali, Pozzi, 1934.

An excellent route on the sunny side of the group giving a good but shorter alternative to the N face routes.

Base hut – Lavaredo 15min to the start 250m 4hr

17.02 Start at the foot of the gully on the L of the face or at a dièdre a few m
VII R.
V+/A0
81 1 35m Climb the wall on the R side of the gully (V) to reach a ledge. A traverse on all fours leads in 15m to a stance below a corner. The more popular alternative start goes straight to this stance (V-).

2 20m Climb the corner diagonally R (IV) and move R to a good ledge below the vertical yellow walls

3 25m Move R and climb a yellow groove for 12m (V-) to an OH. Move R for 4m and climb another corner for 10m (VI or V/A0) to a stance on the R

4 20m Climb up and R (V) to reach a rotten open groove which narrows to a crack (IV+)

5 25m Move R 2m and climb the OH above direct (VI+ or A0) to reach an exposed yellow slab (V+) leading to a short crack (VII- or A0) and a flake stance

6 25m Climb an OHing dièdre on the L for 5m to a horizontal fault and traverse 20m (V) to a better stance below the obvious corner

7 35m Bridge up the corner (V+) to a stance on the pillar on the edge of the face

8 35m Continue up easier rock on the L of the edge (IV)

9   35m Go direct to a yellow OH (IV) and climb it (VI or A0) then a
    higher bulge still in the crack leads to a good ledge. There is an
    easier variant to the L and it is possible to traverse L from here to
    reach the descent route (17.03)

10 20m Slant L to the summit (III).

DESCENT BY DULFER COULOIR

17.03 There is a real danger from stonefall on this descent. All abseil pegs
    are cemented in place. Descend by ledges on the W face, traversing to
    a ledge on the NW corner which overlooks the col between this peak
    and the Punta Frida. Abseil to the col and continue abseiling down
    the couloir SE. Most abseils are under 25m, pegs not always obvious
    but usually on the W wall. 45m abseils make the descent quicker and
    safer (2hr).

Punta Frida 2792m

SOUTH-EAST RIDGE
Del Vecchio, Zaccaria, 1948.

*This route may be found to be less busy than its more notable neighbours. It
is exposed and quite sustained.*

Base hut – Lavaredo 15min to the start 300m 6hr

17.04 Start at the L side of the gully on the R of the face, just L of 17.02, on
VI/A1 a grassy ledge which leads L.

 1   20m Climb over two dark steps (IV) to a ledge

2   25m Climb the grey-yellow dièdre on the L of the arête obliquely
    to below a roof (IV,V)

3   30m Climb the yellow OH (VI-) and go diagonally round the edge
    (IV) to a grassy ledge

4   30m Climb a slanting corner on the R of the edge (III,IV)

5   30m Continue on the L by an OHing crack for 20m (V) and at its
    end go L to a narrow ledge. Climb a 6m wall to a higher ledge

6   60m Two pitches up the vertical black crack cut by two yellow
    OHs well seen from below (V,VI,IV,V) to reach a stance on a
    pinnacle a little L of the arête

7   20m Climb a corner (III,IV)

8 35m Move R to a very exposed crack up the edge (V)

9 40m Continue up the edge (IV,III)

10 20m Continue in the same line (IV,V,VI) on solid rock to reach a ledge below a big yellow roof

11 20m Climb the loose OH direct and continue up the exposed slab above (V+/A1)

12 20m Continue up the edge and climb a higher OH (V) to a terrace

13 40m Easily to the summit.

SOUTH-EAST FACE DIRECT
Comici, Fabian, Cottafavi, Pompei, 1934.

A fine route up the lower walls, with an easy descent.

Base hut – Lavaredo 15min to the start 300m 4hr

17.05 Start 50m L of 17.04 near a memorial plaque.
VI+ Zig-zag up a series of short, steep walls for three pitches to the
V+/A1 foot of a yellow OHing dièdre. Make an exposed traverse 6m R to a
81 small ledge at the foot of a parallel dièdre. Climb the dièdre for 40m (VI+ or V+/A1) going R near the top to avoid poor rock. Continue L by a marked chimney for 50m to reach easier ground. Descent route is L if required, or take a line of loose cracks and chimneys on red rock direct to the summit (IV).

DESCENT
17.06 From the summit descend towards the W by a chimney and then little
79 rock steps to the col between the Punta Frida and the Piccola (F d Frida). From here follow an easy rock ramp down the S face L (E) to reach a ledge leading back R (W) towards the foot of 17.07.

Follow this to a scree hollow, and with one 20m abseil reach a horizontal ledge leading to the screes near the start of 17.07. (1hr to the screes)

Cima Piccola (Kleine Zinne) 2856m

SOUTH ARETE (YELLOW EDGE – SPIGOLO GIALLO)
Comici, Varale, Zanutti, 1933.

This famous route takes a line up the almost vertical arête of the lower summit of the peak (the Anticima). The original route kept very near the arête all the way, but most modern ascents use variations on the face to the R to a greater or lesser degree. This easier line is the one described.

Base hut – Lavaredo 20min to the start 350m 5hr

17.07 Start just L of the line of the arête at a steep corner starting near a
VI horizontal ledge.
V+/A1

1 20m Climb the corner to a ledge on the R (V)

2 30m Continue up the corner passing an OH on the R (V+) after 15m, and another direct

3 20m Follow the corner to climb a large OH by a crack (V) to a stance R

4 50m Trend R up easier ground to the foot of a shallow groove (II)

5 60m Climb the groove for two pitches until the wall steepens (III,IV)

6 20m Climb the wall to reach a traverse line (V-)

7 25m Traverse L and step up to a niche

8 20m Climb the edge above to the foot of an obvious yellow dièdre which leans slightly R (IV+)

9 25m Climb the dièdre (VI or V+/A1) and traverse L to a good stance on the edge

10 50m Continue up the arête, first R then L (V), to a good stance below a final vertical section

11 20m From the R-hand side of the ledge climb a crack (V-) to a belay amongst detached blocks

12 20m The top section of the arête is rather loose in places but climbable (V+). It is better to traverse R to reach a line of cracks and chimneys

13 60m Up these (V-,IV) to the top of the Anticima.

From here either climb the main peak by 17.08 or join the descent (17.11).

SOUTH-WEST FACE (ORDINARY ROUTE)
Innerkofler, Innerkofler, 1881.

The usual route up and the normal way down.

Base hut – Auronzo 25min to the start 300m 2hr

17.08 Walk direct up the screes from the little Alpine chapel aiming for the
III   scree gully between Cima Grande and Cima Piccola.

79

Climb the gully for a short distance until about 30m below the start of 17.16 and then follow the rocky spur (SW) which leans against the vertical walls of the Piccola. Follow a short ledge R then up a small chimney, followed by a series of steps leading diagonally R to another chimney and then easy steps to reach the scree-covered slope at the top of the buttress.

Climb slightly R by an easy staircase of scree and chimneys as far as a horizontal fault which traverses the whole wall. Climb two chimneys for 10m to a niche and then climb obliquely L to reach the start of the famous 'Traversata'. Follow this L for 40m until a corner is reached. Climb the dièdre for 5m then the rib on its L, then a crack between the vertical summit walls and the rib, and finally by easier rocks diagonally R to a small chimney, which leads to the shoulder between the main summit on the L and the Anticima on the R.

Climb up to the 'Pulpito' on the final wall and then go L up the wall to the foot of the Zsigmondy Chimney. Follow this for 20m, exposed with good holds, past a little red OH (III) to the summit. (Two other chimneys to the R from the pulpit are both harder.)

NORTH-WEST RIDGE
Comici, Mazzorana, 1936.

A spectacular route with hard free climbing on poor rock. Not often done.

Base hut – Lavaredo 140min to the start 280m 9hr

17.09 Start up 17.08 and traverse L to the col between Cima Piccola and
VI+/   Cima Grande, or climb the gully all the way. Descend 40m below the
A1   col (F d Piccola) on the N side.

80

Climb past two caves in the wall (1914-18 blockhouses) and reach a ledge which is traversed for 15m to the L. From here climb a loose OHing chimney for 25m to a ledge (IV). Climb 15m to another ledge (III) and then 25m to a large loose ledge (IV). From here ascend

30m to a yellow groove (V, loose). The groove ends with a larger ledge. Continue to climb straight up for 10m (V) and traverse 15m across a yellow wall. Climb down a few m towards the R (V) to reach an OHing dièdre. Ascend this for 10m (VI) to beneath a small roof. Traverse beneath it for 7m to an OHing dièdre beneath a large roof (VI). Climb the dièdre for 15m to beneath the great roof (VI).

Traverse R beneath the OH for 7m to reach a good ledge. Climb R for 10m to another ledge (III) and then up for 15m (IV) to a narrow ledge that runs round the rib. Move on to the N side of the arête and climb the OHing wall for 10m (VI). Then climbing R reach the arête and continue straight up it for 15m to another narrow ledge under a small roof on the arête (VI). Climb the OH on the R of the arête and return to the arête. Continue up this for 15m (VI) to reach a ledge under two yellow OHs. Climb 10m to the first roof and pass it on the R (VI) then return to the L to below the second roof. Climb this on the L to beneath yet another OH (10m,VI). Surmount this on the R, climbing towards the rib for 10m (VI). Go straight up the rib, then to the L for 10m (IV) to another small ledge. Continue up the arête for 20m to a large platform (VI). Go straight up the arête for another 20m (VI) and continue up the OHing section (10m,VI). Traverse on to the N face and climb R to regain the arête after 15m (VI).

Continue up the OHing arête (VI) and after 15m reach a narrow ledge (VI). Follow the ridge, now somewhat easier (VI), to another ledge (15m). Climb L to the foot of a narrow OHing chimney which leads to the top in 20m.

NORTH FACE (EAST CHIMNEY)
Innerkofler, Innerkofler, Helversen, 1890.

A classic route with a steep upper section, impressive for its time.

Base hut – Lavaredo 20min or 40min to the start 350m or 450m 2hr or 2½hr

17.10 The route proper starts from the Forcella di Frida. This point is
IV reached either up ledges leading L out of the gully between Cima
80 Piccola and Cima Grande, on the N side, at II in 1hr, or by climbing up 17.06, with a pitch of IV up a 20m black wall at the start and then II or III, in 1½hr. Some stonefall danger on the approach from the N.

The route now follows the prominent chimney line directly above the col. (A harder route – Fehrmann, Perry-Smith (V) follows the chimney well to the R.)

From the shoulder below the wall climb a crack L to a ledge below the chimney. Climb a grey slab (IV, crux) and climb for

275

12m a little L then R in the deep chimney. Climb the chimney to a stance on a ledge with perched blocks below a yellow OH. The OH has been climbed on the R by bridging, but it is more usual to traverse R for 10m passing a block, & then return to the chimney above the roof. Continue up the chimney until it is closed by yellow rock. Make an exposed traverse R onto an arête & follow this to a small ledge & the final chimney. Climb this to a notch on the ridge & the summit.

DESCENT BY ORDINARY ROUTE

17.11 Descend S 10m below the summit and abseil from a peg for 20m to reach the shoulder. Now descend R towards the Cima Grande by a series of abseils which at first follow the Ordinary route (17.08). After two abseils traverse out onto the wall L (S) then continue to abseil down to the couloir below.Descend this S to the hut. (2hr)

Cima Grande (Grosse Zinne) 2999m

WEST FACE

Dulfer, Von Bernuth, 1913.

A fine route up a shallow corner and chimneys on the narrow W face. It gives classic Dolomite chimney climbing with opportunities for photographs. Good for a short day by avoiding the summit and thus shortening the route to about 230m.

Base hut – Auronzo 45min to the start 350m to summit 3¹/₂hr

17.12
V
80
Start by climbing screes to the F d Grande between Cima Grande and Cima Ovest.

Move L from the col via a scree terrace to below the line of the route. Go diagonally R for 5m then traverse a few m L to a yellow crack which leads to a stance. Next obliquely R towards a ledge, up a steep yellow step to finally reach a stance at the foot of the obvious weakness. Climb the groove/chimney line (pegs and stances every 20/25m, mostly V) to a stance under a big jammed block well seen from below. Now climb through a tight hole to reach a slippery, often wet, final chimney with various chockstones, and climb this to a terrace. If the hole is iced up traverse R and slightly down along a narrow ledge, past a leaning flake, to reach the SW arête (Spigolo Mazzorama, VI) and climb the final section of this (V).

Once on the terrace either continue up the SW arête, or move R and climb easier rock, or go further R to find Camino Mosca (III) and climb this (see 17.16). The next terrace cuts right across to the descent route (17.17) or easier rock leads to the summit.

NORTH FACE (COMICI ROUTE)
Comici, Dimai, Dimai, 1933.

A spectacular and deservedly famous N face climb. It is a very popular climb and an early start is advised; in fact the first 50m are possible in the dark and this is recommended. Originally a fair amount of aid was used and in the past it often became over-pegged. In recent years the number of pegs has decreased and it is possible free, or more usually with only one short aid section.

Base hut – Lavaredo 40min to the start 500m 8hr

17.13 Start at the R-hand side of the face at a rocky tower.

VII
VI/A1

80

1   40m Climb up from the L up easy rock and a little chimney to a ledge below a crack (II,III)

2   10m Climb the crack (IV) to a good stance at the start of the difficulties

3   25m From the L end of the ledge climb a steep crack and traverse L for 5m (VII or A0) until it is possible to move up on to a slab. Climb this (VI) Lwards for 12m until a crack leads back R (V) to a stance

4   40m Continue Rwards (VI+ or A0) to the bottom of a loose yellow dièdre. Go up it a little (V+) and then move out onto the wall on the R and climb this (V) to a stance

5   40m Move L and then up a few m (VII- or A0) then L again to reach an OHing crack in a shallow corner. Up this (V+/VI) to a stance R

6   30m Climb the OH dièdre above (V+/VI) to a better stance on the R

7   30m Continue up the corner above (VI+ or A0), move R (VI) and then climb another OHing section (VI+ or A0) to a stance on the R

8   35m Climb direct up the open groove above the stance on black compact rock (VI+ or A0) then move out R and traverse (VII or VI/A1) on dark rock to reach another corner. Up this (VI+ or A0) to a stance

9 40m Climb the corner near a red pillar (V) traverse R below a roof (VI) to reach and climb a new crack in black rock. Up this for 15m (V/V+) until easier rock (IV) leads to a big ledge and an easing of angle

10 20m Move down and across L to reach the foot of a chimney (II)

11 50m Climb the chimney (V+/V) and easier slabs above (II)

12 50m Continue up a ramp (III) to a narrow chimney and up this to a ledge (V)

13 10m Do not continue direct but move R (IV) to a stance below a dièdre

14 40m Climb the corner crack on good holds up yellow and black rock (V) moving R after 20m. Continue up the next corner (V+/VI-)

15 20m Do not go L across the yellow wall below a black roof but continue up the corner (IV/V) to a ledge and a niche at the foot of a final black corner

16 40m Move up out of the niche L to the start of a traverse line. Traverse high (IV) or 3m lower (V/V+) to a corner and go round this (V-)

17 50m Climb an open dièdre and a slab (IV) to a ledge. Next move L up a ramp (III)

18 30m A short chimney (III) and broken rock (III) leads to the circular summit band. Now either move 15m R and climb chimneys (III/IV) for 70m to the summit or, if time is short, walk round the band to find the way off (17.17).

NORTH FACE DIRECT (BRANDLER-HASSE)
Brandler, Hasse, Lehne, Low, 1958.

Hard free and artificial climbing in magnificent situations. Usually many pegs and bolts but some are often missing or loose, raising the free standard which is possibly above VI anyway.

Base hut – Lavaredo 40min to the start 500m 12hr

17.14 Start about 75m L of the start of 17.13 at a large block on the path
VI/A3 where a crack formed by a detached flake starts a few m up the wall.
80•   Climb 8m up a small vertical wall (V) then layback a steep crack for 15m (V). The crack widens becoming easier (IV) then narrows

again at the top (V). From the stance traverse R for 12m, climb vertically up some easy cracks (III) and return L to a stance above the first. This point can also be reached up the easier pillar of the Winter Super Direct (an aid route) by a short traverse from the R. The hard climbing starts here.

Traverse several m L then climb direct tending slightly L (V+,VI,V/A1) to a small ledge. Climb 10m direct to a horizontal roof (V+) and climb it (A2) and continue direct to belay on a small flake. Climb 20m first R then trending L (V+) to a wide groove (VI/A1) leading to a better stance. Climb direct for 30m (A2) and continue for 30m more (A2,V) to reach a stance on a traverse line L.

Traverse horizontally L just below the stance for 10m (V/A1 but bolts may be missing) and climb a crack for 9m (V) to reach a good ledge. From here traverse L, descend a crack for 3m (III) to a comfortable ledge below great roofs. Climb a flake (IV) then a vertical wall (V) to reach the beginning of the roofs.

The route now climbs the diagonal OHing dièdre strenuously for four pitches of 35m, 20m, 25m, 35m (all A2/A3), with the first two stances hanging, and finishes on a better stance. At the end of the roofs climb a groove (V) which leads to an excellent platform (bivouac site and route book).

Above and a little L climb a very OHing dièdre for 30m (V,A2). Continue for two pitches (IV+,V) to reach the foot of a wide chimney with two large jammed blocks. Get inside via a letter box and belay on the lower block. Climb outside the second block (V). A final pitch (IV,V) leads to the circular summit band.

Either traverse round the band L to the descent route (17.17) or continue up dièdres and cracks for 60m (III,IV) to the summit.

NORTH-EAST RIDGE (SPIGOLO DIBONA)
Dibona, Stubler, 1909.

A well situated climb up the L edge of the N face. The rock is a bit loose and parties above can cause stonefall but it serves as a good introduction to the type of climbing and the area. Variations abound, usually to the L at a lower standard.

Base hut – Lavaredo 40min to the start 550m 4hr

17.15 Start at the foot of the ridge on the screes below the gully leading to
IV the F d Piccola, or at a chimney 40m L.

Climb the steep arête by cracks, in parts OHing, for 100m (IV) to reach a rocky shoulder, or attain the same point up chimneys and grooves further L (III+). Now climb direct up the ridge for 150m passing a slab, a steep crack, a short traverse R and a broad scree ledge to the point where the ridge becomes an OHing wall.

The wall is avoided by traversing 30m L (III) and climbing chimneys obliquely R to exit onto a large ledge. A variant avoids the wall by an excursion onto the N face and then follows the arête direct (IV).

Continue R as far as a gap in the NE ridge. Then traverse R 2m and climb a 20m yellow crack (III) to reach the ledge which traverses the whole E face. Climb cracks above (III+) and then slant L (III) on the E face to arrive at a traversing ledge.

Cross the ledge to a col on the L (S) and climb an awkward section (III+). Finally climb diagonally R over a minor summit and go up a scree gully to the summit.

SOUTH FACE (MOSCA CHIMNEY)
Mosca, Stuger, 1903.

A classic way up this famous peak. Linked with the descent by the Ordinary Route (17.17) it makes a fine day out.

Base hut – Lavaredo 40min to the start 200m of climbing 2½hr

17.16 Walk up the screes above the Alpine Chapel towards the col between
III Cima Grande and Cima Piccola until about 70m below the col where a
79 gully goes L (red triangular marking on the rock).

First climb the gully for 50m by a ramp (II) and then zig-zag up 80m L (red marks) to a little col between the main peak and a subsidiary tower (II). From the col go diagonally L up a wall with good holds (II+) to a ledge, and then by a gully to a scree-covered shoulder. This is the lower terrace, which cuts the whole face. (The Ordinary Route now goes a little R and then up chimneys, keeping near the SE ridge, with one 15m pitch of III up a smooth chimney near the top.)

However for this route traverse about 80m L to near the middle of the S face. Climb obliquely L on ledges to reach the bottom of the chimney where it is quite narrow (40m,III). First climb on the L of the chimney, then in it by back and foot climbing for 40m (III). Easier climbing to a fork (30m,II,III) then bridge up the R branch for 30m (III) to a ledge. Finally climb looser rock to the upper terrace and walk 60m R to reach a gully (Ordinary Route) which leads L to the summit blocks (50m,II).

DESCENT BY ORDINARY ROUTE

17.17 Descend an easy gully and follow it to the upper terrace. Go along this
II L(E) for 80m to a cairn and red mark near its end. Climb down a little
[79] ridge to a lower ledge and continue down until 20m above a little col.
Abseil down to this and then descend a chimney facing SW (abseil
15m) and then zig-zag down to the lower terrace. Go down a gully to
the E and abseil 20m to a ledge a little below a col on the SE ridge. Go
through the col, which is easy to miss at night or in mist! Descend an
easy gully, with one abseil if required, to the screes below F d Piccola
and follow these to the hut. (2½hr)

Cima Ovest (Westliche Zinne) 2973m

NORTH-EAST RIDGE
Demuth, Lichtenegger, Peringer, 1933.

*A good climb in a fine situation. Route finding is complex; mainly keep just
L of the edge of the ridge.*

Base hut – Lavaredo 45min to the start 500m 5hr

17.18 Start a little way up the gully between the E face and a secondary
VI+ pinnacle. Walk out along an easy ledge for 20m to near the ridge.
V+/A0

  1 35m Climb a crack immediately L of the edge which leads L
[80]   beside a pillar. Step R to a stance behind the pillar (III,IV)

  2 35m Move a few m R and up steep rock (IV) to reach a ledge.
     Traverse 10m L (II)and climb back R (IV) to a stance above an
     OH (direct is VI-)

  3 40m Move R and climb an open corner (IV,V) to a stance below a
     line of yellow OHs

  4 25m Traverse R below the OHs (III,V)

  5 45m Break through the roofs on the R and continue up a steep
     flake (V+) to a niche at the bottom of the large scoop in the ridge.
     Continue to a stance (III)

  6 40m Move direct up the base of the hollow on slabs (IV)

  7 35m Move R across a slab (IV+) and then direct to a ledge (IV)

  8 40m Climb 6m over a bulge on the R near the arête (VI+ or A0)
     and continue R up an OHing dièdre past a loose OH

9 40m Climb a corner (V-) and a slab L (IV+) to a scree ledge

10 45m Move L 12m on the ledge and climb a grey compact wall close to the black water stripes on the R (IV). Pass an OH on the L (V+) and continue L (IV/V) to a stance below a corner

11 45m Climb the corner (III) and a ramp (IV) to a ledge below a big red chimney

12 50m Climb up diagonally R of the chimney (III+) and then direct up a ramp (IV) to a ledge

13 50m Climb a groove above (III,IV) to a stance on the edge of the ridge behind a pinnacle

14 40m Slabs L then R (IV+,V,IV) lead to the big circular ledge below the summit. A traverse L leads to 17.22 and the descent.

15 60m Continue up the ridge to the summit (III).

NORTH FACE (CASSIN ROUTE)
Cassin, Ratti, 1935.

An enjoyable and satisfying classic climb with a high standard of difficulty. Long traverses necessitate a strong party. Some poor pegs and a little loose rock.

Base hut – Lavaredo 1hr to the start 450m 9hr

17.19 Start on the R of the face below easier rocks just round the edge of the
VIII– face.

VI–/A2
80

1 60m Climb none too solid rock on the R of the edge of the NW ridge to reach a grey pillar (II,III+)

2 30m Climb a yellow wall (IV+) move L and then direct (V-) to a ledge on the L

3 15m Climb a deep crack to the top of a flake (IV+)

4 35m Climb a steep wall tending L (V+) and then go straight up a crack (V) to a large ledge with blocks

5 35m Move L for 8m (V) then climb direct for 12m on OHing rock (VI+ or A2) and finally L to a narrow ledge at the start of a horizontal fault which crosses the N face (VIII- or A2)

6 50m Traverse 20m L (V+ or A0) then descend 5m (VII or A1) and continue L (VI-) to a small ledge. Move up and L again to a stance 15m R of a black couloir running down the centre of the face. A

good alternative avoids the 5m descent by a bold, strenuous hand-traverse (VI+). (An easy traverse leads to a good bivouac under roofs in the centre of the face – Kasparek bivouac)

7   40m Climb direct on grey rock, for a few m, then tend L and continue to a good stance below yellow/black OHs (VI+ or A1/V+,V+)

8   25m Climb up to the black roof (V) and pass it (VII or A2)

9   25m Move L for 10m across wet black rock then back R to a good ledge (IV+).

10 20m Continue below and L of black roofs (V+,IV+) to the base of the final chimney/dièdre

11 150m Climb in or near the corner with sections on the L wall (IV,V with one section VI or A0).

Now either slant up R on a loose ramp to reach a horizontal band which leads round to the S face and the descent (17.22), or continue for 90m direct (V), or take cracks on the L to the NE ridge and follow this to the summit (III+).

NORTH FACE – AID ROUTES
The main OHing area of the N face has at least three aid routes up it, and a variety of finishes up the walls to the L of the Cassin Route (17.19). These are only described briefly and are not that popular at present.

Base hut – Lavaredo 1hr to the start 500m

17.20 All start fairly close together on the big ledge which crosses a few m
A3/A4 up at the base of the face.

80

      a. Couzy Route. Demaison, Mazeaud, 1959. This starts furthest L below a yellow roof and OHing crack. 230m of sustained aid climbing, with stances in étriers, until the second big roofs are passed to the R, with only one possible bivouac ledge. The second section is easier free climbing on grey rock direct to the top (IV/V) although some parties traverse to the NE ridge (17.18) and escape. Usually two days. Take plenty of liquid. Any retreat would be extremely difficult.

      b. Swiss Italian Routes. Bellodis, Franceschi, 1959. Start in the middle of the ledge directly below the black central groove of 17.19. This is a route of sustained aid climbing, first passing a red roof on the L at about 80m and then by a white corner leading up to the L side of the big roofs. It is usual, after about 190m, to slant R towards the Kasparek bivouac on 17.19 and to finish up this route. However two other finishes are possible, the first taking the line of the black stripe falling from a black chimney near the summit, the other going direct from the bivouac up grey rock just L of the upper part of 17.19. One bivouac usual.

c. Bauer Route. Bauer, Rudolph, Rudolph, 1968. This route starts where the ledge meets the screes and accepts the challenge of the great roof below the famous traverse of 17.19. It leads direct in 200m to the Kasparek bivouac and finishes as for 17.19. Many bolts and pegs. First ascent took 30hr of climbing but subsequent ascents have been much quicker.

NORTH-WEST RIDGE (SQUIRRELS RIDGE)
Lorenzi, Michielli, Ghedina, Lacadelli, 1959.

Mainly aid climbing in a superb position. A slow party may have to bivouac.

Base hut – Lavaredo 1hr to the start 450m 8-15hr

17.21 Start as for Cassin Route (17.19).

A2/V+

80

1 140m As for 17.19 pitches 1 – 4

2 50m Climb L to the top of a loose pillar, then vertically for 15m, then again slightly L to a large roof. Climb this on the L and continue direct for 15m on OHing rock, then climb towards the arête, with less difficulty, for 15m to a stance on the crest (A2/V/V+)

3 30m Traverse L for 3m, climb vertically for 3m then slightly R to reach a good peg crack. Climb this for 15m and traverse L for 6m. Poor stance. (A1/A2/V)

4 25m Climb vertically for 6m then slightly L to reach a good stance below a roof (A1/A2/V)

5 40m Climb the roof (A2) and after 8m climb a cracked dièdre slanting R for 10m (V). Go L under a roof then continue on the crest of the ridge for 22m (A1/A2) to a narrow ledge

6 20m Climb a small OHing crack for 15m then slant L (A1/A2)

7 45m Climb a crack past several small roofs for 20m (A2) to a small niche. Continue by the OHing crack above (A2/V-, A1/IV+) to a spacious ledge

8 150m Follow the crest easily (II/III) to the traversing ledges and then the summit.

ORDINARY ROUTE
Ploner, Innerkofler, 1879.

Also the descent route.

Base hut – Auronzo 45min to the start 350m 3hr

17.22   Approach as for 17.12 to the F d Grande, a col with wartime shelters
II   cut in it.

      About 10m before the col climb L up a rock-filled gully which
cuts across the whole of the S face of Cima Ovest. Pass another gully
on the L and turn large blocks on the L until a little higher the gully
splits. Climb a step in the R branch of the gully then, immediately, a
second higher step (6m, not easy, but an alternative is possible up
rocks on the L). The col at the top of the gully is now near and a few
m before it, on the R, a short ledge and 15m chimney lead to a large
ledge which cuts across the E, S and W faces.

      Traverse W and reach the middle of the W face. Leave the
terrace and climb easy but friable rock, first L then direct up small
chimneys to a final arête. Follow this to the top with 3m of harder
climbing just before the summit.

      In descent go down SW for 100m from the summit with an early
awkward move and then descend little chimneys and ledges, fairly
well marked, to the middle of the W face. Follow tracks on a large
ledge round L to the S face and a little further along it descend a 15m
chimney to a ledge which leads into a main gully. Descend this gully
past an awkward step of 6m, or move out onto the rocks to its E to
reach, by branching L, another gully running E. Follow this over
blocks to reach the screes below the F d Grande and so to the hut.
Usually many cairns. (1½hr)

Geografica 1:25000 sheet 2

These groups lie to the E of the Tre Cime di Lavaredo and the whole is often referred to as the Dolomiti de Sesto or Sexten Dolomites. Whilst Paterno is well served with via ferrata, Cima Una and Croda dei Toni are big isolated peaks.

HUTS

Lavaredo and Locatelli Huts As for Tre Cime di Lavaredo (group 17)

Zsigmondy-Comici Hut 2224m. Well situated in the hollow surrounded by Cima Una, Croda dei Toni, Monte Popera and Cima Undici. Very popular. Approaches– i)from Sesto (Sexten) by car to Capanna al Fondo Valle (1526m) in the Val di Fiscalina or bus to Hotel Piano Fiscalino and 45min walk. Continue on 103 SE to the hut, ii)by 101 from Locatelli hut (2hr) iii)by 104 from Lavaredo hut (2½hr)

*Pian di Cengia Hut*2528m. A very small private hut at the foot of the Via Ferrata delle Forcelle which leads W up Paterno. Approaches– i)by 101 from Locatelli hut (1hr), ii)by 104 from Lavaredo hut (1¾hr)

Paterno (Paternkofel) 2744m

NORTH-WEST RIDGE
Bolte, Wolf, 1930.

A good route with fine views.

Base hut – Locatelli 1hr to the start 350m 3hr

18.01 From the hut walk across by path 101 below the N ridge. Do not
IV+ descend below the foot of a spur but go up screes and a short gully to
82 pass behind a subsidiary tower and so get into the scree chute leading up to the col where 18.02 starts. Do not climb the gully but cross over and climb a subsidiary gully leading up to the NW ridge and joining it above its lower rocks. Climb a final short crack and chimney (II) to a small platform on the ridge.

1   35m Climb R up a grey wall past a peg then direct to a stance
     (III+,IV)

2   35m Climb an OHing crack (IV), move R to a ring peg and go
     direct over an OH (IV+)

3   20m Climb the ridge (II)

4   30m Traverse L round the arête to a steep chimney. Climb this for
     10m to a stance.

5   40m Move R round the ridge and continue R until beneath a grey
     wall (II)

6   25m Climb the grey wall for 15m (III+) staying near the arête,
     climb it for 10m over a steep section (III) to reach a ledge

7   50m Follow the easy ridge to the summit (II).

NORTH-NORTH-WEST RIDGE
Innerkofler, Innerkofler, Biendl, 1896.

A fine exposed climb on good rock

Base hut – Locatelli 45min to the start 250m 2½hr

18.02 From the hut head for a prominent pinnacle at the foot of the N ridge
III+   (Salsiccia or Frankfurter sausage) and follow a tunnel (Gallerie del
82   Paterno, torch needed) through the ridge to reach a scree gully. It is
           also possible to climb the gully direct but there is a risk of stonefall.
              Continue up the gully to a small col between a tower on the N
           ridge and the start of the NNW ridge which leads from here to join
           the NW ridge near the summit. Take a ledge and gully on the W of
           the ridge to pass various pinnacles and a big block to reach a col below
           the true wall of the mountain.
              Climb a smooth little chimney, a narrow chimney and finally a
           wall on the R to a ledge (II,III). Continue up a crack (III+) and then
           make an exposed traverse R on a narrow ledge to reach the NW Ridge
           (18.01) and finish up this.

DESCENT
18.03 Descend a well marked path E to the F d Camoscio (Gamsscharte).
           Now either descend the E ridge by the Via Ferrata delle Forcelle to
           Pian di Cengia hut or descend N to reach and descend the tunnel used
           by 18.02 or descend S by the Via Ferrata Innerkofler to the Lavaredo
           hut. (1 – 1½hr)

Croda dei Toni (Cima Dódici – Zwölferkofel) 3094m

NORTH-NORTH-EAST FACE
Siorpaes, Dimai, Witzenmann, 1897.

A classic route to the highest summit in the group, climbing the obvious R to L crack line on the NE face.

Base hut – Zsigmondy-Comici 1hr to the start 750m 7hr

18.04 Start midway between the lowest point of the rocks and the gully on
IV the L by an icy cave (possible bergschrund).

  Climb smooth, wet rock to a hollow and then R up a wet gully
(III) to reach an obvious horizontal ledge. Go L 50m, climb up a pitch
(IV) to reach a higher ledge and go back R avoiding the lowest part of
the gully. Now move back diagonally L towards the gully. Climb near
it or climb a chimney and slabs to its R (IV) crossing an ice gully at
one place. When a direct ascent seems impossible make a strenuous
traverse L for 35m to reach easy ground and above this climb an
OHing crack (IV). Continue up exposed short steps moving gradually
L until a gully leads to a terrace. Climb wet slabs above to a higher
ledge (cairn) and move R to reach an obvious chimney leading to the
N ridge and by this over blocks to the summit.

NORTH RIDGE DIRECT
Schranzhofer, Schranzhofer, 1932.

An excellent climb up the superb sweep of slabs leading from the start of 18.04 direct to the summit. There is a harder start if required.

Base hut – Zsigmondy-Comici 1hr to the start 700m 8hr

18.05 Start as for 18.04 to reach the obvious horizontal ledge which cuts the
VI–/A1 base of the whole N wall.

  Climb the crack on the R (III) then the noticable crack line up
the centre of the big grey slab (II,III) which finishes just R of a snow
or scree terrace in the corner about 200m from the start. Continue up
slabs for 50m to a higher ledge (III). Now move up and R to climb a
steep rib (IV). The main corner on the L now bends L and a traverse
L leads for 20m past a small stance with a cairn to a 250m chimney.
Climb 40m up damp OHing rock on poor holds to a good stance (V).
Continue for 40m to a higher stance where the chimney opens out.
After 50m it narrows again and it is best to climb on the R wall for
20m to reach a stance on a big block. Continue on the R wall for 30m

to reach a narrow ledge which is followed for 8m to reach an obvious crack. Climb this all the way (IV+) then return to the chimney at a large jammed block. Continue for a short distance, climb easier ground first L then move R by ledges to below the final walls of the peak. After an initial crack leading to a shoulder, climb diagonally R for 5m below a big block and continue to a higher shoulder. Descend 5m and traverse 20m R. Continue going round large pinnacles with possibly a short rope move to reach the true ridge (bivouac site & cairn).

Climb the edge for 4m and then continue up the OHing red wall for 40m (A1) to a small ledge. After a few easier moves climb a second wall (VI-/A1) for 35m to a small scree-covered ledge and continue for 40m, still vertical (V+) to a large ledge. Continue up a crack on very steep rock (V+/A1).

The route now relents and after a 15m wall on good holds, easier rock leads to the summit.

ALTERNATIVE START
Del Vechio, Mauri, 1947. Happacher, Brandler, 1959.

In order to avoid the easy lower section and the 250m chimney it is possible to climb direct up the lower walls starting just L of an obvious water stripe on the steep wall of the Anticima (the lower R-hand peak when seen from the hut).

Walk 50m L along the traversing ledge (move of V) and climb the hidden chimney just L of the water stripe. Ten pitches with at least eight sections of VI or A1.

Now cross easier ground to reach the start of an OHing crack leading up just on the arête and climb this and the edge above (first pitch VI, the rest V) to join the main route near the upper pinnacles. (This variation is not often climbed but is recommended by R.Messner!)

DESCENT BY NORMAL ROUTE

18.06 This descent climbs down ledges and gullies on the W face and has some stonefall danger. Start down the E face for 120m to reach the traversing ledge and follow this R (S) round the peak to the prominent col (F Alta Croda dei Toni). It may be possible to abseil down the R bank of the 55 degree snow gully leading down the W face but it is usually better to continue the traverse round to the middle of the face directly below the summit (a direct descent to here is possible) and then descend a long diagonal line back to the base of the couloir. Cross this and descend on the far side. At least eight abseils of 20m, all from fixed pegs. (3hr)

Cima Una (Einserkofel) 2698m

SOUTH FACE (NORMAL ROUTE)
Innerkofler, Happacher, Eötvös, 1879.

This is also the usual descent route.

Base hut – Zsigmondy-Comici 1½ to the start 250m 1hr

18.07 Follow path 103 down for a few minutes until a green ledge leads off
II N below Il Pulpito. Take this ledge and get into the valley on the R of
Il Pulpito to reach a cirque (Cadin di Cima Una). Climb a green
tongue NW towards the col between Cima Una and Crode Fiscaline (
pleasant walking peak from the SE) until a large block is reached in
the snowy gully.

   The S face is crossed by two obvious ledges. A lower one which
rises and falls and an upper ledge 70m below the summit. Follow the
lower ledge R until just short of a gully and climb up and R to enter
the gully. Climb it until it widens out at half height and then slant L
to reach a scree terrace. Climb a black wall above this terrace bearing
L to reach the upper terrace. Traverse L and climb a gully to the ridge
and the summit. Many variations are possible.

NORTH FACE DIRECT (ORIGINAL ROUTE)
Dibona, Rizzi, Mayer, Mayer, 1910.

*The N face has at least ten routes and variations on it. This route and
18.09 take the same line for the lower part of the wall. Then it heads for
two cols on the ridge R of the summit whilst 18.09 takes the challenge of the
steep nose direct to the summit. Both routes give route-finding problems.*

Base hut – Val di Fiscalina 1¼ to the start 800m 7hr

18.08 Start at the top of the westernmost of the three scree-filled bays which
V can be seen at the base of the N face. Above the bay is a gully which
83 goes diagonally from R to L and higher up appears to be continued as
a wide, high-angled terrace.

   The start of the climb is reached over steep snow. Cross the
terminal crevasse and climb a smooth step of rock to gain entry to the
mouth of the gully. A little higher the walls of the gully meet to form a
cave (below and to the L of this is the Loschner Stone). Above, an exit
maybe made on to the face through a narrow opening. An exposed
wall leads to a broad easy gully which terminates in a vertical step
flanked by a slippery crack. Climb the crack to half-height then move
out on to the slab on the L to reach a stone-covered ledge.

Follow this easily L until it ends. Traverse on good holds to reach a smooth narrow crack and climb it (IV) to a small stance below black slabs. Traverse R, descend a gully until a step is reached and move R on to the wall. A narrow ledge leads to a thin crack splitting the vertical wall, climb this (IV, very exposed). Do not take the gully which follows but move R to the next crack. This is smooth at first but becomes easier and leads to a narrow ledge going off L wards. At this point the route leaves the original N Face Route of Langl, Loschner and Hartl which moves R.

Follow the ledge L wards up a yellow step (V). Climb grooves, steep slabs and a final step, trending R to gain a terrace also reached by the Langl Route further R which provides an easier way of getting there.

From a recess on the terrace descend slightly L wards to an OHing corner. Climb this over blocks for 30m and at the top move L and climb a slab (V) to reach a small ledge. Climb the steep wall above (less difficult) to another ledge and traverse horizontally R for 10-15m along the narrow crumbling ledges which form its continuation (V). Go L wards up a slab (V) to an ill-defined corner where the rock is poor. Climb this moving L at the top and continue to a wide ledge sloping towards the E. A little to the L climb the OHing wall (6m, V) and go up to a slabby terrace (visible from the valley) which overlooks a wall. Go R as far as the rocks which form the edge of this and make a long traverse L by means of a poor ledge (exposed) to reach a 150m chimney. This is damp and contains several OHs. Climb the chimney (V) until it is possible to take to the rib dividing the two gullies which descend from the cols, E and W respectively, of the point on the ridge between the summit and the fore-summit. Both gullies and the rib between have been climbed. The rib is the most pleasant but hardest. It is easy at first then more difficult until two OHs and a section of rotten rock have to be overcome to reach a small gap. Climb R wards up the smooth OHing wall to a knob (V) and continue up the next wall (V, very exposed) to a good ledge. (Height of final wall from gap, 70m, crux).

Move R easily along the ledge to the col lying W of the point in the middle of the ridge. Traverse below the subsidiary point to the col immediately below the main summit and then climb to the summit.

NORTH FACE – RIGHT HAND SUPER DIRECT (VIA DELLA GIOVINEZZA)

Steger, Weisinger, 1928.

Another long serious route up this sombre face.

Base hut – Val di Fiscalina or Locateeli 1¼hr to the start 800m 9hr

18.09
VI–/
A0
83

Start as for 18.08. From the point where 18.08 branches off from the Langl-Loschner-Hartl Route traverse L as for 18.08 but continue Lwards across steeply inclined ledges until just below the huge OHing yellow wall, bounded to L and to R by OHing cracks, in a direct line below the summit. Go R up a scree-filled gully to reach a large scree terrace (cairn). From the cairn trend R for 40m to a cracked dièdre. Climb the edge of the crack for 12m to a small stance (V). A wrinkled slab with poor holds leads in 15m to a crack which rises L. Climb this on poor holds (VI-/A0) to reach a shelf (cairn, peg) which is followed L to another crack. Climb this on poor holds until it widens out into a chimney (cairn) and go up the chimney, very narrow at first, to a scree-covered platform. Climb the OHing wall on the L of the platform to a bulge (cairn) from which a steep groove of 8m leads to a sloping stone-covered ledge in an amphitheatre formed by a huge OHing yellow/black wall bounded by cracks.

Above here much of the climbing is V with short sections of VI-/A0 but it eases to IV near the top. Start up the L-hand crack/dièdre which widens to a chimney after 15m. Cairn and small stance. Climb the L-hand wall of the chimney then the chimney itself to a peg and finally take the OHing L wall again to a sloping scree-covered ledge. In this section the chimney is shallow and rounded and hardly distinguishable from the wall. Now take the R-hand crack on whitish/yellow rock. It slopes outwards and is moss-covered, making it hard and strenuous (20m, two pegs). From the upper peg traverse into the L-hand crack and climb it to where, as a thin chimney, it divides. Take the R branch then a wrinkled slab to a scree-covered ledge and move R to the foot of a yellow crack. Climb the crack to a small niche then start bearing L to re-enter the L-hand crack (cairn). Follow the crack to a small terrace where the cracks divide again forming a sharp angle between them. (Escape maybe possible L round the E ridge to join 18.07 at the upper ledge.) Take the L-hand crack to reach a gendarme (cairn). Descend a few m to an obvious chimney and climb this to a ledge (cairn). Move R for a few m to a crack which leads directly to the summit.

Index of Climbs

					19
1	**Brenta Group**				
1.01	Torre d'Ambiez	S face	200m	III+	21
1.02		E dièdre	250m	IV+	21
1.03		Descent			22
1.04	Cima d'Ambiez	SE face	350m	V+	22
1.05		E face (Concordia)	350m	VI+ or V+/A1	23
1.06		E face direct	350m	VI+ or V+/A1	24
1.07		Descent			24
1.08	Cima Tosa	NE face direct	750m	V	25
1.09		N canalone della Tosa	1200m	AD	25
1.10		Descent			25
1.11	Crozzon di Brenta	N ridge	1000m	IV+	26
1.12		NNE face (Aste dièdre)	850m	VI+ or VI−/A2	26
1.13		NE pillar (Frenchmans)	830m	VI−	27
1.14		NE face (Preuss)	800m	IV+	28
1.15		ENE face (Guides)	800m	V+	29
1.16		Descent			29
1.17	Cima d Vedretta	E face	350m	V	30
1.18		Descent			30
1.19	Cima d Farfalla	NE wall	380m	VI−/A2	31
1.20		Descent			31
1.21	Cima Margherita	SSW face	300m	III	31
1.22		SSW face (Detassis Crack)	300m	V−	32
1.23		N face	600m	VI/A2	32
1.24		Descent			33
1.25	Croz del Rifugio	SW buttress (Camp Teresa)	150m	IV	34
1.26		Descent			34
1.27	Brenta Alta	NE face	500m	V+	34
1.28		NE dièdre	450m	V+/A2	36
1.29		Descent			36
1.30	Campanile Basso	Ordinary	270m	IV	37
1.31		E face (Preuss)	120m	V	37
1.32		SE ridge (Fox)	200m	VI+ or V/A0	38
1.33		SW dièdre (Fehrman)	550m	IV+	38
1.34		SW ridge (Graffer)	500m	VI+ or V/A0	39
1.35		Descent			40
1.36	Campanile Alto	W ridge	550m	IV+	40
1.37		Descent (NE chimney)			41
1.38	Torre di Brenta	N face	300m	III+	41
1.39		SW face	400m	V	42
1.40		Descent			42

1.41 Cima Brenta	E face (Verona)	500m V+/A3	43
1.42	Descent		43
1.43 Croz d'Altissimo	SW dièdre (Armani)	700m VII or VI/A1	44
1.44	Descent		45
2 Pala Group			**46**
2.01 Campanile Alto dei Lastei	W face	400m VI	47
2.02	Descent		48
2.03 Cima della Vezzana	SSE face	270m I	48
2.04	W face direct	600m IV	49
2.05	Descent		49
2.06 Cimon della Pala	NW ridge	600m III	49
2.07	Ordinary	900m II	50
2.08	Descent		50
2.09 Croda Paola	NE face (Minucci)	150m IV+	51
2.10 Dente del Cimone	W ridge	350m IV	51
2.11	Descent		52
2.12 Pala d San Martino	SW pillar (Gran Pilastro)	600m IV−	52
2.13	Descent	II	53
2.14 Cima d Val di Roda	NW face (Langes)	750m III	53
2.15	Descent		53
2.16 Cima della Madonna	NW ridge (Spigolo del Velo)	450m V	54
2.17	Descent		54
2.18 Sass Maor	E face	1000m VI	55
2.19	SE ridge	700m VI−	56
2.20	SE face direct	600m VIII or VI/A2	57
2.21			57
2.22 Campanile di Pradidali	NE chimney	350m V	57
2.23	NE face	350m IV	57
2.24	Descent		58
2.25 Cima Canali	N face	600m III	58
2.26	Ordinary	700m III	59
2.27	W face (Simon)	700m V	59
2.28	W face (Buhl)	600m VI−	59
2.29	Descent		60
2.30 Torre Gialla	W face	440m VI−	60
2.31	Descent		61
2.32 Pala del Rifugio	NW ridge	700m V	61
2.33	Descent		62
2.34 Sasso d'Ortiga	W ridge	250m V	62
2.35	Descent		63
2.36 Monte Agner	N face	1500m V+	63
2.37	N ridge	1700m V+	64
2.38	Descent		65

Catinaccio Group					66
.01	Roda di Vael	SW face (Dibona)	400m	IV	68
.02		W face (Buhlweg)	350m	VIII or VI/A1	68
.03		W face (Maestri)	400m	V/A2	69
.04		W face (Schrott−Abram)	350m	V/A3	69
.05		W face (Eisenstecken)	350m	VI	70
.06		Descent			70
.07	Cima Sud dei Mugoni	SE face (Zeni−Gross)	350m	V+/A2	71
.08		SE face (Eisenstecken)	300m	V+/A1	71
.09		SE face (Grand dièdre)	300m	V+/A1	72
.10		SE pillar	300m	VI/A2	72
.11		NE face	200m	III	73
.12		Descent			73
.13	La Sforcella	E face	180m	III+	73
.14		W face	300m	IV+	74
.15		Descent			74
.16	Catinaccio	SE face of S peak	500m	IV	75
.17		E face direct of S peak	600m	V	75
.18		Descent from S peak			75
.19		E face direct (Steger)	600m	V+	76
.20		Descent from Central peak			76
.21		SE dièdre of N peak	400m	V+/A1	77
.22		E face direct (Olympia)	600m	V+/A2	78
.23		Descent from N peak			78
.24		W face (Normal)	150m	III	78
.25		W face (Pederiva)	150m	IV+	78
.26		W face (Piaz−Delago)	150m	IV+	79
.27		W face (Dulfer)	150m	IV−	79
.28		W face (Anna Maria)	150m	IV+	79
.29		NW face	300m	VI or V/A1	79
.30	Punta Emma	SE face	400m	V−	80
.31		E face (Steger)	300m	V	80
.32		NE face (Piaz crack)	250m	V or IV/A0	81
.33		N face (Eisenstecken)	200m	VI/A0	81
.34		Descent			82
.35	Torre Delago	SW ridge	120m	IV	82
.36		S face (Preuss/Piaz)	120m	V−	83
.37		S face (Delago chimney)	120m	IV	83
.38		Descent			83
.39	Torre Stabeler	S face	120m	IV	84
.40		Descent			84
.41	Torre Winkler	SE crack (Winkler crack)	150m	IV	84
.42		S face direct	110m	V+	85

3.43		E ridge	100m V	85
3.44		NE face	150m V+	85
3.45		Descent		86
3.46	Vajolet Towers	Traverse	IV	86
3.47	Torre Piaz	SW ridge	60m IV	86
3.48		Descent		86
3.49	Torre Est	SE face (Piaz crack)	450m V	87
3.50		Descent		87
3.51	Croda d Re Laurino	W face direct	500m IV−	87
3.52		Descent		88
3.53	Cima Orientale di Val	NW ridge	450m V	88
3.54	Bona	Descent		88
3.55	Crepa di Socorda	SW face direct	600m V+	89
3.56		Descent		89
4	**Sassolungo Group**			90
4.01	Sassolungo	SW face (Ordinary)	800m II+	91
4.02		N face E tower	900m IV	92
4.03		N ridge	1000m IV	93
4.04		N face direct	1100m VI	94
4.05		N pillar (Esposito)	1100m VI	95
4.06		N pillar (Demetz)	650m IV+	95
4.07		Descent by Ordinary route	800m II	96
4.08	Gran Campanile	NW ridge	300m IV+	97
4.09		Descent by W gully		98
4.10	Il Salame	N face	400m VI or V+/A1	98
4.11		Descent		99
4.12	Spallone del Sassolungo	SE face	800m III	99
4.13		SE face (Ramp)	800m IV	100
4.14		Descent by W ridge		101
4.15	Punta della Cinque Dita	SW ridge	250m IV	101
4.16		S face (Schmitt chimneys)	300m IV	102
4.17		S face (Diagonal crack)	300m IV+	103
4.18		N ridge of the Thumb	250m IV−	103
4.19		Descent by Ordinary route		103
4.20	Sasso Levante	S face and S ridge	600m IV	104
4.21		S face direct	600m V	105
4.22		ENE ridge	350m IV−	105
4.23	Punta Pian de Sass	S face (Rizzi chimney)	500m V	106
4.24		S pillar	500m VI/A3	106
4.25		SE wall (Gran diedro)	500m VI/A2	107
4.26		SE ridge	450m IV	108
4.27		Descent		108

5	**Odle Group**				109
5.01	Piccola Fermeda	W ridge (Normal)	300m	I	109
5.02		SW gully	300m	III	109
5.03		S face	400m	III	110
5.04		S face (Direct start)	90m	VI	110
5.05		SE ridge (Direct start)	100m	VI	110
5.06		SE ridge	400m	III	110
5.07	Grand Fermeda	W face and SW ridge	200m	III	111
5.08		SW face (Yellow chimney)	150m	III	111
5.09		W Fermeda gully connection	100m	III	111
5.10		SW face (Direct start)	150m	III	111
5.11		SW face (Ordinary)	400m	III+	111
5.12		SE ridge	400m	III	112
5.13		NE face	400m	IV+	112
5.14	Campanile di Funes	S face (Delago chimney)	400m	IV	113
5.15	Odle di Cisles	SW face direct	400m	IV	113
5.16		S face (Dulfer crack)	400m	V	114
5.17		S face variation	400m	V+	114
5.18		SE ridge	500m	V−	114
5.19		Normal from E	500m	II	115
5.20	Gran Odla	SE ridge	500m	V	115
5.21	Sass de Mesdi	SW ridge	400m	V−	115
5.22		W face	150m	IV	116
5.23		S face (Hannemann crack)	250m	V	116
5.24		S face pillar	250m	IV	117
5.25		S face cracks	100m	V	117
5.26	Sass Rigais	S face Normal	600m	I	117
5.27		E ridge	150m	I	117
5.28	Il Pulpiti	W face			118
5.29	Furchetta	W ridge (Ordinary)	400m	I	118
5.30		N face (Solleder)	600m	V+/A0	118
5.31		Descent			119
6	**Sella Group**				120
6.01	First Sella Tower	W ridge	100m	IV+	120
6.02		S face (Tissi)	170m	VI or V/A0	121
6.03		S face (Rossi)	170m	VI+ or V+/A0	122
6.04		S face (SW dièdre)	150m	V	122
6.05		S pillar (Pilastrini)	100m	V	123
6.06		S face (Fiechtle crack)	100m	IV	123
6.07		S face (SE chimney)	120m	III	124
6.08		Descent by Ordinary route			124
6.09	Second Sella Tower	NW ridge	250m	V/A0	124
6.10		N face	250m	V−	125

6.11		NW face direct	200m VI−	126
6.12		Descent		126
6.13	Third Sella Tower	SW face	350m III+	127
6.14		W face	300m VI− or V−/A0	127
6.15		Descent by Ordinary route		128
6.16	Fourth Sella Tower	W face direct	250m V−	128
6.17		Descent by Ordinary route		128
6.18	Piz di Ciavazes	Normal and descent route	300m I	129
6.19		SE face (Ramp)	300m IV	130
6.20		SE ridge	170m VII or V+/A1	130
6.21		S face direct	300m VI	131
6.22		S face direct (S dièdre)	300m VI	133
6.23		S face (Italia)	250m VI/A3	133
6.24		SW dièdre	250m VI+ or V+/A1	134
6.25		S face (Schubert)	220m VI or VI−/A0	134
6.26	Sass Pordoi	NW face (Fedele)	750m IV+	136
6.27		S pillar (Piaz arête)	250m V−/A0	136
6.28		W face	800m IV+	137
6.29		SW face	800m V	137
6.30		S face (Galleria)	250m IV	138
6.31		S pillar (Maria)	250m IV	138
6.32	Gran Campanile Del	NE face	450m IV	139
6.33	Murfreid	Descent by Ordinary route		139
6.34	Torre del Murfreid	N face chimney	400m V	140
6.35		Descent by Ordinary route		140
7	**Marmolada Group**			141
7.01	Marmolada di Penia	Normal (Glacier)	700m PD	142
7.02		W ridge	450m I	142
7.03		SW face (Solda)	550m VI or V+/A1	143
7.04		New S pillar	550m VI+	144
7.05		S pillar	550m VI/A0	146
7.06		S face	650m IV+	147
7.07		S face (Ombrello)	680m VI	148
7.08		S face (Sudtiroler)	700m VI/A0 or VI/A2	149
7.09		Descents		150
7.10	Marmolada di Rocca	Normal (Glacier)	700m PD	150
7.11		S face (Gogna)	800m VII− or VI/A1	151
7.12		S face (Modern Zeiten)	800m VII+	153
7.13		S face (Vinatzer)	800m VI+ or V+/A1	155
7.14		S face variation (Messner)	400m VI+ or VI/A1	156
7.15		Descent		157
7.16	Marmolada d'Ombretta	S face (Ideale)	850m VII− or VII−/A1	158
7.17		S face (Fisch)	850m VII/A1	159

.18		S face (Conforto crack)	850m	VI	162
.19	S face (Don Chisciotte)		750m	VI	163
.20		S face (Schwalbenschwanz)	750m	VI	164
.21		S face (Castiglioni)	750m	V	166
.22		S face (Hatschi Bratschi)	750m	VI−	167
.23		Descents			168
	Civetta Group				169
.01	Torre Coldai	NNW face direct	400m	IV+	170
.02		Descent to NE			170
.03	Torre d'Alleghe	E face	400m	IV	171
.04		NW face of S pillar	400m	VII/A0 or VI/A2	171
.05		NW face of N pillar	400m	VII− or VI/A2	172
.06		Descent by E face, NE ridge			173
.07	Torre di Valgrande	NE pillar	250m	IV+	173
.08		NW face	500m	V11+ or VI−/A2	174
.09		S face (Guide)	200m	VII or VI/A0	174
.10		Descent by NE face			175
.11	Pan di Zucchero	E face	370m	V+	175
.12		NW face	600m	V+	176
.13		Descent by NE ridge			177
.14	Punta Civetta	NW face (Andrich)	800m	VI+ or VI/A1	177
.15		NW face (Aste)	800m	VI+ or VI/A1	179
.16		Descent			179
.17	Punta Tiss i	NW face (Philipp−Flamm)	950m	VII or VI−/A1	180
.18		Descent			181
.19	Monte Civett a	NW face (Comici)	1500m	VI or VI−/A1	182
.20		NW face (Friends)	1100m	V+/A2	184
.21		NW face (Solleder)	1300m	VI or VI−/A1	185
.22		Descent			186
.23	Cima Su Alto	NW face (Livanos dièdre)	800m	VI/A2	187
.24		NW face (Ratti)	800m	VI or V+/A1	188
.25		Descent by E face			188
8.26	Cima d Terranova	NW face	700m	VI/A2	189
.27		Descent by N ridge, E face			190
8.28	Campanile Brabante	NW ridge	180m	VI−	190
.29		Descent			190
8.30	Guglia Rudatis	NE and NW face	80m	V+	191
8.31		SE ridge	75m	V−	191
8.32		Descent by E face			191
8.33	Pulpito di Pelsa	W face direct	200m	IV+	192
8.34		Descent by E face			192
8.35	Punta Agordo	W face (Agordo dièdre)	360m	IV+	192
8.36		Descent by E face			193

8.37	Torre Venezia	W face	300m IV	193
8.38		SW buttress	300m V+	194
8.39		SSW face	420m VI−	195
8.40		S face (Tissi)	600m VI− or V+/A0	196
8.41		Descent by E face		197
8.42	Cima del Bancon	E face	450m VII− or VI/A1	197
8.43		Descent to W		198
8.44	Torre di Babele	S ridge	300m VI−	199
8.45		Descent to SW		199
8.46	Cima della Busazza	W face	1000m VI−	200
8.47		Descent by SE face		200
8.48	Castello di Busazza	S face	800m V+	201
8.49		Descent to E		201
8.50	Torre Trieste	W ridge	650m VI or V+/A0	201
8.51		S face	700m VIII− or VI+/A2	203
8.52		SE ridge	700m VII+ or VI/A2	205
8.53		Descent by E face		207
9	**Pelmo Group**			208
9.01	Monte Pelmo	Ordinary from SE	1000m II	208
9.02		SE pillar (Franceschi)	800m VI−/A1	209
9.03		SE pillar (Angellini)	850m IV	209
9.04		N face	850m V+	210
9.05		Descents		211
9.06	Pelmetto	NW ridge	850m V	212
9.07		Descent		212
10	**Bosconero Group**			213
10.01	Rocchetta Alta di	S face	400m V−	214
10.02	Bosconero	W pillar	750m V	215
10.03		NW ridge (Spigolo Strobel)	600m VII or VI/A2	216
10.04		N face (Grole)	700m VI/A1	217
10.05		Descents		218
10.06	Sasso di Bosconero	NW ridge	600m IV+	219
10.07		Descent by S face		219
11	**Schiara Group**			220
11.01	Schiara	Traverse	700m II	220
11.02		S pillar	500m VI−/A2	221
11.03	Second Pala del Balcon	W pillar by S ridge	250m IV	222
11.04		E pillar by S ridge	250m V+	222
11.05	Third Pala del Balcon	E face	220m IV−	223
11.06		Descent		223
11.07	Burèl	SW face (Miotto)	1100m VI/A2	223

1.08 Guśla del Vescovà	Ordinary	40m	IV+	225
1.09	Descent			225
2	**Lagazuoi, Fanis, Cunturines Groups**			226
Piccola Lagazuoi	S faces			226
2.01 Torre di Falzarego	S ridge and S face	300m	IV/V+	227
2.02	Descent			227
2.03 Lagazuoi Nord	W face (Drago)	300m	VI−	228
2.04	WNW face (Consiglio)	300m	IV+	229
2.05	Descent			229
2.06 Cima Scotoni	SW face (Lacedelli)	550m	VIII− or VI−/A1	229
2.07	SW face (Fachiri)	400m	VI	231
2.08	Descent			231
2.09 Col Boccia	W face	250m	V	232
2.10 Cima and Torre del Lago	W dièdre	370m	IV+	232
2.11	Descent			233
2.12 Sasso della Croce	W face (Gran Muro)	550m	VII or VI−/A1	233
2.13	W dièdre	550m	VII− or V+/A2	234
2.14	W face of central pillar	500m	VIII or VII−	235
2.15	Descent			235
2.16 Sasso Nove	S E slab	250m	IV+	236
2.17	S face (Diagonal)	300m	IV	236
2.18	S face (Placche)	250m	V	237
2.19	Descent			237
3	**Tofana Group**			238
3.01 Tofana di Rozes	S face	800m	IV+	238
3.02	Descent to N			239
3.03 Pilastro di Rozes	SW ridge	500m	VI−	239
3.04	S face	500m	VII+ or V+/A2	240
3.05	Descent			241
3.06 Primo Spigolo di Rozes	SW ridge	400m	V	242
3.07 Tofana di Mezzo	E face (Central spur)	450m	VI	243
3.08	E face (Right−hand spur)	450m	VI	243
3.09	Descents			243
4	**Cinque Torri**			244
4.01 Torre Grande Cima Sud	S face (Franceschi)	100m	VI+ or V+/A1	244
4.02	S face (Col Vento)	150m	VII+	245
4.03	S face (Scoiattoli)	150m	VIII−	245
4.04	S face (Miriam)	210m	V	246
4.05	S face direct (Dimai)	190m	VI+/A0	247
4.06	E face (Dimai crack)	150m	V+	247
4.07	Descent			248

14.08 Torre Grande Cima Ovest	WNW face (Armida)	100m	VI or V/A1	24:
14.09	NW face (Olga)	120m	V+	24:
14.10	SW face (Guide)	140m	IV	24:
14.11	Descent			24:
14.12 Torre Lusy	N face	120m	IV	24:
14.13	Descent			25:
14.14 Torre del Barancio	N face	120m	IV+	25:
14.15	S face (Giovanna)	80m	VI	25:
14.16	Descent			25:
14.17 Torre Romana	N dièdre	100m	IV	25:
14.18	S chimney (Normal)	50m	III	252
14.19 Torre Latina	S face	70m	VI/A1	252
14.20 Torre Quarta	E face of Alta	65m	VII+	253
14.21	S face of Bassa, Normal Alta	150m	IV−	253
14.22	Descent			254
14.23 Torre Inglesi	S E face	50m	IV−	254
14.24	Descent			254
15 Pomagagnon, Cristallo Groups				255
15.01 Punta Fiames	SE ridge	350m	V	255
15.02	S face (Central)	200m	VI−	256
15.03	S face (Ordinary)	300m	IV	256
15.04	Descent Via Ferrata Strobel			257
15.05 Testa del Bartoldo	S face (Terschak chimney)	500m	V−	258
15.06	Descent by Fifth ledge			259
15.07 Monte Cristallo	SE face (Normal)	450m	PD	259
16 Sorapiss, Antelao Groups				260
16.01 Punta di Sorapiss	NW face	400m	IV	261
16.02	SE face (Ordinary)	400m	III−	262
16.03	Descents			262
16.04 Punta Zurlon	N face	500m	VI−/A1	262
16.05	Descent by S ridge			263
16.06 Dito di Dio	Normal	500m	II	263
16.07	N face	600m	VI/A1	264
16.08	Descent			265
16.09 Sorelle di Mezzo	NW face	600m	V+/A0	265
16.10	Descent to S			266
16.11 Antelao	NE face (Menini)	700m	AD	267
16.12	SW face	1000m	VI−/A1	267
16.13	Descent to N			268
17 Tre Cime de Lavaredo Group				269
17.01 Cima Piccolissima	NE face (Preuss crack)	200m	V	269

17.02	SE face	250m	VII or V+/A0	270
17.03	Descent by Dulfer couloir			271
17.04 Punta Frida	SE ridge	300m	VI/A1	271
17.05	SE face direct	300m	VI+ or V+/A1	272
17.06	Descent			272
17.07 Cima Piccola	S arète (Yellow Edge)	350m	VI or V+/A1	273
17.08	SW face (Ordinary)	300m	III	274
17.09	NW ridge	280m	VI+/A1	274
17.10	N face (E chimney)	450m	IV	275
17.11	Descent by Ordinary route			276
17.12 Cima Grande	W face	350m	V	276
17.13	N face (Comici)	500m	VII or VI/A1	277
17.14	N face direct (Brandler)	500m	VI/A3	278
17.15	NE ridge (Spigolo Dibona)	550m	IV	279
17.16	S face (Mosca chimney)	200m	III	280
17.17	Descent by Ordinary route			281
17.18 Cima Ovest	NE ridge	500m	VI+ or V+/A0	281
17.19	N face (Cassin)	450m	VIII− or VI−/A2	282
17.20	N face aid routes	500m	A3/A4	283
17.21	NW ridge (Squirrels)	450m	A2/V+	284
17.22	Ordinary and descent route	350m	II	285
18	**Paterno, Croda dei Toni Groups**			286
18.01 Paterno	NW ridge	350m	IV+	286
18.02	NNW ridge	250m	III+	287
18.03	Descent			287
18.04 Croda dei Toni	NNE face	750m	IV	288
18.05	N ridge direct	700m	VI−/A1	288
18.06	Descent by Ordinary route			289
18.07 Cima Una	S face (Normal and descent)	250m	II	290
18.08	N face direct (Original)	800m	V	290
18.09	N face direct (Giovinezza)	800m	VI−/A0	292

1

1

2

2

39

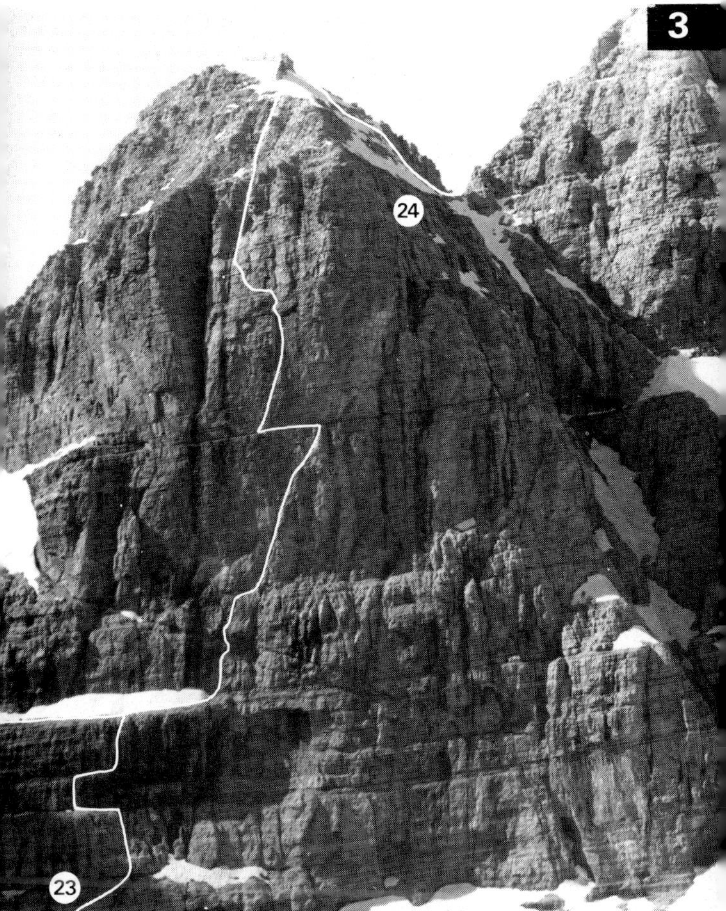
24
23

306 **Cima Tosa and Crozzon di Brenta** NE face
Group 1

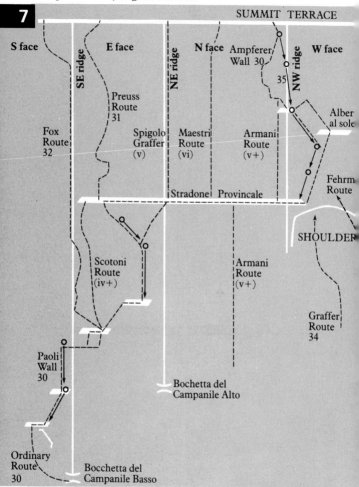

SUMMIT TERRACE

S face

SE ridge

E face

NE ridge

N face

Ampferer
Wall 30

NW ridge

W face

Alber
al sole

Preuss
Route
31

Fox
Route
32

Spigolo
Graffer
(v)

Maestri
Route
(vi)

Armani
Route
(v+)

35

Fehrm
Route

Stradone Provincale

SHOULDER

Scotoni
Route
(iv+)

Armani
Route
(v+)

Graffer
Route
34

Paoli
Wall
30

Bochetta del
Campanile Alto

Ordinary
Route
30

Bochetta del
Campanile Basso

Campanile Basso

Group 1
SW flank

8

Croz dell 'Altissimo

Group 1
SE face

9

Group 2
Sass Maor and Cimon della Madonna **NW flank**

10

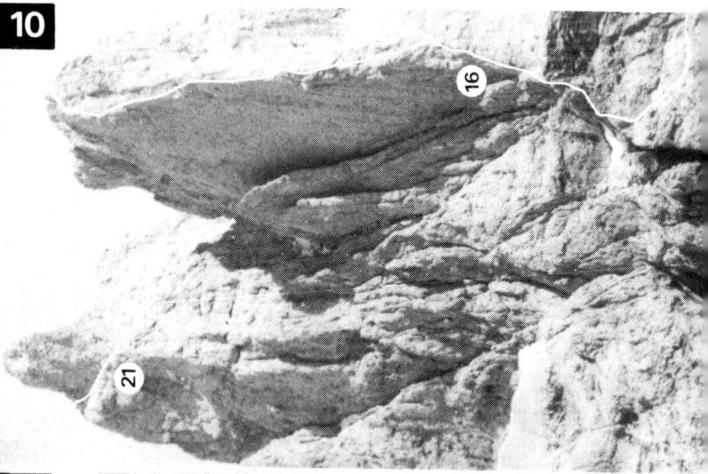

11

 Cima Brenta **NE face**
Group 1

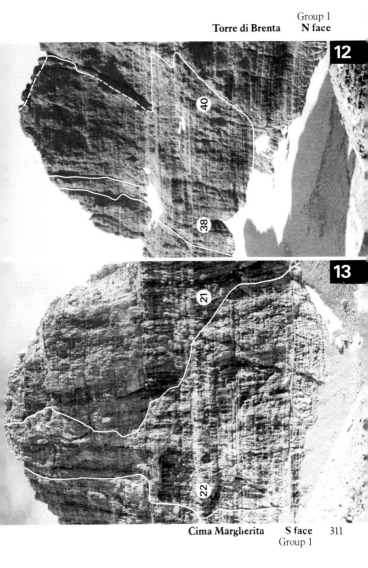

16

20   18

Zagonel ▲   313

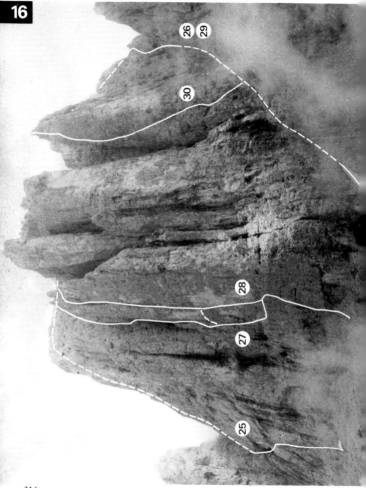

19

4

6

20

16   17   19

24

7   8   9   10

Vin

25

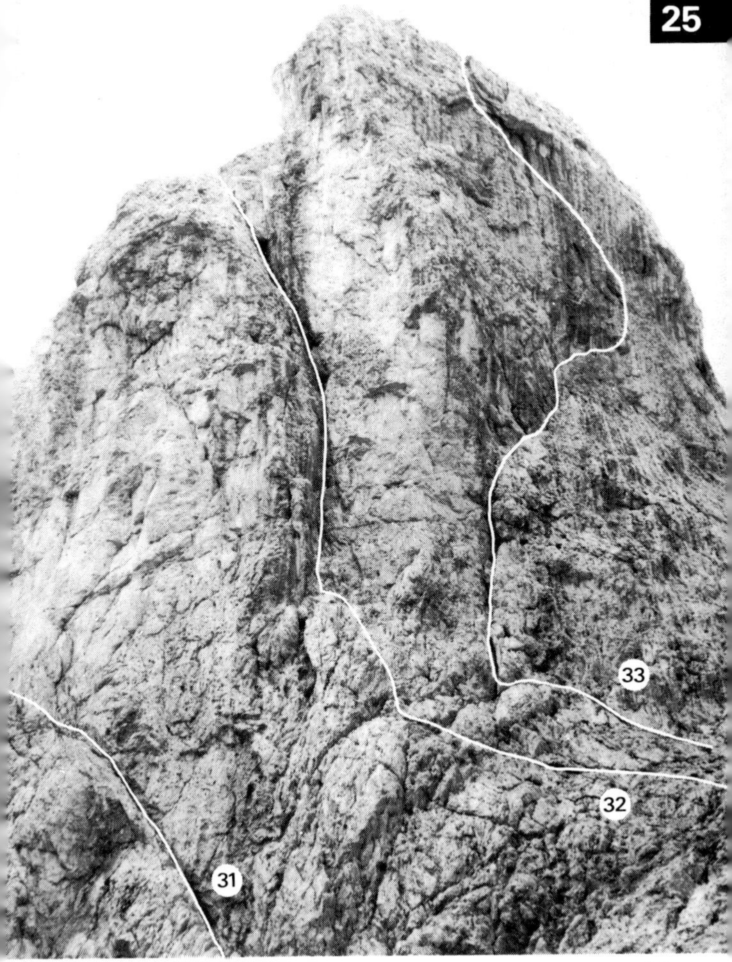

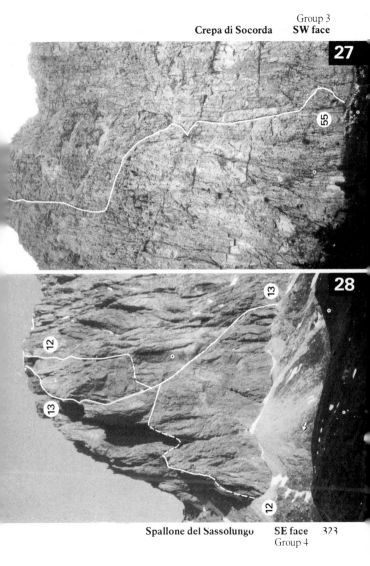

29

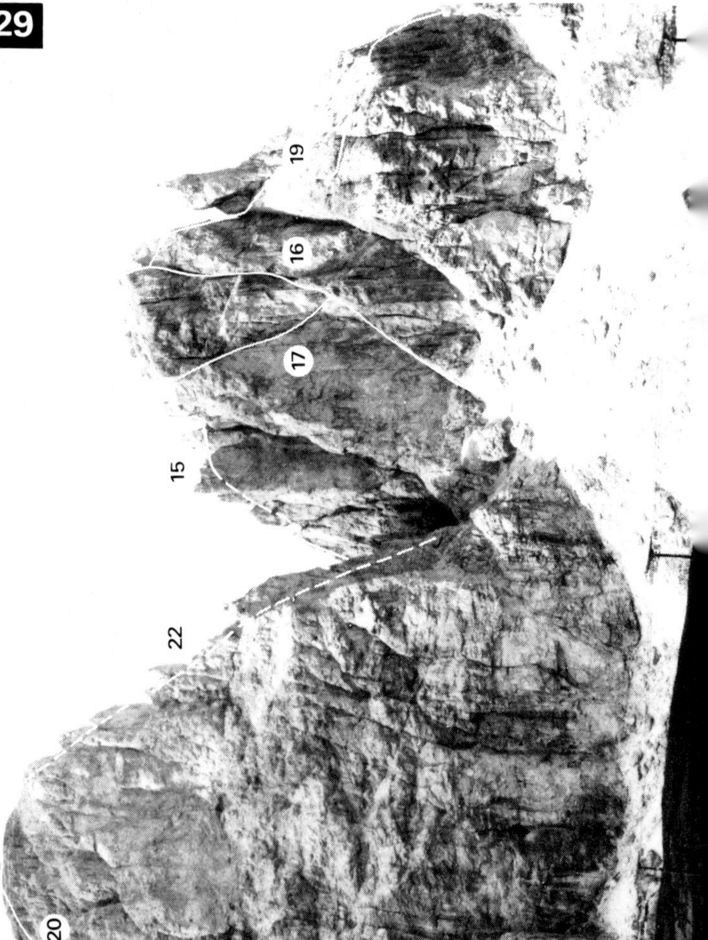

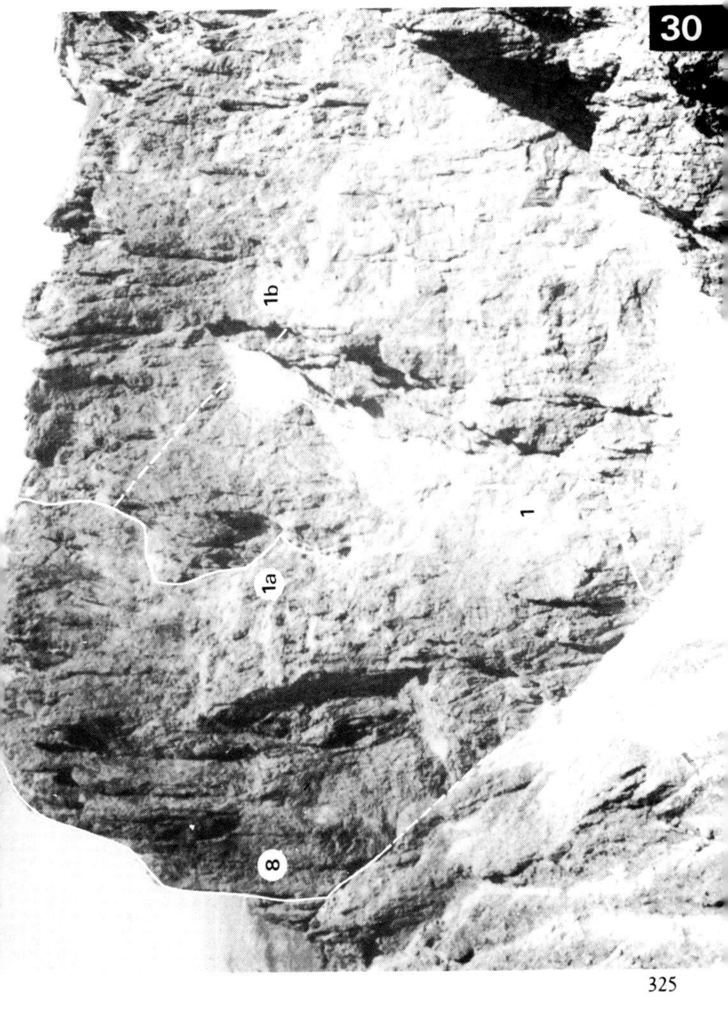
1b
1
1a
8

36

37

9

10

11

38

1

334

40

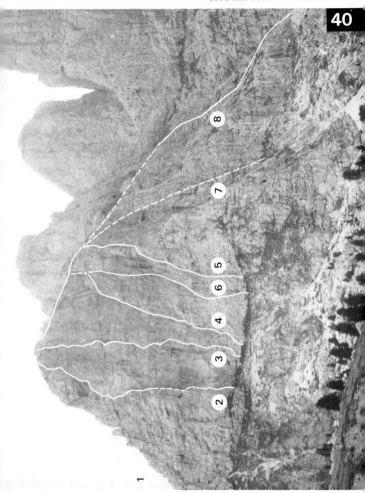

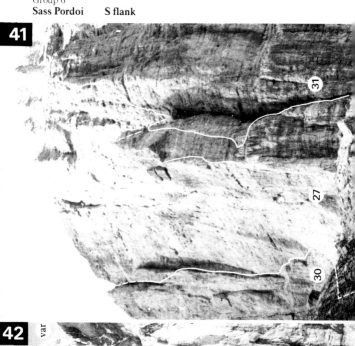

52

53

54

Guséla del Vescovà   NW facc   347
Group 11

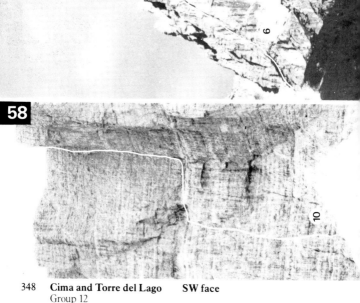

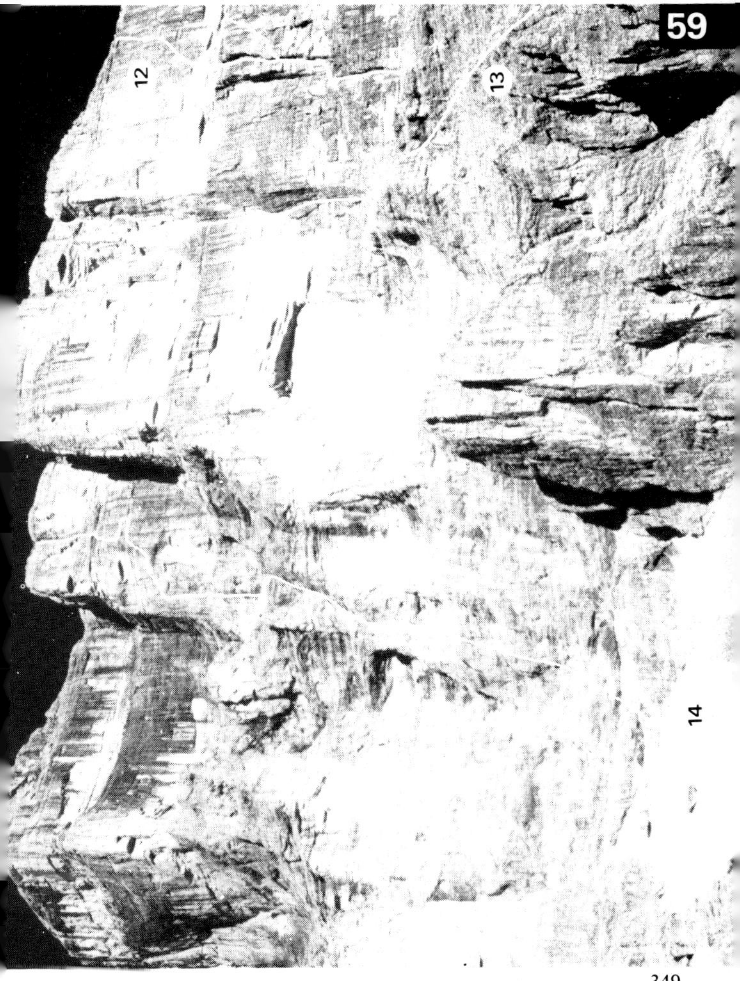
59
12
13
14

60

63

7

8

65

67

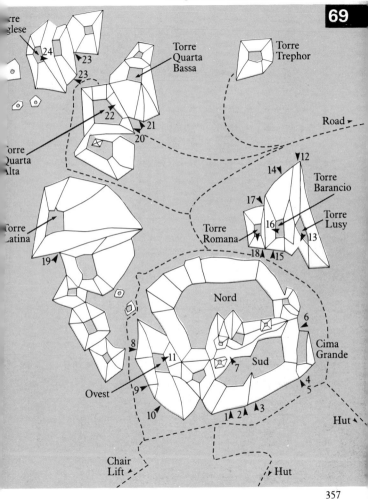

Torre Inglese

24

23

23

Torre
Quarta
Bassa

22

21

20

Torre
Trephor

Road

12

14

17

Torre
Barancio

16

Torre
Lusy

13

Torre
Quarta
Alta

Torre
Romana

18

15

Torre
Latina

19

Nord

6

Cima
Grande

8

11

7

Sud

Ovest

9

4
5

10

1 2 3

Hut

Chair
Lift

Hut

357

358   **Testa del Bartoldo**   S face
Group 15

72

73

23

usual   original

75

76

4

7

77

12

78

9

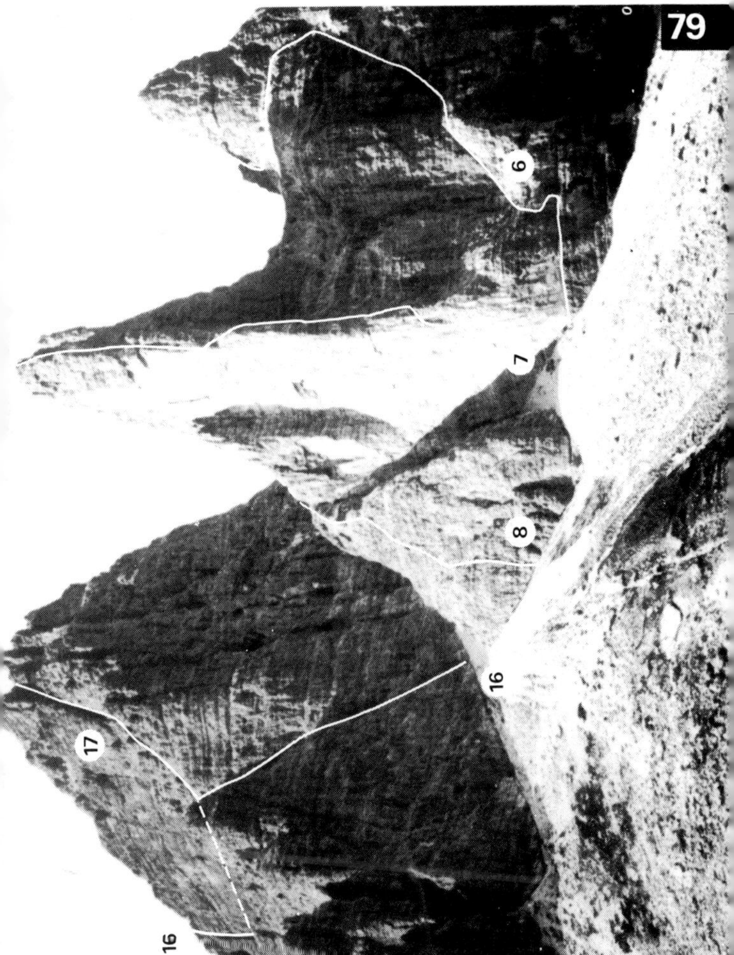
79
6
7
8
16
17
16

80